W9-ADP-795

OLD MEDIA
NEW MEDIA

OLD MEDIA
NEW MEDIA

Mass Communications in the Information Age

Wilson Dizard, Jr.

Georgetown University

Longman

**Old Media/New Media: Mass Communications
in the Information Age**

Longman, 10 Bank Street, White Plains, N.Y. 10606

Associated companies:
Longman Group Ltd., London
Longman Cheshire Pty., Melbourne
Longman Paul Pty., Auckland
Copp Clark Pitman, Toronto

Acquisitions editor: Kathleen M. Schurawich
Development editor: Susan Alkana
Production editor: Victoria Mifsud
Text design adaptation: Betty Sokol
Cover design: Betty Sokol
Cover illustration: Donald Gambino
Text art: Fine Line, Inc.
Production supervisor: Anne Armeny

Library of Congress Cataloging-in-Publication Data

Dizard, Wilson, Jr.
    Old media/new media : mass communications in the information age /
Wilson Dizard, Jr.
        p.   cm.

    Includes bibliographical references and index.
    ISBN 0-8013-1151-9
    1. Mass media—United States—Technological innovations.
I. Title.
P96.T422U634   1993
302.23'0973—dc20   93-25021
                                                            CIP

2 3 4 5 6 7 8 9 10-MA-97969594

For Ithiel de Sola Pool (1917–1984)
who saw it all coming

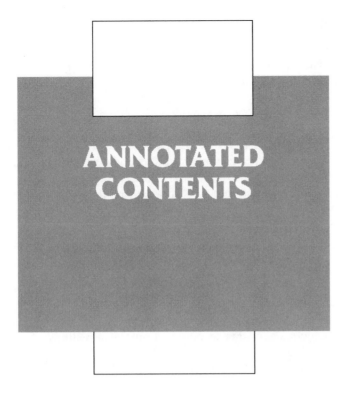

ANNOTATED CONTENTS

U.S. mass communication patterns are changing radically these days with the introduction of a wide variety of advanced technologies along with shifting social and economic conditions. The result is a competitive mix of old and new media together with a different agenda for the role of information and entertainment resources in our personal and working lives.

A primer on multimedia computers, telecomputers, and other advanced information machines: what they are, what they do, and how they are influencing both the old and new media.

FOREWORD
by
Everette E. Dennis

*Director, Freedom Forum
Media Studies Center*

Any true understanding of mass communications in the modern age requires unusual sensitivity to technology and change as well as deep knowledge of history, economics, politics, and sociology for a start. Essential also is grounding in technology and technological change—not simply in what Arthur C. Clarke called "voices from the sky" in the future tense but also in the sometimes anachronistic system of communication as expressed in today's media. Only a person of unusual intellect, experience, scholarly capacity, and communications savvy could manage such a task. But that is just what Wilson Dizard, diplomat, technology and communications expert, scholar, and commentator, has done here.

At the heart of this book is an explication conveyed in overt and subtle tones of media convergence—that condition signifying a united state of media wherein all media forms and instruments come together by virtue of computers and digitization. But even as all media are blurring and blending together into what is really a single system or set of interrelated systems, so are individual media accentuating their distinctiveness. The world Wilson Dizard presents in *Old Media/New Media* connects long-standing, traditional communication media with those only imagined today by futurists. It is this rich weave of durable media forms—along with those currently under siege and still others now being conceived in laboratories—that makes this a unique and valuable source of intelligence for students, media researchers, professionals, and the public.

Correctly recognizing that the future of communications lies at the confluence of old and new media, Professor Dizard has produced a book rich in its range and scope of the present and future shape of mass communication and deep in its understanding of the processes that will, in fact, define and determine the kind and nature of media that people will experience in the twenty-first century. All books are a product of the experience of their authors, and Wilson Dizard has observed and participated in communications around the world both in developing nations and in industrial societies. His understanding of the process and framework of the old media of print and broadcast technologies—including publishing, film, and television—connect and overlap with his expertise about information networks and various new media technologies and data streams.

The story of old and new media cannot be told in technological terms alone, involving only relationships between people and machines but must be seen also through the prism of politics and economics, which grant permission for new entries, such as satellites and computers, to be on the media stage and sometimes allow old-timers, such as newspapers, to stay a bit beyond their prime.

Part of the concern of this book is with the pace of new media determined by the forces of invention, creativity, market demand, and regulatory freedom. The discussion speaks in broad policy terms and zeroes in on new and evolving industry segments, such as cable. It is buttressed by an assessment of old media, such as newspapers and the movies, that are undergoing a remodeling process as they struggle to survive and flourish in the new information age.

All this helps to explain why good ideas and feasible technologies that could liberate people by providing massive information sources and up-to-the-minute graphics and retrieval do not always get transformed into reality. The interceding human factors, as they are called, are cataloged and analyzed effectively by Professor Dizard, who understands that even the finest technological innovation or the most brilliant new media form will not advance from the R&D lab unless market demand, cost-effectiveness, and the political-regulatory climate are favorable. When we hear predictions about the media room of the future or about the prospects of a given media industry, we often forget that pure logic and the magic of invention are not enough to make new media happen. For those reasons and others, this book also makes us appreciate old media, quite ingenious themselves, even more, and it also explains why seemingly obsolete media such as radio have gotten new life, even in the face of television expansion.

Here is the story of the media family, etched against the backdrop of the whole communications system and confined not to a single country or culture but viewed with a global perspective. Old players or "media family" members are observed at various stages of development and appreciated for their contributions both ephemeral and lasting. Gracefully written, this solidly researched book is an exquisite consumer's guide to the future of communications media and has the rare distinction of connecting memories of the past with the present and future. Wilson Dizard can and does hold his own with world policymakers (and has been one himself), debating with technical experts on such issues as cross-data border flow and the future of radio while arguing about what system should govern a given old technology or technological innovation. Mr. Dizard's book is not giddy about the new "toys" on the block, yet it does not underestimate their potential. At the same time, the author appreciates the prowess and staying power of the conventional media and makes sense out of great complexity while offering a coherent theme and framework for unified understanding of mass communication in the information age.

Avoiding the jargon of engineering technology or of policy wonks, the book is eminently practical in its patient explanation of the juxtaposition of economics and politics as determinants of the changing media scene. Neither seduced by the new machines nor underestimating the power of technology both as a societal force and as a metaphor for change, the book is a masterful examination of society's central nervous system and its communication infrastructure, which are presented in a highly accessible form. It will, no doubt, be greeted with enthusiasm by all who are students of the media and of communication whether they are just entering the field or have long occupied the executive suite. Once again, Wilson Dizard has given us an important treatise that is a sensemaker *extraordinaire*.

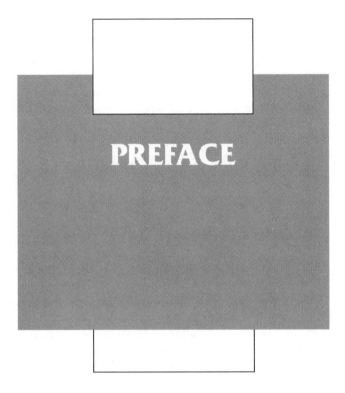

PREFACE

This is a report on the massive changes currently taking place in American communications. It describes the new convergence of economic, political, and technological resources that affect the way we deal with information in our daily lives.

My focus is primarily on the mass media—print, video, and film. For shorthand purposes, the discussion is divided between the *old media* and the *new media,* that is, the traditional forms and the new challengers. A partial list of the latter includes multimedia computers, CD-ROM laserdiscs, advanced facsimile machines, hand-held data banks, electronic books, videotext networks, intelligent telephones, and direct-to-home broadcasting satellites. The shared technology in each of these services is computerization. The result is that the dominant mass medium of the early years of the next century may be DOS (Disk-Operating System)—the most common computer software standard.

The media constitute a ubiquitous presence in American society. We spend more time with them than with any other activity, including work or sleep. Some enterprising researchers at Veronis Suhler Associates, the New York investment firm, have calculated that, out of the 8,760 hours in a year, we allot 3,256 hours—nine hours a day—to the media. (The details are given on p. 4.) The overall impact of this pattern on our lives is enormous. Moreover, this amount of focus on information, through the media and other resources, is increasing. It may not be an exaggeration to suggest that the way we cope with this flood will be the defining factor of the American postindustrial age.

I have tried to draw a line—somewhat shakily at points—between the long-term promise of advanced media resources and what is actually happening now. By and large, I have projected a scenario only to the end of the 1990s. This seems prudent enough, given the changes that will take place in the next few years. By the end of the century, we will have 300-channel cable systems, hand-held electronic newspapers, digital disks that can store a small library, and multimedia telecomputers that can integrate in one machine the personal computers, TV sets, VCR players, and compact disc stereos that now clutter up American homes.

These innovations are part of a larger shift in the use of information resources. Taken together, telecommunications and information technologies are pushing us toward a national information utility. The result will be networks based on computers and advanced circuits that will make information available in any form—voice, print, or video—almost anywhere, just as we now tap into electricity or water utilities. The U.S. information utility is now about half completed, radically changing the ways in which business and government operate. The next decade will see the consumerization of the utility, reaching down to most American homes.

These changes are being driven by technology, specifically the innovations developed by research laboratories in this country and in Europe and Japan. A new range of options is forcing a convergence of the telecommunications and information sectors, that is, the producers and the transmitters of information resources. Inevitably, the mass media will be transformed into something very different from what they are now.

None of this will happen smoothly. Technological options have to be translated into political and economic realities. There are at least as many powerful forces opposed to changes in the status quo as there are those supporting them. The debate is marked by many dissonant voices. In industry, professional cheerleaders see lucrative markets for glitzy new products and services. In public life at all levels, politicians worry about the impact on the governing pattern and, more directly, on their own career. The academic community, which can play a vital role in clarifying the issues, has not always been helpful. It tends to focus on threats in the new prospects, particularly the danger of more centralized control over information resources. The professors are right to keep a critical, even skeptical, stance. However, they also have an obligation to see the whole picture, involving as it does new complexities in which there are no clear-cut villains or heroes.

Finally, there is the ultimate consumer of the new-media resources—the mythical Joe and Jane Six-Pack—who, so far, has exercised commendable caution regarding the hoopla over technologies guaranteed to change his life. There are real questions about how, or whether, multimedia computers and the other promised services will satisfy personal needs. What information do I really want? How much will it cost? What is missing? How much is enough? These questions have been pointedly summarized by media watcher Neil Postman: "Any fool can tell you what technology is good for. It takes real thought to figure out what computers will deprive us of." Too often the debate has been dominated by people who, in Evelyn Waugh's phrase, have never been troubled by the itch of precise thought.

There are, in short, no easy formulas. The ultimate question is how all these prospects can benefit us in a more complex postindustrial democracy. For over two centuries, our lodestar in defining information freedoms has been the First Amendment. Originally, it referred only to printed publications, but its protections have been expanded in recent decades to include the electronic media. Expanding its scope further will be increasingly difficult given the introduction of more complex media technologies.

There are disturbing signs that the new information resources could further strain the American social fabric. This shows itself in a growing division between the information rich and the information poor. If present trends continue, the former will totally dominate the information resources needed by all of us to survive and thrive, and the latter will become a postindustrial lumpenproletariat, relegated to mindless entertainment and other trivia. The guarantee of equitable access to advanced information resources is the most urgent issue we face as we move into the new media pattern.

ACKNOWLEDGMENTS

Many individuals helped me to prepare this study. First, I owe much to the counsel of the late Ithiel de Sola Pool, a teacher and scholar who inspired so many of us trying to make sense of the new-media environment. The title of his last book on information resources, *The Technologies of Freedom*, summarizes all that this study tries to express. My thanks go also to my colleagues at the Center for Strategic and International Studies and at Georgetown University, in particular, to Diana Lady Dougan, chief of the center's communications policy program, and to Peter Krogh, dean of the School of Foreign Service, both of whom gave me space, time, and resources to finish this work.

Among others who helped me were Elena Androunas, Walter Baer, Porter Bibb, Leo Bogart, Hodding Carter, Jannette Dates, Marcia DeSonne, Charles Firestone, Michael O'Hara Garcia, Henry Geller, Cheryl Glickfield, Robert Hilliard, Eri Hirano, Craig Johnson, Leland Johnson, Carol Joy, Montague Kern, Anton Lensen, Lawrence Lichty, Brenda Maddox, Robert Pepper, Marsha Siefert, Anthony Smith, Gregory Staple, John Vondracek, David Webster, and George Wedell. I also want to acknowledge the courtesy extended by Dr. Elie M. Noam, of Columbia University's Institute for Tele-Information, who allowed me to reprint, in an appendix, his imaginative "Principles for the Communications Act of 2034."

Also, I would like to thank the following reviewers for their help:

James Bernstein, Indiana University

Marlan Nelson, Oklahoma State University

Jan Whitt, University of Colorado, Boulder

Thomas Schwartz, Ohio State University

Joseph Turow, University of Pennsylvania

Ronald Garay, Louisiana State University

Travis Linn, University of Nevada, Reno

Gregory Lisby, Georgia State University

Kenneth Harwood, University of Houston

Susan Caudill, University of Tennessee, Knoxville

Patrick Parsons, Pennsylvania State University

Robert Wicks, Indiana University

Christopher Sterling, George Washington University

Maureen Beasley, University of Maryland

Edwin Diamond, Media Critic, *New York* Magazine

Finally, a heartfelt tribute, again, to my resident chief editor and thoughtful critic on works in progress, Lynn Wood Dizard.

OLD MEDIA
NEW MEDIA

Chapter

1

THE EVOLUTION OF MASS COMMUNICATIONS

In December 1991, the unthinkable happened in the American mass media industry. For the first time in their history, the "Big Three" television networks—NBC, CBS, and ABC—ended the year without collectively making a profit. The record was not much better at many of the local stations they served across the country.[1] It was a seismic shock for a business once described by a media executive, in an unguarded moment, as a license to print money.

In previous years, the networks could count on profits of 15 percent or more. Now it was reality time. The Big Three's fall from fiscal grace signaled, in the most attention-getting way possible, that television and other traditional media industries are being transformed. In part, television's money woes in the early 1990s were the result of an economic recession that had affected all business sectors. The networks' profit slide was not, however, due only to a temporary bad patch in the economy. The signs that they were losing their grip on American media habits have been around for years. The warnings were particularly visible in the cold statistics of prime-time network viewing, which dropped from 90 percent to 60 percent in the six years from 1985 to 1991.

In those years, comfortable profits masked long-term changes in television and the other old-line media industries. Increasingly, however, they have felt the pressure from new technologies offering an expanded range of information and entertainment services. The result has been a more competitive market, an erosion of audiences, and, inevitably, lower profits.

The U.S. mass entertainment and information sector is evolving into a new pattern—a mix of old media and new media. The transition has been under way for a decade or more, and it will accelerate throughout the rest of the 1990s. Measuring the change is difficult. The American media industry is too large and spread out to be fitted into easy generalizations. It includes 2,700 television stations, 12,000 radio stations, 11,000 cable systems, and 15,000 newspapers and periodicals, among other resources.[2] The industry stretches from the magisterial *New York Times* to station KPQD in Bighorn, Texas, bringing the best in country music to all those folks out in radioland.

Cable television and home videotape players are the most familiar examples of new technologies in the American media environment. Both have been highly successful in attracting audiences away from television broadcasting and other old-line services. As a result, cable and videotape have become, in a relatively short time, part of the conventional media pattern along with TV, radio, film, and publications.

The older media will be around for a long time as part of the American communications mix. But they will be different. The winds of change have swept away the comfortable assumptions that guided their operations in recent decades. The media have a new agenda. The issue now is: Who will compete with what products for which audiences in a more complex marketplace? There will be many winners and losers in the industry shakeout now taking place. The survivors will be the organizations that adapt to changing technological and economic realities. The losers will be the corporate dinosaurs, large and small, that cannot or will not change—all candidates for mergers, takeovers, or old-fashioned bankruptcy.

The new element in this pattern is the next generation of advanced computer-based services, which will compete in the entertainment and information industries. Such services include high-definition television, digital radio broadcasting, multimedia computers, hand-held data banks, wireless cable systems, CD-ROM (compact disk–read-only memory) laser discs, direct broadcast satellites, advanced facsimile machines, intelligent telephones, consumer computer networks, portable electronic newspapers, and national videotext services. The ultimate mechanism for delivering advanced media services to homes may be the *telecomputer,* a fusion of television and computer technology in a single box, offering a full range of video, voice, and data services.[3] (Each of these technologies is discussed in detail in the next two chapters.)

Can these new technologies be classified as mass media? Not in the current dictionary sense of the phrase. Mass media historically has meant centrally produced standardized information and entertainment products, distributed to large audiences through separate channels.[4] The new electronic challengers modify all of these conditions. Their products often do not come from a central source. Moreover, the new media usually provide specialized services for large numbers of relatively small audiences. Their most significant innovation, however, is the distribution of voice, video, and print products on a common electronic channel, often in two-way interactive formats that give consumers more control over what services that want, when they get them, and in what form.

Purists can argue that the new media are substantially different from the old.

Confusing them with conventional media, the argument goes, is mixing apples and oranges, traditional channels versus the glitzy new electronics. The pragmatic fact, however, is that the dividing line between the two is being smudged every day. Telephone compete with cable systems? Compact disks with books? Facsimile machines with newspapers? In each case, they already do compete. The coming years will see similar changes as advanced media technologies erode the old media's operating styles as well as their audiences and revenues.

In the process, "mass media" will be redefined to reflect the changes. The semantic contest for a new name has already started. Anthony Oettinger, director of Harvard University's Program in Information Resources, suggests that media will become part of the structure of **compunications,** an artful enmeshment of "computers" and "communications." Others propose the expression **information utility,** visualizing vast amounts of media resources flowing together through electronic "information pipes," analogous to natural gas and water utilities. For the present, it remains prudent to use the terms "old media" and "new media," at least until we know more about how they will interact and, eventually, meld into a different pattern.

The new media are currently influencing the information and entertainment sectors in two ways. At one level, their products are distinct from, and competitive with, the industry's present output. At another level, the established media organizations are beginning to adapt the new technologies to their own operations.

This latter trend has been led by a new breed of information entrepreneurs, exemplified by such industry innovators as Robert Edward (Ted) Turner, Rupert Murdoch, Gerald Levin of Time Warner, and Michael Eisner of the Disney organization, among others. They are a giant step removed from the traditional pattern of media executives.[5] Their talents are in multimedia information packaging. Product synergy is their working formula. Each item in their packages—films, books, television, and so on—is designed to bolster the others in ways that produce new and more profitable combinations. The idea is to win a marketing advantage over their single-media competitors.[6] Multimedia synergy has turned out to be a somewhat elusive goal, as we shall see when we look at the major information packagers, but it is an important force in the new media environment.[7]

Increasingly, the old and new media share one resource: a common channel for delivering their services. Both rely on sophisticated national and global telecommunications networks—the old phone system vastly expanded. These networks can relay massive amounts of voice, video, and data/print products as digital signals on the same circuit at very high speeds. (A single communications satellite can transmit the entire contents of the *Encyclopaedia Britannica* in less than a minute.) More than any other factor, electronics are forcing the technical integration of the old and new media, with major impacts on the future shape of the industry.

This integration of the old and the new is in its early stages. Advanced information and entertainment technologies still play a relatively minor role in American media. How and when they will take on a major role is an open question. But it would be a mistake to underestimate their cumulative effect on the ways in which Americans—and the world—will be getting the information they need to survive and thrive as we move into a new century.

The new media are not simply a linear extension of the old. The common link between the two is the ability to offer information and entertainment resources to large audiences, conveniently and at affordable prices. The difference is that the new media can usually perform better because they expand the range of resources and other capabilities dramatically. They can, for example, provide on-line interactive links between the consumer and the information provider. This capability adds a striking new dimension to the present mass-media pattern of one-way products from a centralized source. It permits consumers to query, challenge, and modify media output. Consumers may also bypass the old media structure by setting up their own electronic networks. The result can be a new kind of democratic communications environment, matching media guru Marshall McLuhan's vision, 30 years ago, of advanced information machines that will make Everyman his own publisher.[8] His concept is being realized in the rapid spread of electronic personal communications networks, including 50,000 computer "bulletin board" grids linking millions of Americans.

McLuhan aside, the trail is littered with the bones of academics, think tank consultants, and other self-appointed seers who have made wrong guesses about the arrival of the so-called information revolution. Their instincts were right, but their timing was off. Their mistake was in misestimating the convergence of the technological, economic, and political forces needed to bring the promise of the new media to reality.

These forces are now coming together in ways that affect the role of information in our lives.[9] This is particularly true of the ways in which we use the mass media. A 1992 study by Veronis, Suhler & Associates suggests that Americans spend more time dealing with the media than with any other activity, including work or sleep. The survey estimates that we allot, on average, 3,256 hours in a year—9 hours a day—to media. Television viewing (both over the air and cable) accounts for more than 70 percent of that total, with newspapers, magazines, home video, books, and films sharing very small percentages. (See Table 1.1.)

These media habits have major consequences for the form and direction of American society. The core of every society consists of the folktales it tells about itself and its origins. For most of human history, these tales have been passed on directly by storytellers. The *Iliad,* the Bible, the Viking sagas, and the Hindu *Mahabharata* epic all began as spoken stories that have defined nations and civilizations. Only in the past 500 years was this pattern modified, beginning with the introduction of multiple-copy printed books.

In modern America, and most of the rest of the world, story-telling has been modified once again, this time by the electronic mass media, and particularly by radio and television. Television is the most compelling storyteller of these tales, with its mélange of Dan Rather, "Murphy Brown," soap operas, "Wheel of Fortune," Saturday morning cartoons, Phil Donahue, and the other electronic icons it has created. Debates may rage as to how much television is eroding our cultural heritage by displacing the comfortable old folk stories. But there is little doubt that television's way of telling stories influences the way we see ourselves and the world around us.[10]

The new media will add a powerful dimension to this cultural pattern. Their capacities for creating and distributing information and entertainment go well beyond anything we deal with now. Will these new resources serve us in ways that

TABLE 1.1 Hours Per Person Per Year Using Media

Medium	1986	1987	1988	1989	1990	1991
Television	1,522	1,485	1,490	1,485	1,470	1,515
Network-Affiliated Stations*	985	912	865	835	780	848
Independent Stations*	339	332	349	345	340	265
Basic Cable Programs	126	157	182	210	260	319
Pay Cable Programs	72	84	94	95	90	83
Radio	1,205	1,155	1,165	1,155	1,135	1,115
Recorded Music	173	200	215	220	235	219
Daily Newspapers	184	180	178	175	175	169
Consumer Magazines	109	110	110	90	90	88
Consumer Books	88	88	90	96	95	98
Home Video†	22	29	35	39	42	43
Movies in Theaters	10	11	11	11	10	9
Total	3,313	3,258	3,294	3,271	3,252	3,256

SOURCE: Veronis, Suhler & Associates, A. C. Nielsen, RADAR®, Volume 1, Copyright © Statistical Research Inc.,
1991, Newspaper Advertising Bureau, Magazine Publishers of America, Gallup, Motion Picture Association of
America, Television Bureau of Advertising, Leo Shapiro and Associates, Wilkofsky Gruen Associates. Reprinted
by permission of Veronis, Suhler & Associates.
*Affiliates of the Fox Network are counted as network affiliates in 1991 but as independent stations in earlier
years.
†Playback of prerecorded tapes only.
Note: Estimates of time spent were derived using rating data for television and radio, survey research and
consumer purchase data for recorded music, newspapers, magazines, books, and home video, and admissions
for movies. Adults 18 and older were the basis for estimates except for recorded music and movies in theaters,
where estimates included persons 12 and older.

strengthen our personal and communal lives? Will they reinforce the best parts of our
tradition? Or will they further erode it? These are critical questions for a United States
that is beginning the transition to new forms of postindustrial democracy suited to
the changes that will take place in the next century.

George Gilder, senior fellow at the Hudson Institute in Indianapolis, considers
the transition to a new media environment a liberation:

> A new age of individualism is coming, and it will bring with it an eruption of culture
> unprecedented in human history. . . . The upsurge in artistic output will enhance
> the position of the United States as a center of video production and creation. We
> will discover that television was a technology with supreme powers but deadly flaws.
> In the beginning, the powers were ascendent; now the flaws dominate. The cultural
> limitations of television, tolerable when there was no alternative, are unendurable in
> the face of the new computer technologies now on the horizon—technologies in
> which, happily, the U.S. leads the world.[11]

Even at this early stage, we can see the outlines of the new mass information and
entertainment pattern. It is a combination of old and new media that overlap and
compete. The newer technologies are already cutting into the traditionally strong
position of older ones. The most prominent examples of this, as previously noted, are

cable television and videocassettes. There are, however, at least a half dozen other major media technologies jostling to enter the marketplace.

The competition between old and new media involves a process that was best characterized 60 years ago by Harvard economist Joseph Schumpeter in his analysis of capitalist economies. Capitalism's vitality came from the dynamics of what he called creative destruction. Schumpeter defined this as the ability to adapt to changes in technologies and markets. Creative destruction is as handy a phrase as any to describe the adjustments the U.S. economy is undergoing these days as it deals with postindustrial realities. The pressures are both domestic and global as international trade competition increases. The media business has been slower than most in dealing with these changes. It has been generally content to cycle and recycle its highly successful formats. Product changes have tended to be stylistic—the equivalents of the auto manufacturers' flashy tailfins back in the 1960s. For years, large parts of the media industry were driven by the pervasive attitude that, in a phrase, you don't mess with success.

This attitude was reinforced in the 1970s and 1980s by a series of well-publicized failures involving new technologies. The managers of those projects suffered the fate of most pioneers: they were the ones with the arrows in their backs. The most spectacular losses were suffered by Warner Communications in its attempt to become the leader in the emerging market for home entertainment computers. In 1975, Warner paid $75 million for the company that had developed the Atari computer, a machine that could program interactive game cassettes. By 1982, Atari accounted for more than half of Warner's revenues. Within a year, however, the Atari market had collapsed, resulting in a loss of hundreds of millions of dollars for the company and scaring off other entertainment companies from entering the computer entertainment business for years.[12]

Such formidable businesses as Time Inc., AT&T, CBS, and the Knight-Ridder newspaper chain lost hundreds of millions of dollars during the 1980s in a series of failed ventures involving videotext networks, broadcast satellites, electronic publishing, and the like. In most cases, their mistake was jumping too soon into untested, expensive technologies. They compounded this misjudgment with poor marketing strategies. The result was to make other media companies gun-shy when the next set of proposals for high-technology ventures came along.

There were some successes. A notable one was an inspired decision in 1974 by the top managers of the Home Box Office (HBO) cable television network. They proposed to use satellites to distribute Hollywood films and other entertainment features to thousands of local cable systems across the country. The cable industry originally depended on a simple technology—coaxial cables, strung from telephone poles, which could transmit a dozen or more channels into suburban or small-town homes. Such cable technology had already been in use for 20 years before HBO combined it with satellites to create large-scale continental networks. The industry was quickly transformed from an isolated collection of local mom-and-pop systems into groups of national cable operators dominated by a few firms.

HBO's success was a textbook example of the convergence of technology, economics, and politics to create a major media industry. The shift to satellite distribution technology was a small, albeit crucial, part of the process. The second leg of the convergence triangle was economics. Banks and other lenders fell over themselves in the rush to give money to cable system owners and program distributors. The lenders' instincts were eminently sound. Satellite transmission of Hollywood films, sports events, and other attractions vastly increased cable's consumer appeal. Starting with fewer than 10 million customers in the 1970s, the cable industry now provides services to over 60 million U.S. homes and other outlets.

Politics completed the triangle. At the municipal level, the awarding of monopoly cable franchises was heavily political. (The process was labeled "rent an alderman," reflecting the often flagrant ways in which franchise seekers influenced local politicians.) At the national level, the cable industry successfully fought off most attempts by Congress and regulatory agencies to limit its franchise monopolies. The **National Cable Television Association,** the industry's trade organization, rapidly developed into one of the most powerful and well-funded lobbies in Washington.

The cable industry faces some long-term problems in maintaining its strong position in the media sector, as we shall see.[13] For the present, however, cable TV is profiting from the successful convergence of technology, economics, and politics in its operations. The cable industry's strategy is a model for the rest of the U.S. media establishment as it copes with the introduction of new technologies. The media industries as a whole are overdue for restructuring, a process that may find more losers than winners among the thousands of companies involved. Essentially, media firms have two choices. They can either embrace the new media technologies as an extension of (or replacement for) their present operations, or they will need to refine their present products to make them competitive in a more crowded marketplace.

Either choice will involve massive changes in the present media pattern. The readjustment has been under way for some time. It was first documented in the early 1970s by New York University sociologist Richard Maisel, who examined American consumer information and entertainment patterns from 1950 to 1970. Maisel's findings confirmed that traditional mass media were losing out to newer, more specialized outlets. In research published in 1973, he concluded that

> the rate of increase for consumer expenditures for radio, television, magazines and motion pictures has been far less than the rate of increase in consumer expenditures as a whole. . . . The mass media are actually shrinking in size relative to the total economy.[14]

Maisel's ground-breaking research of 20 years ago has been confirmed by the media sector's performance since then. Maisel argued, prophetically, that the media were becoming a broadened mix of general interest and specialized information and entertainment products. He called the latter the "new media" — possibly the first use of the phrase in communications research.

Neither Professor Maisel nor anyone else at the time could have predicted the stepped-up pace of new media applications in the past 20 years. Maisel was writing before the introduction of personal computers, national cable networks, consumer videotext, and high-definition television. We are beginning to experience for ourselves the transforming impact of those media on the information and entertainment industries. Joseph Schumpeter's creative destruction is alive and well in the media business these days. The signs of change are out there, insistent and pervasive, an electronic version of Old Testamental writing-on-the-wall warnings.

Before an exploration in detail of the future impact of the new media, it may be useful to summarize the current situation in each of the major media sectors: television, radio, cable, publishing, and filmmaking.

First, and most dramatically, television broadcasting is changing. For over 40 years, television was the media king of the hill, with a technology, an attractive product, and a marketing formula that made it appear invulnerable to challenges from other services. The first signs of vulnerability showed up in the early 1980s. It began with a gradual falling off in prime-time network viewing—the first hairline crack in television's seamless facade. The audience loss was dismissed at the time by most of the industry's managers as a bump on the road to greater profits. They could point out, correctly, that their audiences were actually expanding, as measured by a steady increase in HUTs (the industry's acronym for homes using television).

Beyond these cheery reassurances, however, were signs that network television's long reign as the preeminent popular medium was threatened. Taken largely by surprise, NBC, CBS, and ABC found themselves facing significant competition from independent stations—those not affiliated with a network. The number of such stations increased from 86 in 1975 to 390 some 15 years later, accounting for three-quarters of total station growth in that period.[15] The other threat to the networks' audience base came from two upstart technologies: satellite-based cable television and videocassette players.

By the early 1990s, the shaky state of broadcast television's prospects was clearly evident. This was documented in a 1991 analysis of the industry by the Federal Communications Commission (FCC) research staff.[16] The report's gloomy tone was reflected in its estimate that average prime-time network viewing might fall to 15 percent of the potential audience by the end of the decade—a precipitous drop from the then-current 60 percent and the 90 percent of the mid-1980s. This audience decline, the FCC report projects, will result in a major downsizing of the industry. Many local stations face the prospect of insolvency. The report predicts that the New York networks will probably become three program packagers among a large number, supplying more materials to cable systems or other media rather than to their traditional local affiliates.[17]

Television's more innovative managers are already looking at new outlets for their products. One of them is Ted Turner, the industry's chief maverick. In 1991, Turner inaugurated a new service, beaming programs to public places where people line up, such as supermarket checkout stands, airports, train stations, and fast-food restaurants. His screens feature news, entertainment, and lots of advertising.[18] A more specialized TV operation is the American Transportation Television Network (ATTN), a satellite-based service beamed to truck stops around the nation. In addition to entertainment features, the network offers news, health and safety tips, traffic and weather reports, and a regular feature on missing kids, who often turn up at truck stops. Said ATTN's founder, Jim Rutledge, "We want this to be the CNN for truckers."[19]

Increasingly, television broadcasters must look beyond their present television operations to stem their declining fortunes. One possibility is to team up with cable industry program producers, an option that all of the major networks have begun to exercise. The networks also have a major stake in the prospects for **high-definition television** (HDTV), scheduled for limited operation by the mid-1990s. HDTV will require the eventual replacement of every television set in the country, as well as most of the industry's production equipment. In return, it will open up a new market for program services, with a greatly enhanced television screen picture, stereophonic sound, and other advanced features.

The television industry's interest in HDTV is pitted against that of cable systems, direct-satellite broadcasters, and even telephone companies. All are competing, as we shall see, in what promises to be, by the end of the 1990s, the biggest economic bonanza in the history of American media. Telephone companies, in particular, have positioned themselves strongly to compete in using HDTV and other new technologies for advanced entertainment and information services for homes, following the removal of many of the legal restrictions on their activities in the field in recent years.[20]

Television is the most visible example of the shakeout that is taking place in the media industry. The only media sector to avoid most of the economic turmoil so far has been cable television, which is the chief beneficiary of the mass audience migration from broadcast television, at least for the present. In the early 1990s, cable penetration of American homes was over 60 percent, a figure that will probably level off at about 70 percent by the end of the decade. In the process, cable TV monopoly franchises have replaced television station ownership as licenses to print money. Not only do cable companies extract an increasingly hefty monthly fee from each of their subscribers, but they also are experiencing a steady rise in advertising revenues on their systems. By 1989, cable's share of all cable and broadcast advertising dollars, together with its subscription revenues, was 42 percent, although cable accounted for only 32 percent of the total viewing audience.[21]

Nevertheless, even the cable TV industry shows early-warning signs of diminishing growth. A threatening problem is the decline in audience shares by many cable program services. The reason for this is an increase in the number of competing channel services, a number that can be expected to rise sharply as the 54-channel capacities of many local cable networks expand to 150 channels or more in the coming years. The issue has been described succinctly by cable executive Scott Sassa:

> It's kind of like opening Pandora's box. The (television) networks started getting eaten up by independent stations. Then the first big wave of cable channels came along. Now there's a second wave. The viewing has to come from somewhere. Viewing is a zero-sum game. It's arrogant to believe that we have this size of an audience and we're always going to have it.[22]

One difference between the cable industry and other media sectors is that the cable operators are fighting new competition from *within* the industry, at least for the present. The other media sectors are dealing increasingly with outside competition. In cable, the big services like HBO, Cable News Network (CNN), and MTV will probably each hold onto their present viewing audience but not expand it substantially, as they had become accustomed to doing. For smaller cable services, the prospect looks somewhat dimmer, with the likelihood of substantial audience losses in a more competitive industry environment.

Cable television's future lies in the development of new services. In the short term, the likeliest candidate for such expansion is **pay-per-view** (PPV) services, which provide cable subscribers with new Hollywood films and special events on demand. PPV capabilities have been installed in most major cable systems and will be available on all systems in the mid-1990s. Cable's long-range prospects lie, however, with its ability to become a full-service information and entertainment resource, supplying a wide range of multimedia products to homes. As noted earlier, the cable industry is already engaged in a political and economic battle with telephone companies to become the primary supplier of services (videotext, stereo sound, etc.) beyond its present schedule of video entertainment programs. "Cable television has become a medium that passes by 90 percent of American households," Columbia University communications expert Elie Noam points out. "It is unrealistic to assume that it will remain confined to video transmission."[23]

Given these prospects, the cable industry can probably look forward to a period of strong, steady expansion. The same cannot be said for other media sectors. Radio stations, for example, are in trouble as over 11,000 of them compete for increasingly fragmented audiences. In the Washington, D.C., area, there are 40 stations with more than 30 different program formats (soft rock, all news, classical, etc.), each designed to capture a thin and hard-to-identify slice of the local audience. With the decline of national radio networks in the 1960s, most radio stations have become local juke boxes. About half of the music they play consists of canned recordings, prepared by anonymous program packagers and delivered to the stations by satellite or telephone lines from New York and Los Angeles.[24]

The print publication industries—newspapers, magazines, books—are too varied to allow many generalizations about their future. Their common challenger can be identified, however. It is the computer. As Apple Computer's Alan Kay points out, "The computer is a new kind of medium. Gutenberg has come and we haven't recognized him yet."[25] Although the computer as a mass medium may still not be fully appreciated, the print industries have recognized its value in their internal operations. They have spent hundreds of millions of dollars in recent years computerizing the production and distribution of their standard products. A newspaper story is literally untouched by human hands these days from the time it is typed on a word processor by a newsroom reporter until it comes off the press. The entire process is computer driven.

Increasingly, the print industries are seeking electronic niches for services that can compete with such technologies as facsimile machines, consumer data networks, and compact disks that can store vast amounts of information. As we shall see, newspaper and magazine managers are actively experimenting with a wide range of techniques for delivering products to consumers via computers, television screens, and telephone networks.

The most unlikely group looking at the new electronic prospects are the old-line book publishers. A few years ago, they would have summarily dismissed any notions that their books could, or would, be read on a television screen or a computer monitor. Since then a small but growing business has developed, selling "books" transferred to compact-disk-read-only-memory (CD-ROM) devices. Hundreds of books have been published in the new format, most of them business reference or educational titles. The consumer market includes a half million or so personal computer owners whose machines are hooked up to CD-ROM drives—a potential audience of electronic book readers that is expected to number in the millions in a few years. Industry analysts estimate that a mass market will develop by the end of the decade as television sets become routinely equipped with CD-ROM capabilities.[26]

Among the print media, newspapers are in the most trouble in dealing with new competition. Their long-term woes are obscured by the fact that, overall, the industry is still profitable. In the past 20 years, newspaper managers have made some important adjustments, particularly in upgrading their production methods. Some have discovered how to adapt their product to the changing demographics and tastes of their readers.

The textbook example, of course, is *USA Today,* sent by satellite to printing plants all over the world. The paper's short, snappy stories and features are designed for an audience raised on radio and television news bulletins. Even its street dispensers are designed to look like a television set. *USA Today*'s bite-sized editorial formula has been adopted, with varying results, by other newspapers. It is clear, however, that such cosmetic changes have only a limited effect. The stubborn problem facing the newspaper business is that it is losing its future readership at an alarming rate. Many young people have never had, or have lost, the habit of reading a daily paper. Moreover, the chances of changing their habits appear slim.

This prospect was documented in a 1991 study of the industry's future commissioned by the American Society of Newspaper Editors (ASNE). Significantly, the study's title is "Keys to Our Survival." The report finds that 55 percent of all American adults read a newspaper every day. They are classified as "loyal readers," with a high regard for their daily paper and a preference for hard news. Another 26 percent are "at risk" or "potential" readers who are not regular readers. The rest—19 percent—are poor prospects or nonreaders.

The significant finding, as far as the industry's economic health is concerned, is that young people (aged 18–34) make up only 28 percent of the loyal-reader category. Speaking to the industry, the report concludes:

> Going after the at-risk and potential readers is a must. The loyal audience of regular readers is aging—mostly over 35. The at-risk and potential readers are mostly under 35. If we don't turn them into loyal readers somehow, our audience is going to disappear.[27]

The options set out in the ASNE report include recommendations that newspapers put greater emphasis on editorial materials and delivery systems tailored to the life-styles of younger people.

Among other options, the industry is looking at electronic delivery of customized editions of newspapers. The *Daily Times* becomes, in effect, the *Daily Mr. Smith.*[28] Connecticut's *Hartford Courant,* the oldest paper in the country, faxes a specialized edition of the next day's paper to subscribers each evening, with materials keyed to their individual interests. The editorial menus for such services by newspapers could include a selection of local news, financial tables, sports, and (why not?) the comics. The fax editions of the *Courant* and other newspapers are designed to meet the competition from hundreds of specialized newsletters and other news services that send materials electronically to consumers every day.

Fax delivery of newspapers may, however, be displaced by an even more advanced technology—papers delivered electronically to customers who own notebook-sized, pen-based computers. A varied menu of news and features will be offered, transmitted to subscribers through cable TV networks, direct broadcast satellites, and high-speed telephone circuits. A number of major newspaper chains are experimenting with portable electronic newspapers, in the expectation that the service will be available to the public in the late 1990s.

Finally, there is that uniquely American institution—Hollywood. Its product is shadows on a screen, a metaphor for an industry that has defied rational analysis for almost a century. Predictions of Hollywood's demise as the world's largest dream factory have been around for decades, only to be contradicted by the talents of an unlikely combination of movie executives, directors, writers, actors, and other creative artists. With less than 10 percent of global film production in any year, Hollywood still sets the pace, tone, and profitability of the movie business worldwide. Its continuing strength is a product that filmmakers in other countries have consistently attempted, and failed, to copy successfully.

Hollywood will survive and thrive through the 1990s and into the new century. Its products and prospects will, however, be different. One important factor will be a new audience profile. Young people have been the industry's ace in the hole in recent years. But that audience is shrinking demographically at a time when its attention is turning to alternative attractions. Added to this is the danger that the industry may be pricing its product out of the market in an era of $7 admission tickets.

At another level, Hollywood's dependence on outside financing has become shaky as bankers and other money sources recoil at the inflating costs of moviemaking. For example, *Jurassic Park,* the 1993 blockbuster hit, quickly recouped its $100 million costs and more. *Hudson Hawk,* an earlier Bruce Willis superflop at $50 million, did not. Moreover, this preeminently American institution may be losing control over its own management. In the early 1990s, three of the six major studios were controlled by foreign interests—two Japanese and one British.[29]

Whoever is in charge, Hollywood will have to deal with the impact of new media technologies. Forty years ago, the industry pulled itself up from potential decline by becoming a major production center for the new television industry. More recently, it has cashed in on the videocassette and cable boom. Down the road, Hollywood sees a new bonanza in the production of high-definition films for television, cable, and its own theater outlets. The latter includes the prospect of transmitting films directly to theaters by satellite, thus eliminating projection booths, duplicate prints, and other costs involved in handling conventional film distribution. Another possibility is to deliver its products by satellite to videocassette-rental stores, a project that is being tested in Japan.[30]

High-definition video is only one of the new media technologies Hollywood is looking at these days. By the end of the decade, its output will be a mix of entertainment films and some very different products. In Burbank, a division of Time Warner Inc. is developing interactive multimedia packages of books, magazines, films, and music for distribution by laser disc and cable television.[31]

Farther north, at the Skywalker Ranch near San Francisco, George Lucas, of *Star Wars* fame, is in the education business. His Lucasfilm learning division produces curriculum materials for elementary school classes. Lucasfilm educational productions combine a full range of multimedia techniques for its media-savvy audiences. The American history program includes 1,800 displays and film clips of primary source materials. It also has Map Rap, a geography lesson featuring rap music, which describes the nation's expansion from the original thirteen colonies to Alaskan statehood.[32] Map Rap may offend those who question the value of razzle-dazzle electronics to teach children. Their doubts have wider implications as similar techniques are used to market other kinds of information Americans will need in order to deal with complex issues and events in the coming years.

The film industry's most lucrative long-term prospect may lie in direct delivery of its products to home television screens on a PPV basis. PPV is already a thriving part of the cable TV business. Eventually, it will become part of a larger two-way information and entertainment delivery service, which will include interactive shopping, educational programs, and video phone calls. In 1993, Time Warner, the largest U.S. media operator, teamed up with U.S. West, a regional telephone company, in a joint venture to develop such a network.

In summary, the old-line media services are in transition to a different technological, economic, and social environment. Eventually a new mix of information resources will emerge, with many new players entering the field. Predictions about the terminal decline of present-day broadcasting, publishing, and other media sectors are, however, decidedly premature. Media managers are not going to self-destruct, lemminglike, at the thought that their products may be overtaken by new technologies. By and large, they will adapt and survive. Increasingly, their survival will depend on innovative strategies for marketing the new high-technology services. As previously noted, the memory of previous expensive failures is still very much alive in the industry. Moreover, there is no great rush of customers to embrace the new services.

A case in point is consumer data networking, which provides access to a wide range of electronic information services (shopping, banking, timetables, etc.) delivered to homes via personal computers or telephones. The often-cited success story is that of **Minitel,** a consumer data network that has been operating in France since the early 1980s. Minitel service is available in over 7 million French homes through a small computer terminal attached to the telephone. Its users have access to thousands of information services, from local train schedules to daily horoscopes. The service is cheap, paid for as part of the monthly telephone bill. Attempts to replicate Minitel's success as a mass consumer service in the United States have so far met with only modest success. Computer information networking is a large and growing industry, but it serves primarily the business community. Of its $9 billion in revenues in 1990, less than 3 percent came from home consumers.[33]

Is there a mass audience in this country for consumer data networks and related services? The question presents a chicken-and-egg dilemma. On one hand, the customers will not show up in force until a full range of services is available. On the other hand, the industry will not invest in the necessary equipment and services without reasonable expectations for a mass audience. So far, that audience has not materialized despite considerable investment in videotext projects by media firms.

The solution, more often than not, lies in innovative marketing. In the early years after World War II, the television broadcasting industry captured its mass audience initially by way of TV sets placed in bars, bowling alleys, and other public places. In the 1990s, the new media may find its audiences in equally unlikely locations, namely, the classrooms of America, from kindergartens to graduate schools. There are over 2 million computers in U.S. schools. Millions of students also have access to other computers at home. An entire computer-literate generation has grown up with Pac-man and Nintendo games, data banks, automated cash machines, videocassettes with interactive keypads, and other new-technology products. Most young people are moving into jobs in which dealing with computers, directly or indirectly, is the norm.

This is the natural audience for the computer-based media as new services are put on the market. The result will be a very different pattern of old and new media services, which can revitalize the information and entertainment industries. The London *Economist* has described the media sector as the last great all-American industry. It is no accident that the United States is the world's information bank. The roots of this accumulated wealth go back two centuries to the Bill of Rights, prohibiting government interference in the media. The First Amendment's reference point was the press, the only technology available at the time. In the intervening years, constitutional protection has been widened by law and tradition to include everything from computer data banks to rock music. Columbia University communications scholar Elie Noam proposes an updated version of the First Amendment, which would protect the right of the people to assemble electronically.

The evolving pattern of old and new media can be a powerful force for strengthening and expanding First Amendment liberties. The changes taking place open up choices about how, or even whether, the expansion will continue. Only a Pollyanna will see automatic onward-and-upward benefits. There are no guarantees that the new media mix will lead us to an information age nirvana of freedom and prosperity. Many of the signs point in other directions. Whatever their faults and failings, the older media have played a critical role in producing and distributing massive amounts of information. They have also served as agenda-setting institutions, helping to define national purpose and consensus.

Will the new mix of old and new media play a similar role? More specifically, will the vast proliferation of increasingly specialized information resources and channels be a clear benefit? Media critic Douglass Cater has some questions:

> Is the fractionalization of audiences a net social gain? . . . What happens when each minority group can tune in to its own prophets? When there are no more Walter Cronkites each evening to reassure us that despite all its afflictions the nation still stands?[34]

His questions are important in weighing the impact of current media changes. The new technology applications tend to segment and divide audiences. Are 500 cable channels—a distinct possibility by the late 1990s—an improvement over the 3 national television channels that have dominated media habits until recently? Probably yes, but the question remains.

There is a dark side to the flood of new entertainment and information resources. Media critic Neil Postman suggests that it could result in a spate of trivialized products, whose effects are to anesthetize us to realities rather than energize us to understand and act upon them.[35] He and other critics see disturbing signs that the expansion of media channels, competing for attention in a crowded market, could be dominated by a narcissistic mélange of lightweight services—"entertaining ourselves to death," to use Postman's phrase.

The new technologies may widen the distance between the information rich and the information poor in American society. The former know how to use the new resources for their personal and professional advancement. The information poor might settle for the hyped-up entertainment diversions the new channels will offer. The result could be further fragmentation of community, an increasing sense of disengagement, and greater distrust of government and other institutions that need broad consensus to be effective.

Economist Robert Reich sees that fragmentation already happening. The top fifth of working Americans take home more money than the other four-fifths combined. This affluent group is composed largely of "symbol analysts," to use his awkward phrase. In plainer English, they are the professionals who create or otherwise deal with information. In the process, Reich adds, they

> inhabit a different economy from other Americans. The new elite is linked by jet, modem, fax, satellite and fiber-optic cable to the great commercial and recreational centers of the world, but it is not particularly connected to the rest of the nation.

With their control over information, they are the movers and shakers of the country, increasingly isolated from the rest of the society, in Reich's opinion.[36]

The ultimate scenario could be a sort of benign, information-based fascism in which the elite is in effective control of the facts and figures needed to keep order in a disintegrating society. This prospect was once caricatured, not wholly in jest, by Columbia University law professor Alan Westin, who envisioned a single national data bank center in Philadelphia, run by an elite Establishment. The facility is attacked by democratic dissidents, the Fold, Staple, Spindle, and Mutilate movement. The dissidents are defeated, and the Establishment decides to program every event in every citizen's life to prevent further disruption. Professor Westin's scenario lets the dissidents win eventually, but not without some sobering insights about the relevance of information to the democratic process.

These issues of information access are often pushed aside in the rough-and-tumble of changes taking place in the media and other information areas these days. Technology and economics drive most of the decisions. It is critical, however, that machines and markets be guided by a new social consensus on the future of information resources, rooted in First Amendment traditions. The overriding issue is whether the new media are going to make us freer and more competent, individually and collectively, to deal with the complex problems of postindustrial democracy.

More than 70 years ago, Walter Lippmann, a leading journalist of the day, dealt with a similar set of issues in his book *Public Opinion,*[37] a trenchant criticism of the role of media in a democracy. Lippmann was wary of claims that citizens make their political and social decisions after an objective study of the facts. Most of our decisions are based on what he called "the pictures in our heads," that is, fixed perceptions and prejudices. The idea of informed public opinion influencing issues and actions, he argued, is largely a wishful fantasy; the business of running the country is done by elites. He was critical of American journalism in particular for failing to provide even the basic information needed to sustain a viable democratic society. Mass media can never do the job itself, Lippmann said, but it has a great responsibility to serve as both an adequate information provider and as a watchdog of the public interest. He saw the best hope in a media sector that would identify and monitor what he called "the governing forces" as a check on the ruling Establishment.

The questions Walter Lippmann raised those 70 years ago take on new meaning in the current transition to a more complex media environment. There is a sense of urgency in dealing with the issues he raised. Vincent Mosco points out that computerization—the common module for all the new media—is in its infancy: "There are still many degrees of freedom left on how to computerize. . . . Now is the time to ask hard questions since some social options remain."[38] Another media scholar, the late Ithiel de Sola Pool, summarized this imperative in his last book, *The Technologies of Freedom:*

> The onus is on us to determine whether free societies in the twenty-first century will conduct electronic communications under the conditions of freedom established for the domain of print through centuries of struggle, or whether that great achievement will become lost in a confusion about the new technologies.[39]

In the chapters that follow, we look at the technological, economic, and social forces affecting the new media environment in which these choices will be made.

NOTES

1. "Big Three's '91 Financial Results Advertise a Bad Year," *Broadcasting,* 13 April 1992, p. 4.
2. The most convenient survey of the current state of American information industries can be found in the annual *U.S. Industrial Outlook,* published each January by the International Trade Administration, U.S. Department of Commerce, Washington, D.C.
3. George Gilder, *Life After Television* (Knoxville, Tenn.: Whittle Direct Books, 1990), 23–37.
4. For an interesting discussion of the complicated nature of mass communications, see Robert Escarpit, "The Concept of 'Mass'," *Journal of Communication* 29, no. 2 (Spring 1977): 44–47.
5. For a useful description of the new media packagers, see Anthony Smith, *The Age of the Behemoths,* a Twentieth Century Fund Paper (New York: Priority Press Publications, 1991); also Greg MacDonald, *The Emergence of Global Multi-Media Conglomerates,* Working Paper No. 70, Multinational Enterprises Program (Geneva, Switzerland: International Labor Organization, 1990).
6. Multimedia information packaging is not a new idea. The original media packager was William Randolph Hearst, early in this century. Beginning with a large chain of news-

papers, he expanded his operations to include Hollywood films, newsreels, magazines, and other enterprises. See Leo Bogart, *The American Media System and Its Commercial Culture,* Occasional Paper No. 8 (New York: Gannett Foundation Media Center, March 1991), 4.

7. For a useful survey of the leading information packagers, see Bronwen Maddox, "Headline Makers," *Financial Times* (London), 17 December 1991, p. 16.
8. McLuhan's prophetic views on the new media are scattered throughout his books, including *The Gutenberg Galaxy* (Toronto: University of Toronto Press, 1962) and *Understanding Media,* 2d ed. (New York: New American Library, 1964).
9. The most comprehensive study of the new information impact on American society is *The Information Economy,* 9 vols., Office of Telecommunications Special Publication 77-12, U.S. Department of Commerce, 1977. See also "Too Many Words," *Economist* (London), 20 August 1983, p. 79.
10. For a useful discussion of this issue, see "Children and Television: Growing up in a Media World," special issue of *Media & Values* no. 52-53 (Fall 1990/Winter 1992).
11. Gilder, *Life After Television,* 36.
12. Richard Clurman, *To the End of Time* (New York: Simon & Schuster, 1992), 114–121.
13. "Cable Networks See Dimmer Future," *New York Times,* 7 July 1991, p. D-1.
14. Richard Maisel, "Decline of the Mass Media," *Public Opinion Quarterly* 37, no. 2 (Summer 1973): 159–170.
15. Florence Setzer and Jonathan Levy, *Broadcast Television in a Multichannel Marketplace,* OPP Working Paper No. 26, Federal Communications Commission, Washington, D.C., June 1991, p. 15.
16. Ibid.
17. Ibid., p. ix.
18. "Turner Aims to Line Up Captive Audience," *Wall Street Journal,* 21 April 1991, p. B-1.
19. "One for the Good Buddies," *Washington Post,* Washington Business supplement, 17 September 1992, p. 3.
20. "Judge Allows Phone Companies to Provide Information Services," *New York Times,* 26 July 1991, p. 1.
21. "The Advertising Market," in Setzer and Levy, *Broadcast Television,* 112–134.
22. "Cable Networks See Dimmer Future."
23. Quoted in "Cable TV Battling Phone Companies," *New York Times,* 29 March 1992, p. 1.
24. "Format Suppliers' Future in Fragmentation," *Broadcasting,* 8 July 1991, p. 40.
25. Frank Rose, "Pied Piper of the Computer," *New York Times Magazine,* 8 November 1987, p. 56.
26. "Lean, Green and on the Screen," *Economist* (London), 13 July 1991, p. 96.
27. *Keys to Our Survival,* American Society of Newspaper Editors, Reston, Va., July 1991, p. 4.
28. Norman Macrae, "The Next Ages of Man," special section of *Economist* (London), 24 December 1988, p. 15.
29. For a useful summary of overall changes in the film industry, see "In Hollywood, Big Just Gets Bigger," *New York Times,* 14 October 1990, p. F-12.
30. "Japanese Vidstores to Get Pix via Satellite, HDTV," *Variety,* 21 October 1991, p. 57.
31. Kim Sudhalter, "Warner New Media Leads Hollywood into the Computer Age," *Instruction Delivery Systems* 2, no. 1 (July–August 1991): 10–13.
32. Fred Bonner, "IVD Learning: Design for Discovery," *Instruction Delivery Systems* 2, no. 1 (July-August 1991): 14–16.
33. "'Baby Bells' Explore Phone's Future," *Washington Post,* 27 July 1991, p. F-1.
34. Douglass Cater, "A Communications Revolution?" *Wall Street Journal,* 6 August 1973, p. 18.

35. Neil Postman, *Amusing Ourselves to Death: Public Discourse in the Age of Show Business* (New York: Penguin Books, 1986).
36. Robert Reich, "Secession of the Successful," *New York Times Magazine,* 20 January 1991, p. 16. See also "The Information Gap," a special issue of *Journal of Communication* 39, no. 3 (Summer 1989).
37. Walter Lippmann, *Public Opinion* (New York: Harcourt Brace, 1922).
38. Quoted in Vincent Mosco, *The Pay-Per Society: Computers and Communications in the Information Age* (Norwood, N.J.: Ablex Publishing Co., 1989), 67.
39. Ithiel de Sola Pool, *The Technologies of Freedom* (Cambridge, Mass.: Harvard University Press, 1983), 10.

Chapter

2

NEW MEDIA TECHNOLOGIES: THE INFORMATION MACHINES

The scenario is a familiar one: predictions about the glittering future that advanced media services will play in our lives. They suggest an electronic Utopia, where we sit at home or in offices with our multimedia consoles plugged into a world of vast information resources. It is a crisp, clean world, full of the promise that most, if not all, problems are solvable because we have full access to the facts.[1] The prospect is intriguing but decidedly premature. Dramatic changes are indeed taking place in mass communications, but the road ahead is marked with as many pitfalls as opportunities. In this chapter, we look at the information technologies that will determine the shape and direction of the mass media in the coming decade.

The current changes are the third major transformation in mass-media technologies in modern times. The first took place in the middle of the past century, with the introduction of steam-powered printing presses and cheap pulp paper. The result was the first true mass media—the "penny press" newspapers and large-scale book and magazine publishing industries. The second transformation occurred earlier in this century with the introduction of over-the-air broadcasting—radio in 1920 and television in 1939. The third mass-media transformation—the one we are now experiencing—involves a transition to computer-based production, storage, and distribution of information and entertainment. It brings us to the world of multimedia computers, compact disks, hand-held data banks, national fiber-optic networks, advanced facsimile messaging, and other services that did not exist a dozen years ago.

This new media pattern is qualitatively different from earlier ones in several ways. One technology—computerization—is now the module for all forms of information production: sound, video, and print. As a result, computers are forcing a massive restructuring of older media services and, at the same time, creating a new set of competing services. Traditional lines between one medium and another erode when they share a common computer module. Fax machines are newspapers. Compact disks are books. Satellites are television transmitters. The old distinctions are smudged as computers transform traditional products and add new ones. Technology has always been important in defining the mass media and how they perform. It will become more so in the coming decade as the media industries adjust to new operational and product opportunities.

Until now, new information technologies served mainly the needs of big business and big government—the institutions that could pay for (and, in effect, subsidize) the electronic expansion of the American information structure in the past 30 years.[2] The coming decade will, however, see the rapid consumerization of these advanced information resources. The mass media will be a primary beneficiary of this change as communications networks are expanded to supply electronic services to homes and other consumer locations.[3]

This shift to consumer services is paced by the technological merging of two familiar machines—computers and television sets. Computers are becoming more like television sets; television sets are being computerized. The result is a new kind of electronic hybrid, the telecomputer. A consumer-friendly device, the telecomputer will eventually replace old-fashioned TV receivers, as well as personal computers, videocassette recorders, game machines, digital record players, and the other electronic gadgets that clutter up American homes.[4]

Television sets will be transformed from passive receivers of distant pictures into multimedia interactive instruments, capable of handling all types of video, data, or sound services. The primary channel delivering these services to homes will probably be fiber-optic cables, each with a capacity of hundreds of interactive video channels and thousands of two-way data links. For the first time, a full range of media, both old and new, will be available electronically to home consumers.

What will this new technology-driven pattern look like? We can see its broad outlines with some rough certainty for perhaps a decade into the future. Beyond that, the vision blurs. Predicting the impact of new technologies is a risky business. Even the astute managers at IBM, that bastion of sophisticated technologies, sometimes get it wrong. In the late 1940s, they predicted the worldwide market potential of their newfangled mainframe computers at about a dozen machines. More recently, in 1981, when IBM marketed its first personal computer (PC), company executives projected that overall sales would be about a quarter million machines. Since then, over 50 million of the small computers, built by IBM and its competitors, have been sold in the United States.[5] IBM's corporate blind spots in measuring the market for its products put the firm in good company. Alexander Graham Bell saw only a narrow usefulness for his telephone invention. He thought its primary value was as a transmitter of musical concerts and other entertainment into homes. It was the relatively unknown Theodore Vail, an early president of Bell's telephone company, who recognized the possibilities for a national telephone network connecting people. Vail understood, as Bell did not, the wider social and economic implications of telephone technology. The critical decisions in the adoption of any technology, in fact, are made overwhelmingly on political and economic grounds.[6]

This is a point to keep in mind as we survey the range of technologies available for expanded mass-media services in the coming decade. Many promising technologies will fall by the wayside because they do not fit a clear economic or social need. In the competitive scramble to exploit new techniques, there will be both corporate winners and corporate losers. None of the players involved knows for certain the size and shape of the market for new services.

Their doubts are reinforced by a record of failures in recent years to sell the new electronic services. In most cases these projects ran up against a stone wall of consumer resistance to the glitzy new products, no matter what advantages they promised. Despite that experience, most major media firms are committing large amounts of money and other resources to advanced services. Increasingly, media executives are caught up in tough decisions on how to manage the new opportunities. Whatever their private hesitations about the prospects for success, they know that they cannot afford to be left behind in an increasingly competitive, technology-intensive marketplace.

Two basic technologies are forcing these decisions—advanced computers and high-capacity telecommunications circuits. Together they are creating an information structure that is reshaping American society and, by extension, the rest of the world. Michael Dertouzos, chief of the Massachusetts Institute of Technology (MIT) Laboratory for Computer Sciences, predicted awesome results from the growing integration of computers and communications:

> This relentless compounding of capabilities has transformed a faint promise of synergy into an immense and real potential. . . . These two giants, computers and networks, can be fused to form an infrastructure even more promising than the individual technologies.[7]

Mass media are a small part of the social and economic institutions being shaped by this change. Banks and other financial organizations, for example, are almost totally dependent on the new computer/communications links. The media sector is just beginning to catch up. Increasingly, it sees its future role as that of an electronic supplier of information and entertainment products.

The key to this shift is a fingernail-sized device shared by computers and communications machines. It is the semiconductor chip, the building block of the information age. Most electronic advances in recent decades are based on improvements in chip technology. A new generation of more efficient chips has emerged every two years on average since the first silicon semiconductor devices were developed in the 1960s. Theologians once pondered the question of how many angels could dance on the head of a pin. Semiconductor engineers now ask how many transistors can fit on a silicon flake. Currently, an ordinary commercial chip can accommodate 4 million transistors. And that capacity will increase to hundreds of millions within the next decade.[8]

Advanced chip technology is responsible for the steady shrinkage of computers from room-sized boxes to hand-held devices, simultaneously increasing their computing power a hundred times over. A recent technology—the **flash-memory chip**—will result in even smaller computers. Unlike earlier chips, flash-memory chips retain information when the computer is turned off. This makes it unnecessary to use bulky disk-drive storage systems in lightweight devices such as laptop and hand-held computers. In 1992, a major semiconductor producer, Intel, introduced the flash card, an array of flash chips on a two-ounce plastic card, which can hold as much data as a PC hard disk. The result will be to put enormous amounts of media and other information resources literally into the hands of consumers. By 1993, Sony Corp. had introduced a hand-held, chip-filled Data Discman, an early version of the scaled-down storage devices to come.[9]

The prototype for consumer information-storage devices may be Newton, Apple Computer's entry into the sweepstakes to move computer power from the desktop to the coat pocket. Introduced in 1992, Newton is a videocassette-sized machine designed to be a notepad, diary, fax machine, and data terminal. In addition to its built-in storage capabilities, Newton plugs into a vast array of computer networks. It is designed for easy information access, allowing users to retrieve directly the data they want, without going through the step-by-step procedures needed with older computers.[10] In promoting Newton, Apple will compete in the mid-1990s with a "personal communicator"—a combined pocket telephone and computer—developed by an international consortium that includes AT&T and Matsushita, the Japanese electronics giant.[11]

Chip-based technologies are transforming the media industries in two ways: first, in the computerization of information production and second, in the distribution of media products over high-capacity communications circuits. Although these functions will eventually converge in a single information utility, they are still distinct enough to be looked at separately.

In this chapter, we will survey the technologies that are changing the way media services are produced. In the next chapter, we will examine the role of high-tech communications channels in distributing these services.

First, computers in their many forms: Until recently, media organizations generally lagged in supplying computer-based products to consumers. The reason, in large part, was that home computers and related equipment have not been available on a mass scale. This is changing as computers become a taken-for-granted consumer product. As a result, the market prospects for a new range of computer-based media products have improved dramatically.

Before that happened, the media industries had used computers primarily to improve their internal operations. This began with routine administrative chores such as payrolls, customer billing, and inventories. By the 1980s, however, computers were being put to use extensively in media production. Newspapers took the lead by introducing word processing terminals in newsrooms, replacing typewriters. Stories could be written and edited more quickly, then sent electronically to production facilities as part of a continuous computer-driven process. In recent years, newsroom computing has become more sophisticated, with electronic mail and on-line data retrieval added to conventional word processing capabilities.

Another change has been the increasing use of portable computers. Reporters carry them along to news events, punching in their stories as they happen, then transmitting them directly via telephone lines to their editors. A striking example of laptop journalism took place during the 1991 Persian Gulf war. Print reporters in the war zone made use of an ingenious small suitcase, known as Mascot Nomad. It contains a minicomputer, an omnidirectional aerial, and a telex printer. The aerial permitted direct transmission to a communications satellite 2,000 miles away in space, which relayed news reports to telex printers at news organizations around the world.[12] Meanwhile, television journalists covering the war sent live video reports to their home offices from small, portable Earth terminals via a satellite stationed above the Indian Ocean.[13]

Editorial computerization has been expanded with the introduction of desktop publishing—the editing and layout of newspapers and other publications on small computers. Text, photos, and graphics are assembled electronically in a variety of page layouts, then transmitted for final printing. Desktop publishing techniques are used widely by most newspaper, magazine, and book publishers, but it has been a special boon to small publishers by cutting costs and providing a more attractive product.

A newer, high-tech variation on desktop publishing is video composing. Used extensively in the television and film industries, this technique goes beyond ordinary desktop manipulation of print and graphics by incorporating sound and video. As a print reporter rearranges sentences and paragraphs on a word processor, a video composer can assemble sight, sound, and print materials in any combination, creating different versions (including a choice of hundreds of colors) and storing them on a compact disk before selecting the best combination for the finished film or videotape product. Video composing, also known as nonlinear editing, may eventually replace videotape in television and film studios. By 1993, a number of companies were marketing tapeless recording machines, capable of storing animation, graphics, and video for news, entertainment, and other programming.[14]

Meanwhile, print publishers are turning to computers to store information both for internal editorial uses and for new consumer sales opportunities. Newspapers and magazines, in particular, have accumulated vast amounts of data over the years, which can be marketed in new ways. Traditionally, this information was stored in file cabinets, with a high probability that much of it would be misplaced or otherwise lost and forgotten. A generation ago, microfilm technology brought a measure of efficiency to such information storage, but it tended to be an awkward means of retrieving information.

Microfilm archives are now being replaced by videotext, stored in computers or on compact disks. In the process, a new and potentially profitable revenue source, videotext publishing, is opening up for the newspaper and magazine industries. The pioneer in exploiting this resource was the *New York Times,* whose managers decided in the late 1960s to store the contents of the newspaper in a computer and to market the information as videotext. The New York Times Information Bank provides summaries or the full text of all stories immediately after their original publication in the *Times*. When an Information Bank subscriber requests material, it is sent by phone line to the subscriber's computer. The bank has been expanded to include videotext materials from dozens of other newspapers and magazines as well.[15]

In the 1980s, a number of news organizations followed the *New York Times* lead in marketing information electronically. An early and successful entrant was Dow Jones, publisher of the *Wall Street Journal* and other financial publications. The Dow Jones News/Retrieval Service offers 60 on-line financial and business data services. McGraw-Hill makes most of its magazines and newsletters available in electronic formats. Another major videotext provider is Reuters. This old-line British news agency has developed its computerized financial data videotext services to the point where its news operations account for less than 10 percent of the firm's revenues.

Supplying business firms and other organizations with on-line data services is a thriving part of the publishing business these days. The next step is to expand electronic delivery of news and related information into a wider consumer market. The interest of publishers in this subject has been spurred, in part, by the profitable data bank activities of companies outside the traditional media sector. One of the largest, Mead Data Central, was primarily a paper manufacturer before it became a power in the on-line-data business. Mead Data now manages, among other data services, the New York Times Information Bank. The company claims that its basic data service, Nexis, is the world's largest commercial videotext library, with more than 650 full-text sources of news, business, and trade information. Other firms operating data bank networks are several aircraft manufacturers such as Boeing and McDonnell Douglas. General Electric (GE) was an early entrant into the field. Its GE Information Services may be the most extensive commercial on-line data networker in the world, operating on all continents.

Each of these organizations supplies videotext data that are accessed by computers over ordinary telephone lines or private-line networks. Until recently, most of their customers have been business and government organizations, which could afford the relatively high costs of these services. However, the market picture is changing. Electronic data delivery is evolving as a consumer service, which represents both a competitive threat and a product opportunity for print publishing and other media.

The potential extent of the shift to consumer-based networks is illustrated by the activities of the largest publisher in the world—the United States government. Traditionally, the government has distributed a great number of printed publications, from its best-selling *Baby Care* manual to NASA's maps of Mars, through the U.S. Government Printing Office (GPO). By the early 1990s, however, only 35 percent of government publications were still available in print through the GPO; the rest could be accessed only electronically through 1,200 dial-up videotext services.[16]

Given these changes in the information market, newspapers and other publishing firms are taking a fresh look at consumer electronic services. They want to avoid the mistakes of the early 1980s, when a number of American media groups made premature forays into electronic publishing. Time Inc., the Knight-Ridder newspaper chain, the *Los Angeles Times-Mirror,* and CBS, among others, invested millions of dollars in computerized data services. In each case, they were unsuccessful, bedeviled by inadequate technology, weak products, and massive consumer indifference.[17]

The new entrants hope to repeat the initial success enjoyed by a number of recent European ventures into large-scale consumer videotext services. The most extensive of these ventures is Minitel, managed by France Telecom, the French national phone system. Minitel technology consists of a small computer monitor attached to home telephones. The Minitel service was originally intended only to supply phone-directory information, replacing printed directories. More recently, Minitel has expanded into a full-scale videotext service, with over 7 million installations in homes, businesses, and other locations. Subscribers have access to data banks run by over 17,000 information services, ranging from daily horoscopes to weather reports.[18]

The new American videotext services are counting on two recent developments to spur their plans for marketing videotext services on a mass scale. The first is a rapid increase in the number of data banks oriented to consumer interests. The second is the presence in American homes of over 20 million personal computers, most of them capable of accessing videotext sources. By 1993, almost 3 million households subscribed to computer-based information services delivered via phone lines, doubling the number that had access two years earlier.

This potential market has attracted new investors, most notably Sears Roebuck and IBM. The two firms have made a major commitment to Prodigy, a full-scale attempt to establish a national data service oriented to consumer needs. Prodigy offers such features as home shopping, travel guides, restaurant ratings, an encyclopedia, games, news, stock prices, weather reports, bill-paying services, and an electronic-mail network.[19] It is the largest of the consumer videotext services, subscribed to by about 6 percent of the households with computers that could run Prodigy in 1993. Its competitors include **CompuServe,** a division of H&R Block, General Electric's Genie, and America Online. In 1993, GTE Corp. entered the competition with its Main Street system, a data service delivered to homes via cable TV networks rather than over telephone lines. Main Street uses a remote-control device that connects subscribers to a wide variety of services, including interactive games, data banks, and electronic banking. Main Street's managers are betting that most electronic information customers will prefer to interact with large-screen TV monitors rather than with computer terminals. GTE's plans call for 20 percent penetration of the country's 60 million cable homes by 1997.[20] Main Street will face formidable competition from Prodigy, whose managers plan a similar menu of interactive services delivered to TV sets.

Telephone companies have also entered the competition to provide similar services. In 1991, a federal court canceled most of the restrictions on their participation in such activities.[21] Immediately after the decision, U.S. West, a regional phone company, announced a joint venture with France Telecom to provide Minitel-type services in the Midwest. The first installation involved a million phone subscribers in the Minneapolis–St. Paul area. By 1993, most of the other regional Bell telephone companies had similar plans to offer videotext services to their customers.[22] We take a closer look at the commercial prospects for these ventures in the next chapter. Here we survey the technological structure within which advanced information networks, competing with the older mass media, will operate.

The variety, as well as the availability, of these networks is expanding steadily. One of the newest types consists of information kiosks—computer booths located in public places. Equipped with colorful graphics and sound, the kiosks provide various services, from supplying consumer information to allowing users to order up goods and services by touching the computer screen. The state of California has experimented with a kiosk system (Info/California) that provides its citizens with a range of resources, including job listings, information on AIDS testing, an electronic application for a fishing license, and a summary of state recreational facilities. One 1992 survey indicated that there were about 60,000 kiosks in use throughout the United States, many of them in shopping malls.[23] An advanced electronic kiosk, developed by the Xerox Corp., was demonstrated at the 1992 summer Olympics in Barcelona. Over 600 Xerox Information Points were installed at Olympic sites, each with a touch-sensitive screen permitting users to call up information in four languages on the progress of the games.[24]

For the present, electronic data networks do not represent a serious economic threat to traditional information media. Prodigy, the biggest of the new videotext services, had fewer than 2 million subscribers by 1993. By and large, its services are seen by subscribers as additions to, not replacements for, newspapers and other media sources.[25]

This may change as more sophisticated electronic information services become available later in the decade. Prodigy and similar networks provide a useful but essentially static product (i.e., print videotext with color graphics on a small computer screen). A combination of two newer technologies could change this, transforming Prodigy-type services into more direct competitors of newspapers, television, radio, and cable systems. The two technologies are multimedia computers and advanced **compact disks** (CDs). Taken together, they add a dramatic dimension to electronic delivery of information and entertainment services to mass audiences. Both technologies are poised for full-scale entry into consumer markets by the mid-1990s. Given this prospect, it is useful to look at their technical capabilities and their prospects for becoming an innovative force in the mix of old and new media.

First, CDs, already a familiar consumer item as a provider of high-fidelity music recordings: By 1993, almost half of U.S. homes had a CD audio player. The CD music business will continue to flourish, but it represents a very limited use of disk technology. Disks can also store enormous amounts of print data, as well as graphics and video programming. The entire contents of the *Encyclopaedia Britannica* can be put on a single disk, using CD-ROM technology. One commercially available disk includes a directory of 9 million U.S. business firms. A flourishing industry for putting printed materials on CDs already exists. One of its customers is the U.S. Navy, which has transferred to a handful of CDs the 26 tons of technical documents previously required for each of its cruisers.[26] CD technology also makes it easier to store photographs, charts, and other images. About 10,000 images can be stored on a single disk the size of a compact music disc.[27]

In the early decades of the next century, such information storage capacities may be eclipsed by a light-sensitive plastic memory device the size of a sugar cube. An early prototype, developed at the University of California's Irvine campus, has the potential for storing 6.5 *trillion* bits of information—the contents of a million books. This is roughly 2,000 times more data than can be stored in one of today's commercial computers.[28]

Another competitor to disk storage, already in production, is the laser-based tape system, whose storage capacities represent a quantum leap over present-day magnetic tapes. A 12-inch laser-tape reel can store the same amount of data as 170 CDs or 5,000 magnetic-tape cartridges.[29]

Increasingly, videotext disks are being marketed as a mass-consumer product. By 1992, the cost of adding a CD-ROM drive to a PC had dropped to $500.[30] The number of PCs with built-in CD-ROM drives reached over a half million units by 1993. As a result, book publishers and computer software firms are offering consumer-oriented disks for the first time.[31] Microsoft Corp.'s "library" includes a full range of reference works such as *American Heritage Library* and *Bartlett's Quotations.* The Oxford University Press offers its 12-volume *Oxford English Dictionary* on a single disk. Another firm sells the complete works of Shakespeare on two disks, priced under $50.

In addition to CD attachments for PCs, manufacturers are marketing portable CD-player devices. Sony's Data Discman, a hand-held device, provides printed text as well as CD-quality music, still pictures, and speech. Data Discman's software library includes, among other features, 11 dictionaries, language lessons, travel guides, quiz games, and the Bible. Meanwhile, Sony has developed a "subminiature disk," about half the size of present ones, which can hold the equivalent of 32,000 pages of double-spaced typed pages.[32]

The greater promise for the media industries, however, lies in a more advanced disk format that can supply a full range of sound, video, and data information on a single disk. This is multimedia CD-I, the abbreviation for **compact disk interactive.** CD-I uses computer and laser technology to produce high-quality sound, pictures, graphics, and text through an attachment to a television set or a computer. The user interacts with the device, using a keyboard or remote-control pad to access "pages" of multimedia information stored on the disks.[33]

By the early 1990s, multimedia disks were already being used extensively in the business sector as a training aid. Schools and libraries also began to see the educational possibilities of the technology. One of the more innovative early experiments in this field is being carried out by the Library of Congress. Its American Memory project puts significant parts of its American history collection on disks for distribution to schools and libraries as teaching aids. The disks offer a multimedia panorama of U.S. history, including nineteenth-century photographs of the opening of the West, films of President William McKinley, and sound recordings of Presidents Warren Harding and Calvin Coolidge.[34]

Another unusual multimedia educational project is the *Interactive Encyclopaedia of Jewish Heritage and the Holocaust* at the Museum of Jewish Heritage in Washington, which opened in 1993. The encyclopedia integrates computers, CDs, videotape, and film in an exhibit designed to acquaint visitors with the museum's holdings. Visitors can "browse" through the materials or go directly to a subject of individual interest. For example, someone interested in a particular Jewish community in pre–World War II Poland could read its history, view a film and photographs of the community, hear a popular song from the region, and study street maps of the town.

Multimedia technologies are expanding quickly beyond business and educational uses. Consumer-oriented disks are being marketed that cover a wide range of information and entertainment applications, including the next generation of Nintendo-type games and Walkman-type data storage units. Charlotte Wolter, editor of *Video Technology News,* predicts an annual multimedia market of $24 billion later in the decade.

The introduction of the first consumer-market CD-I player in 1992 by Holland's Philips Company quickened media industry interest in the technology. Marketed as the "first family-oriented multimedia system," the Philips CD-I disks can be displayed on ordinary home TV receivers. Along with its interactive machines, Philips developed an impressive array of disks, heavily weighted toward children's interests. One disk, *Children's Bible Stories: Noah's Ark,* tells the traditional story, adding related interactive games, puzzles, and coloring exercises. Describing another disk, *Cartoon Jukebox,* the Philips CD-I catalog stated:

> Children color characters from favorite tunes, then watch each cartoon come alive
> in these colors in dazzling original animation and song! Over 50 pages of cartoons,
> plus interactive games and features.

In 1993, Philips expanded its catalog of CD-I offerings to include Hollywood films on 5-inch disks.

Philips will face strong competition from Japanese companies that are targeting the market for CD-I players. In late 1992, Sony and Nintendo joined forces to sell a CD-I player designed specifically for the popular Nintendo video games. Among the U.S. companies that have begun producing CD-I entertainment and information disks are Time Warner, ABC–Capital Cities, Turner Broadcasting, and the Children's Television Workshop.[35] ABC News Interactive is focusing on the education market. Turner is recycling its vast store of archival news material as software for interactive digital and CD-ROM products.

This first generation of multimedia products has demonstrated the technological possibilities of the disks, as well as some problems. Consumer resistance to the high price of CD-I players is a major barrier. When it was first introduced, the Philips player cost nearly $1000. By 1993, that price had been lowered to around $500 in discount stores. Another problem is lack of electronics industry agreement on technical standards for CD-I machines. The result could be a replay of the 1980s battle for technical dominance between Betamax and VHS formats in videocassette recorders. Failure to get industry agreement on a common standard could slow down introduction of advanced CD products.[36] Meanwhile, production of CD products is booming. By 1992, the *CD-ROM Periodical Index* listed over 30,000 periodicals and books issued by 2,000 organizations.

Multimedia disk technology will become a strong challenger (and product opportunity) for the traditional media in the latter half of the 1990s. One force propelling it will be the parallel development of a new generation of computers. In *Alice's Adventures in Wonderland,* Alice wonders, "What is the use of a book without pictures or conversation?" Neither she, nor Lewis Carroll, could have imagined multimedia computers, a stunning advance on today's one-dimensional machines, limited to storing and processing words or simple graphics. Multimedia computers are a high-tech hybrid, providing still photographs and moving images on the same screen with text, as well as high-fidelity sound and other features.[37] The technological key to the new computers is high-capacity chips, which can handle prodigious amounts of graphic or video images for instant replay. Built-in speakers supply stereo music or the spoken word, including synthesized voice. Multimedia computers can be linked to data, voice, or video networks. Their storage capabilities can be upgraded with CD-I disks, each with a greater memory capacity than dozens of conventional disks.

The major weakness of the first multimedia disks was their inability to provide sustained full-motion color video. The problem was in the large memory requirements for storing video images on chips. That limitation is being steadily reduced by new techniques for producing multimedia effects on conventional computers. Kodak and Sony have each developed equipment that links the videocassette and computer technologies. Sony's product, known as V/Box, allows a Macintosh or IBM PC to control a number of separate video systems simultaneously.

In a related development, Apple Computers has introduced a multimedia software standard, *Quicktime,* for its Macintosh computers. Quicktime adds such capabilities as film animation, video teleconferencing over standard telephone lines, and video images for later playback. In 1992, Warner New Media issued the first of a series of CD-ROM entertainment disks based on Quicktime technology. Entitled *Funny: The Movie in Quicktime,* the disk features a hundred film and TV personalities telling their favorite jokes and stories. Although Apple has been a pioneer in multimedia hardware, other computer firms jumping into the market include IBM, Microsoft, and the ever-present Japanese firms. Radio Shack—the Tandy Corporation's electronics stores—took an early lead in marketing low-priced computers to support the new multimedia standards.[38]

These developments will introduce multimedia computing to a large consumer audience, made up initially of individuals who are experienced PC users.[39] This will not, however, create a new mass market for multimedia products very quickly. Only about 25 percent of U.S. homes were equipped with PCs in 1992. The percentage is increasing steadily, but it will take the rest of the decade before a significant number of home computers have multimedia capabilities. A different kind of multimedia delivery is needed to bring a full range of information and entertainment services to a mass audience. For the media industries, this prospect is an important key to expanding their consumer markets in the next decade.

What will the new machines look like? Until now, multimedia technology has evolved largely as a high-tech extension of conventional computers. The next generation of computers will, of course, contain many multimedia applications for business and professional uses. However, multimedia machines for home entertainment and information purposes will probably not look like computers. They will more closely resemble television receivers, albeit with capabilities well beyond today's primitive sets. The consumer market for advanced media services will not emerge fully until video, sound, and data technologies are integrated in a single household machine.

The result will be the telecomputer, supplying multimedia services to homes via high-capacity cable or satellite channels. In addition to these links from outside the home, telecomputers will be equipped with interactive CD capabilities. Consumer telecomputers (or "smart TV" as they are sometimes called) could become the master link, supplying both conventional and new media services to mass audiences at home and in other locations.[40] Telecomputers will come in different formats. One possibility is to hang them on a wall. In 1993, Xerox Corp. announced that it had developed a flat panel no thicker than a pad of paper that combined HDTV and multimedia computer functions.

When will telecomputers be available? MIT's Media Lab, among other research units, has been working on prototype versions of telecomputers since the early 1980s. In 1991, the lab's associate director, Andrew Lippman, declared that telecomputing's time had come:

> Forget television sets. In three years, there won't be any. Instead there will be computers with high-quality display screens. Inside, there will be digital instructions allowing them to receive ABC, HBO, BBC and anything we can dream up.[41]

Other computer enthusiasts are not as optimistic about the timing of telecomputing's arrival on the scene. No one in the media industry seriously questions that consumer multimedia resources will be increasingly common by the end of the decade. Whether telecomputers will become the dominant deliverers of multimedia services is still an open question. These doubts do not extend, however, to the computer industry. Its leaders see multimedia in all its forms as their chance to replicate the successes they have had with small computers.

John Sculley, former head of Apple Computers, summarizes these hopes: "Multimedia will change the world in the 1990s as personal computers did in the 1980s." Microsoft Corporation's William Gates, the wunderkind of the computer industry in recent years, is even more expansive: "Multi-media will be bigger than everything we do today."[42] IBM has been the laggard in the race to multimedia. By 1993, however, it had set up a multimedia division and was actively negotiating with film and television companies for joint ventures in interactive media services.[43]

The prospects for a large-scale multimedia market were enhanced in October 1992, when a consortium of 13 technology companies, including Apple Computer, Eastman Kodak, and Corning, formed a consortium to develop multimedia products for American homes.[44] Skeptics question, however, whether home telecomputers and other multimedia machines will attract customers quite as fast as industry enthusiasts suggest. They point out that the first generation of telecomputers will be priced well above the average consumer's reach. One early version, put on the market in 1991 by Frax Inc., a California firm, had a $7000 price tag.

A number of technological problems must be mastered before telecomputers become an affordable mass-consumption product. One of these is the technology of digital compression—the squeezing of data into a more compact form for electronic storage and transmission. The data can be in video, audio, or print form or any combination of the three. Video displays, in particular, call for enormous compression power, involving millions of calculations every second.

As we have seen, chip technology has advanced rapidly to meet the storage needs of advanced multimedia devices. The problem now is upgrading the networks that will link telecomputers to information and entertainment resources outside the home. This requires replacing most of the present equipment in telephone, broadcasting, and other telecommunications systems—an expensive and time-consuming process. Many of these systems still transmit analog signals, a nineteenth-century technology that gave us telephones and broadcasting but that is increasingly obsolete in the computer era. Analog signals can handle only one application at a time, say, a music record, a TV show, or a phone call. They copy the shape, timing, and type of signal they record, in effect tying the receiver (phone, TV set, etc.) to the transmitter in lockstep fashion.

The digital signals needed for telecomputers and other high-tech machines are more flexible. Based on binary digits—the on-off codes manipulated by computers—they make no distinction between video, sound, or data transmissions. They can handle them all in a single stream, originating, storing, editing, transmitting, or receiving messages at increasingly faster computer speeds.[45] Eventually, all the world's telephone, broadcasting, and data networks will be digitized. The changeover has important implications for telecomputers and for the mass media—both old and new—which will supply information and entertainment programming to them.

The process will be hastened as a result of breakthroughs in digital television technology. Until very recently, digital television was regarded as a long-term prospect given the enormous computational requirements involved in video images. In order to achieve smooth motion, digitized video must be displayed at a minimum of 30 frames per second. One minute of digitized video requires about 2 *billion* bytes of storage on semiconductor chips. It takes hours, using older chip technology, to transmit a useful amount of video programming. The problem is being resolved with a new generation of chips that compress the digitized video signals (expressed in symbolic ones and twos), which are then transmitted electronically through cables or over the air to be decompressed at the receiving end. What is being transmitted is a series of still-image frames, which are displayed in quick succession. The human eye cannot pick out the changes from one frame to another, seeing, rather, a running picture.

Digital television receivers for household use are now emerging from the research labs and on to production lines, the forerunners of the new generation of multimedia telecomputers.[46] Digitization will transform television in much the same way that digitized CD technology has changed the musical recording world. Present-day TV sets will become relics. The new sets will not only display a much better television picture but also serve as an all-purpose telecomputing system, offering a wide range of information and entertainment services piped into homes from outside suppliers or from interactive CD resources built into the set. The telecomputer will be a central feature of what industry enthusiasts call "the smart house," in which computerization becomes an essential part of domestic life.[47]

Media companies are only beginning to identify the opportunities (and pitfalls) in adjusting to consumer markets based on telecomputing in the home. What was once a media executive's pipe dream is now a direct challenge. The critical technical component—the semiconductor chips that can handle the massive compression requirements—are already in production. One California company, Integrated Information Technologies, began delivering such chips commercially in 1991, with a $150 price tag per chip.[48] Predictably, the big Japanese companies that have dominated the American consumer electronics market for years are racing to produce telecomputer products.

These developments speed up the timetable for the introduction of consumer telecomputing. Until recently, it was scheduled to take place sometime after the turn of the century. That estimate is currently being revised in favor of an earlier date. The prospect was enhanced in the early 1990s when the FCC set new rules for introducing HDTV, the technology that will provide dramatically improved TV displays. At that time, the FCC, which must decide on HDTV's technical standards, was saying it would give preference to proposals that were based on digital technology. Until that time, it was assumed that the first generation of HDTV technology would be analog based. The FCC's digital HDTV standard will eliminate the need for electronic reconversion between the two types of signals (analog and digital) in television monitors.

The commission's decision to favor a digital standard was motivated in part by economics, specifically the problem of the U.S. international trade deficit. The global market for HDTV products and services will involve tens of billions of dollars annually by the end of the decade. By favoring the more advanced digital standard, the FCC hopes to give U.S. manufacturers an advantage over Japanese and European competitors, whose governments have generally supported the analog standard.[49]

HDTV will be an integral part of telecomputer technology, providing a video image twice as good as the picture currently available on American television sets. Despite HDTV's attractions, however, media firms face barriers in developing and marketing high-definition multimedia products. One hurdle to surmount is their limited experience with multimedia techniques. Another is the enormous amounts of money they will have to invest to develop advanced products, whose appeal to consumers is still untested. No one, in or outside the media industries, knows for certain how HDTV programming will be made available to consumers. Technically, it can be transmitted by cable TV systems, satellites, or over-the-air broadcasts. Another likely candidate is an HDTV videocassette. In 1992, Toshiba, the Japanese electronics company, demonstrated a prototype of an HDTV videorecorder.[50]

HDTV will not become widespread until after the turn of the century. Television production facilities will have to be reequipped at great cost to handle the new technology. HDTV sets will be expensive consumer items for a long time to come; the first HDTV receivers sold in Japan had a price tag of over $20,000. As an interim measure, TV equipment manufacturers are promoting home theater television, featuring large-screen projection capabilities with assorted add-on features. Mitsubishi's Instant Home Theater provides a special decoder attached to a TV set's audio terminal. The decoder directs the signal to speakers in front and back of the viewer, making the sound appear to move, thus matching the action on the screen. Another Japanese offering, JBL's Synthesis One, has a video projector that casts a wall-size image, with large audio speakers creating wraparound sound. Synthesis One's price tag in 1992 was $48,000.[51]

Despite their hesitations about moving into an expensive, untested field, major U.S. media firms know that their future will be determined by HDTV and similar advanced technologies. Telecomputers and other multimedia outlets will compete for the time, attention, and dollars now being spent by consumers on conventional media equipment and services. At one level, this will mean lost business for the old-line media. At another level, it will open new opportunities to supply information and entertainment programs for telecomputers and other multimedia machines.

Every major media company, and many of the smaller ones, are currently probing these prospects. One of the major players will be IBM, which announced a $100-million project in 1992 to develop an interactive digital network supplying video, software, and other information to business and home entertainment customers. The project includes joint ventures with major media companies to supply programming for the network.[52]

At the same time, media firms are getting ready for the new multimedia environment by upgrading their internal operations through computerization. Television, in particular, is in the midst of a sweeping automation of its news-gathering, recording, archiving, and studio operations. TV studios now use robot cameras operated entirely by program directors rather than by camera operators. Program directors are also making greater use of computers to program videocassettes, hundreds of which are needed daily for programs, advertisements, and station announcements.[53]

Hollywood is also turning to computers for cinematic effects that will make its products more attractive. Filmmakers are particularly interested in computer-generated imaging (CGI). CGI produces scenes programmed by advanced microchips for feature films or television programs. The technique was first introduced in the early 1980s in the science fiction film *Tron,* which relied heavily on computer-generated scenes. The flaw in these early CGI applications was poor integration between computerized sequences and live action. That problem has been largely overcome by the use of more advanced microchips. In the 1991 science fiction hit, *Terminator 2,* a liquid-metal robot metamorphosed into a live-action actor. In another scene, Los Angeles evaporated under a nuclear attack, an illusion created by images generated on a Macintosh PC. Initial successes with CGI technology have led some Hollywood entrepreneurs to predict a new consumer market: film productions on chips, stored in home telecomputers and available in real time.[54]

Cartoons and other animated products have benefited greatly from computerization techniques. Computers can be used to move cameras precisely for inking and drawing and for designing three-dimensional effects. In the 1991 Disney full-length cartoon, *Beauty and the Beast,* a cartoon-sequence ballroom comes alive thanks to computer graphics.[55]

Another innovative media technology, **virtual reality** (VR), will become part of the multimedia pattern in the coming years. Virtual reality is a new kind of human-computer interface, offering a fantasy world in which games and other entertainment will be available to home consumers. Also known as **cyberspace** (a term borrowed from William Gibson's 1984 novel, *Neuromancer*), VR allows the user to create and experience fantasy situations that are generated by computers filled with interactive software. Its one-of-a-kind effects are limited only by the imagination of the individual user. Instead of keyboards, users give instructions by voice commands, head nodding, finger pointing, and other natural gestures.[56]

The ultimate goal of VR engineers is to simulate an environment in which one can walk around and manipulate objects at will. Current technology is based on data gloves, which project a user's hand into a three-dimensional, computer-generated environment. Another technique is data goggles, which uses stereoscopic view-screens, worn like a helmet, to take the wearer into a virtual-fantasy world.[57]

VR is more than a science fiction game. It is also a small but active subdivision of the U.S. media industry. It has its own newsletters and journals, trade shows, and a penchant for describing itself as the virtual reality profession. One VR enthusiast, Dr. Sandra Key Heisel, describes VR's emergence as "the most profound gestalt shift of the twentieth century." She and other practitioners see important applications for their devices in the education and training fields. Bill Travers, a British conservationist, suggests that VR techniques might create a different kind of zoo in the next century, one without animals, which would use high technology to bring people to animals, rather than animals to people. Among other techniques, his zoo would use VR to create animal images. Travers also envisions live satellite linkups to all parts of the world, with experts talking directly to zoo visitors from an African rain forest or the Gobi Desert.[58]

The National Aeronautics and Space Administration (NASA) is currently using VR techniques in its Virtual Planetary Exploration project at Ames Research Center in California. NASA's purpose is to create, in computer imagery, a three-dimensional terrain of Mars and other planets based on the thousands of still photographs sent back by satellites. Among other experiments, it has assembled a *trillion* bytes of data from satellite photographs to create a "virtual Venus" landscape, which is the closest any earthling will get to a planet where the surface temperature is 460 degrees centigrade.[59]

VR's first major test may come in business applications. One early test involves Wall Street stocks. Using VR equipment, a stockbroker wanders through a surreal computer-generated landscape made up of colored squares. The squares change color as the market changes: blue squares can signify a rising stock; red ones, losers. The advantage is that traders can see how individual stocks are performing relative to others. Such information, available more quickly than studying lists of prices, could mean the difference between turning a profit or sustaining a loss in today's fast-paced financial markets.[60]

Whether VR will become a media force or remain just another interesting technological device will not be known for some time. As an information tool, it could literally add new dimensions to our understanding of the world around us.[61] As an entertainment device, it could be the super-Nintendo toy that would put all other computer gaming in the shade. A British firm, W Industries, has had considerable success marketing VR units in game arcades throughout the world at a cost of $40,000 per unit.[62]

Virtual reality aside, we are moving into an environment in which computer-based information machines are changing the ways in which we produce and store information. After years of tentative experiments with these new techniques, the mass-media industries are adapting them to present services and seriously examining their potential for new products. The one clear trend is that we are moving into a mass-communications environment, which will be dominated increasingly by multimedia services in both the information and entertainment sectors.

In the next chapter, we look at the changes taking place in the communications channels that will distribute these services.

NOTES

1. The social impacts of an increasingly computerized society are discussed in Kevin Robins and Frank Webster, "Cybernetic Capitalism: Information, Technology, Everyday Life," in Vincent Mosco and Janet Wasco, *The Political Economy of Information* (Madison, Wis.: University of Wisconsin Press, 1988), 44–75.
2. For general descriptions of this transformation, see two special surveys of telecommunications developments in *Economist* (London): "Netting the Future," 10 March 1990, and "The New Boys," 5 October 1991. See also "Communications, Computers and Networks," a special edition of *Scientific American* 265, no. 3 (September 1991).
3. For a survey of current and potential home services, see "Home Tech Fever," *U.S. News & World Report,* 25 November 1991, pp. 68–83.
4. The implications of telecomputer technology are discussed in "Retina Projection, Tactile Fields and Other Toys," *Broadcasting,* 9 December 1991, pp. 66–67.
5. "The Computer Age: Still a Work in Progress," *New York Times,* 11 September 1991, p. E-3.
6. The point is documented, with interesting examples, in Carolyn Marvin, *When Old Technologies Were New* (New York: Oxford University Press, 1988).
7. Michael Dertouzos, "Communications, Computers and Networks," *Scientific American* 265, no. 3 (September 1991): 63.
8. "Denser, Faster, Cheaper: The Microchip in the 21st Century," *New York Times,* 29 December 1991, p. F-5.
9. "Era of the Tiny PC is Nearly at Hand," *New York Times,* 23 March 1992, p. D-1.
10. "Apple Inspired by Newton," *Economist* (London), 30 May 1992, p. 67.
11. "US-Japan Consortium Plans Communications Revolution," *Financial Times* (London), 1 October 1992, p. 20.
12. "How the News Is Sent Back Home," *Financial Times* (London), 18 January 1991, p. 25.
13. "Getting Video Home from the Persian Gulf," *Broadcasting,* 3 September 1990, p. 23.
14. "Closing in on a Videotape Replacement," *Broadcasting,* 4 November 1991, p. 29.
15. For a survey of the development of electronic publishing, see Walter Baer and Martin Greenberger, "Consumer Electronic Publishing in a Competitive Environment," *Journal of Communication* 37, no. 1 (Winter 1987): 49–63.
16. Bob Dixon, "Recent Developments in Network-Produced Information," *Cast Calendar,* Center for Advanced Study in Telecommunication, Ohio State University, June 1991, p. 7.
17. For an analysis of early U.S. attempts to develop videotext networks, see Gary Stix, "What Zapped the Electronic Newspaper," *Columbia Journalism Review* 26, no. 1 (May/June 1987): 45–48; also "Ruling May Not Aid Videotext," *New York Times,* 15 September 1987, p. D-1.
18. Minitel and other European videotext ventures are surveyed in "The Dynamics of Videotext Development in Britain, France and Germany: A Cross-National Comparison," *European Journal of Communications* 6, no. 2 (June 1991): 187–212.
19. "Can Prodigy Be All Things to 15 Million PC Owners?" *New York Times,* 2 June 1991, p. F-4.
20. "Can GTE Outdo Prodigy?" *Business Week,* 28 December 1992, p. 42-D.
21. "A Foot in the Door for Telcos," *Broadcasting,* 29 July 1991, pp. 23–24.
22. "Venture to Allow PC Subscribers to Tap into Phone Book," *Washington Post,* 10 September 1992, p. D-1.

23. "The Kiosks Are Coming, the Kiosks Are Coming," *Business Week,* 22 June 1992, p. 122.

24. "A Race for Publicity," *Financial Times* (London), 2 August 1991, p. 7.

25. John C. Schweitzer, "Personal Computers and Media Use," *Journalism Quarterly* 68, no. 4 (Winter 1991): 689–697.

26. "CDs Store the Data, but Sifting's a Chore," *New York Times,* 4 August 1991, p. F-9.

27. "New Technology for Old Pictures," *Financial Times* (London), 12 October 1992, p. 6.

28. "Imagine Storing Proust in Just a Crumb of Cake," *New York Times,* 1 September 1991, p. 43.

29. "The Best of Tapes and Disks," *New York Times,* 1 September 1991, p. F-9.

30. "CD-ROM: A Cost-Effective Alternative," *Instructional Delivery Systems* 2, no. 4 (January–February 1992): 21–23.

31. "Big Media Firms Try 'Publishing' in CD Offshoot," *Wall Street Journal,* 18 March 1991, p. B-1; "Lean, Mean and on the Screen," *Economist* (London), 13 July 1991, p. 78.

32. "Disks for Tiny Computers," *New York Times,* 5 April 1992, p. F-7.

33. "Now CDs Emit Sights as Well as Sounds," *New York Times,* 12 May 1991, p. C-1.

34. "Putting a Nation's Story Within Fingertip Reach," *Washington Post,* 11 November 1991, p. D-6.

35. For a useful survey of entertainment CD-ROM and CD-I prospects, see "The CD-ROM Frontier," *Variety,* 9 March 1992, pp. 51–73.

36. "Cacophony," *Economist* (London), 1 June 1991, pp. 63–65.

37. "Mixing Up the Revolution: Multi-Media's High Tech Blend of Sight, Sound May Reshape the Information Revolution," *Washington Post,* 28 July 1991, p. H-1.

38. "Mouse! Movie! Sound! Action!" *New York Times,* 27 October 1991, p. F-11.

39. "CD-ROM for the Common Man," *New York Times,* 28 November 1989, p. C-5.

40. George Gilder, *Life After Television* (Knoxville, Tenn. Whittle Direct Books, 1991), 23–37.

41. Quoted in "Now or Never," *Forbes,* 14 October 1991, p. 188.

42. "It's a PC, It's a TV—It's Multi-Media," *Business Week,* 9 October 1989, p. 153.

43. "The Lucie Show: Shaking Up a Stodgy IBM," *Business Week,* 6 April 1992, p. 64. See also "IBM Considers Investment in Time Warner Division," *Financial Times* (London), 7 May 1992, p. 16.

44. "Thirteen Firms Plan Multi-Media Consortium," *Washington Post,* 1 October 1992, p. D-13.

45. For a description of the transition from analog to digital technology, see "When Analog Meets Digital on a Single Chip," *New York Times,* 13 October 1991, p. F-11.

46. "The Digitization of TV Continues," *Broadcasting,* 28 October 1991, pp. 34–43.

47. "Your Digital Future," *Business Week,* 7 September 1992, p. 56.

48. "Digitizing TV into Obsolescence," *New York Times,* 20 October 1991, p. F-11.

49. "Setting the Standards for High Definition TV," *Washington Post,* 16 June 1991, p. H-1. For a survey of the international trade implications of HDTV, see Leland Johnson, *Development of High-Definition Television: A Study in U.S.-Japan Trade Relations,* Report R 3921 (Santa Monica, Calif.: Rand Corporation, July 1990).

50. "All-New HDTV at NAB," *Broadcasting,* 13 April 1992, p. 43.

51. "Home Theater Makes Its Pitch," *New York Times,* 5 July 1992, p. H-14.

52. "Sony, IBM Unveil Efforts to Create Interactive Systems," *Washington Post,* 17 September 1992, p. B-10.

53. "Computers Coming of Age in TV Studios," *Broadcasting,* 17 October 1988, p. 46.

54. "T2 Effects Microchip away at Future," *Variety,* 22 July 1991, p. 3.

55. "Computer Generation: It's Almost Grown Up," *Variety,* 11 November 1991, p. 45.

56. Virtual reality is developing a special literature of its own. For an authoritative layperson's view of the subject, see Howard Rheingold, *Virtual Reality* (New York: Summit Books, 1991). For a media-oriented account of the subject, see Richard B. Cutler, "Calling Up

Cyberspace: On the Threshold of Telecommunications Research," Center for Research on Communications Technology and Society, University of Texas at Austin, July 1991. See also "Virtual Reality: Is It an Art Yet?" *New York Times,* 5 July 1992, p. H-1.

57. "Video Immersion: Programming Virtual Worlds," *Broadcasting,* 9 December 1991, pp. 64-72.
58. "London Zoo Is Falling Down," *Washington Post,* 2 September 1991, p. D-1.
59. "Planet of the Mind's Eye," *Economist* (London), 9 November 1991, pp. 99-100.
60. "Virtual Reality," *Washington Post,* 16 September 1992, p. H-1.
61. For a useful discussion of VR's potential, see "Virtual Reality: A Communications Perspective," a collection of seven articles in *Journal of Communication* 42, no. 4 (Autumn 1992): 5-172.
62. "Making Virtual Reality a Certainty," *Financial Times* (London), 14 April 1992, p. 10.

Chapter

3

NEW MEDIA TECHNOLOGIES: THE NETWORKS

Despite the many improvements in media technology, the industry still delivers most of its products the old-fashioned ways. Newspapers are tossed up on front porches. Magazines make their uncertain way through the postal system. Hollywood films are shipped in reel cans. Until recently, the only significant breach in these horse-and-buggy practices has been the use of communications satellites for product delivery by radio, television, and cable-TV networks.

In the 1990s, however, the older media are catching up with the high-tech telecommunications revolution. One reason is that older distribution methods are expensive and often unreliable. A more important reason is the need to compete more effectively with the new breed of computer-based information services. Advanced telecommunications facilities are a critical element in the media industries' plans to upgrade their operations, from product production to final delivery to consumers.

"Telecommunications has made information into a weightless commodity," says former London *Economist* editor Norman Macrae, surveying the role of communications technology in the modern world.[1] Increasingly, information travels at the speed of light, as digitized binary digits, which are symbolic ones and zeros that can represent any combination of voice, video, or print information. A fiber-optic cable can deliver a signal across the United States in 30 milliseconds. Computers and the networks that connect them share a common electronic module—the **semiconductor** chip. As a result, they are converging technologically into a single machine: an integrated information utility.[2] For the first time, the media industries will have the high-tech resources to deliver both old and new services electronically to mass audiences. The advanced communications networks that have been built in the United States over the past two decades to serve business and government needs are now being consumerized, reaching down to homes and other locations.

American media industries face complex decisions regarding adaptation of their operations to this new structure. As recently as 20 years ago, such decisions were relatively simple, because the options were fewer. U.S. public telecommunications were almost synonymous with one company's name—AT&T. Since 1934, AT&T had enjoyed a near monopoly on national communications services, granted by the federal government in exchange for a promise to provide universal phone service—a promise the company fulfilled. By the 1970s, as computer usage spread, it was apparent that a system dominated by a single telecommunications company could not fully serve national needs. In the next chapter, we look at the events that led both to more open competition in the telecommunications structure and to the breakup of AT&T in 1984.[3] This competitive environment has had a significant effect on the media industries, particularly on the widening of their distribution choices.

The new telecommunications system is essentially an expanded, higher-performance extension of the old telephone system. Americans dial into the telephone network a billion and a half times a day. Telephones are more ubiquitous than ever, as exemplified by the explosive growth of mobile-telephone services. Originally intended for use in automobiles, mobile phones are now found in shirt pockets and handbags as well. In 1991, Motorola Corporation introduced an eight-ounce portable model, which can make connections with any of the world's 800 million phones.[4] Newer models, developed by AT&T and other firms, will combine telephone and computer capabilities in a small, hand-held unit.

The phone system's primary usage is still what the engineers call POTS—Plain Old Telephone Service, meaning, two people talking. Increasingly, however, the system also provides other services: computer-data links, fax messages, and even television. Phones are now routinely equipped with sophisticated semiconductor-chip technology that makes them, in effect, limited computer terminals.[5] Phone-based communications services such as voice mail, 800 numbers, and voice-response services are already a multi-billion-dollar industry.[6] These innovations have an impact on the old media as phone services compete with those traditionally supplied by newspapers, magazines, newsletters, and radio. A new term, "telemedia," has been coined to describe information resources available by telephone.[7] The most familiar are 800- and 900-number services. From small beginnings 20 years ago, 800 numbers have become a competitive threat to publishing and broadcasting. Ten *billion* calls were placed to 800 numbers in 1991. By 1993, there were more than 1.3 million 800 numbers available throughout the United States, providing telephone companies with an estimated $7 billion in revenues.[8] A notable 800 number was the one that, until recently, enabled Eskimo tribes in the Arctic to report the presence of Russian submarines.[9]

The opportunity to order up goods and services through free phone calls is attracting more and more consumers and at the same time, cutting into traditional media advertising revenues. The pay-per-call 900-number industry is also booming. In 1991, Americans dialed $975 million worth of 900-number calls to almost 15,000 numbers.[10] The most popular 900 services were information data banks, ranging from the *Official Team NFL Insiders Hotline* to *Jeane Dixon Horoscopes.* A variation on 900-number service is a "desktop news service," developed in 1993 by a joint venture managed by IBM and NBC. The service provides video news and information on demand via PCs. Designed initially for use by business firms, the service will eventually be marketed to a potential audience of 35 million PC owners.[11]

Another telephone-based technology affecting media operations is the facsimile machine. It is both an important operational tool within the media industry and a newly competitive service. Facsimile is a 30-year-old technology that has blossomed in recent years because of the introduction of low-cost, chip-filled machines with more sophisticated capabilities. Originally used to transmit documents from one business office to another, the fax machine has been consumerized.[12] It is the fastest-growing service in the new telemedia environment. Although fax is still used primarily for direct messages between individuals, it is rapidly becoming a distribution device for all kinds of information products.

"Junk fax" advertising mail—uninvited and generally unwanted—is a familiar example. More useful is the proliferation of information services that offer fax-on-demand information as a public service or for a fee. One typical commercial service, FaxFacts, supplies technical support, marketing information, and installation instructions from industrial companies to its customers. FaxTicker, introduced in 1991, allows callers to access information on a portfolio of 15 stocks by using their personal identification number.[13] The National Cancer Institute in Washington offers callers to its CancerFax lines a listing of cancers and their symptoms.

The success of these information services has encouraged traditional media operators to experiment with fax delivery in order to reach old customers and attract new ones. The biggest users to date are newsletter publishers whose stock-in-trade is their ability to deliver specialized information to customers as quickly as possible. Fax delivery is fast replacing post office delivery as the communications channel of choice for newsletters. A variation of these services is "broadcast fax," a technique whereby messages can be sent simultaneously to thousands of fax machines across the country. Broadcast fax was used extensively by both the Clinton and Bush campaigns during the 1992 presidential race to get their partisan messages quickly to newspapers, broadcasting stations, and other media outlets.[14]

More recently, newspapers have been testing fax delivery. One of the earliest services began in 1989 when the *Hartford Courant* began sending *FaxPaper,* a 1,500-word summary of stories appearing in its next day's regular edition, to paying subscribers. "Rather than recycling information, in a sense we are precycling it," the *Courant*'s publisher, Michael Davies, said.[15] Other news organizations have followed up on the *Courant*'s experiment. Gannett New Media, the research and development arm of the Gannett publishing chain, began fax transmittal of specialized news summaries it was already supplying on-line to customers with computers. In 1991, a Gannett newspaper, the *Honolulu Star-Bulletin,* added a Japanese-language edition, called "Facts Hawaii," which is faxed to Japanese-owned businesses in the state.[16]

The *New York Times* delivers its daily TimesFax news service for readers in places where the daily *Times* is not readily available. The service includes a six-page fax newspaper for guests at hotels in Japan, an international edition for Australia, and one for cruise-ship passengers.

Newspaper fax services have grown slowly in recent years. By 1992, only 10 U.S. dailies were offering or experimenting with weekday fax editions. Some papers, including the *Chicago Tribune,* the *Knoxville News-Sentinel,* and the *Minneapolis Star-Tribune,* abandoned fax experiments they had started in the early 1990s. "There was interest in the product, but not enough to make it profitable," according to *News-Sentinel* editor Harry Moskos. Other newspapers and database sellers are limiting the use of fax technology to specialized services.

Standard & Poors, the financial data firm, offers its Credit Wire by Fax service, which provides a ratings profile on any one of 3,000 corporations. The *St. Paul Pioneer-Press* provides the prices of up to 15 stocks in a fax summary issued each afternoon. The *Washington Post,* the *Atlanta Journal,* and Dow Jones News/Retrieval Service also offer specialized information services by fax for a fee. The *Post*'s offerings include Capital Fax, a one-page daily bulletin targeted toward Washington political insiders who are willing to pay $1.50 for an advance peek at the next day's big stories. Launched in 1993, Capital Fax supplies them with a half dozen summaries of stories featured in the first edition of the newspaper.

A variation on big-city newspaper facsimile experiments has been under way for several years in two Illinois towns, Effingham and Bloomington. The publications, known as *Fax Today,* have been modestly profitable. The service is free to subscribers and is supported by advertisers.[17] Like most experiments with fax journalism, these publications use telephone circuits to deliver their product. A recent variation is to send the fax signal via radio waves rather than over telephone lines. By hooking a fax machine to a radio receiver costing less than $100, customers could get news reports, sports, weather maps, financial data, and other timely information.[18] In 1991, a New York firm, Montauk Communications, asked the FCC for authorization to start up an advertiser-supported fax news service using this technology.

No one expects facsimile to compete actively with traditional print products in the forseeable future. Most experiments in delivering faxed information to the general public have not been financially successful. The successful experiments have been those that have identified a relatively small niche market and then provided faxed information for a fee in response to specific requests. This technique, known as fax on demand, has been used by the *Detroit Free Press* and other newspapers around the country.[19]

Fax delivery of news and other information may be overtaken by a technology based on the very small computers known as laptops or notebooks. The prospect is that these machines will serve, among other functions, as portable electronic newspapers. A notebook-sized, pen-based computer, first demonstrated in 1992, displays a sharp, 8½-by-11-inch newspaper-style page, including color capabilities, on a thin flat panel. The electronic newspaper's contents can be delivered to subscribers by cable TV networks, direct-broadcasting satellites, or high-capacity telephone circuits. The subscriber makes a selection from a "front-page" menu of news and features, tapping the display with an electronic pen to pick stories or sections for viewing, and then has the option of reading, printing, or storing the information. Eventually, electronic newspapers will have interactive capabilities. The reader could, for instance, tap an advertisement on the computer screen to order goods or services from the advertiser.[20]

Electronic newspapers are only one type of the advanced information-delivery techniques being developed by telephone companies and other electronic networkers. These developments are made possible by recent improvements in transmission technology, involving both the circuits that carry the traffic and the switches that control them. The critical improvement has been the transition from **analog** to **digital** signaling, an extension of the changes taking place in computer technology, described in the previous chapter. The world's communications networks are being rapidly digitized, permitting a common standard for linking digital-based computers, telephones, and other electronic machines with one another. Words, pictures, and sounds are reduced to binary digits (**bits**), usually described as ones or zeros. Uncounted trillions of symbolic ones and zeros flow every hour through communications networks, each a coded part of a message that may involve a phone call, a credit-card transaction, or a TV program.

Today's advanced communications circuits are generally one of two types — wireless microwave or wire cable. Microwave circuits travel through the atmosphere or (in the case of satellites) in outer space. Thanks to improved digital switches, their capacities have increased dramatically in recent decades. A communications satellite is, in effect, a microwave switch in space, simultaneously handling the equivalent of 40,000 telephone calls and data circuits, plus many TV programs.

The most dramatic change in telecommunications circuits, however, involves fiber-optic cables. Fiber circuits transmit information in optical form (i.e., in light waves) along a silicon wire as thin as a human hair.[21] Fiber wires have enormous information-carrying capabilities. A single cable can transmit tens of thousands of phone calls or dozens of television programs. These cables also have many other useful attributes. Unlike conventional copper wires, they are unaffected by heat, moisture, or corrosion. Their light source — lasers — may be no larger than a grain of salt and may emit continuously for a hundred years.

Fiber-optic networks have a special role to play in the changing pattern of American mass media industries. National fiber-optic networks have been in place for a number of years and are heavily used by the media industries for internal operations. Fiber networks are also replacing copper-wire links internationally. The first round-the-world fiber network was inaugurated in 1991, dubbed the Global Digital Highway by its builder, Britain's Cable & Wireless (C&W).[22]

The next step is to extend the network into homes and other mass market locations, creating new opportunities for the delivery of advanced information and entertainment services to consumers. Although there are other competitive technologies such as cable television and satellites, it is probable that fiber-optic cable will be the dominant technology providing these media services in the coming years.[23] Building a full-scale fiber-optic network will be a massive construction project, involving the rewiring and upgrading of the consumer telephone system. Many cable TV operators are also replacing their old low-capacity cables with fiber cable.[24]

Such networks involve a major economic gamble. Estimates of the cost of wiring

American homes with fiber optics run as high as a trillion dollars.[25] Despite confident assurances from fiber-to-the-home enthusiasts, many experts are not sure that the average American home needs the enormous circuit capacities that fiber cables can provide. Experimental fiber-optic networks serving households have been authorized by the FCC in some communities since the late 1980s. The results of these tests have been mixed. Surveys show that most consumers think they get enough information and entertainment from their present media services—television, newspapers, and the like. They are generally reluctant to pay for access to more channels, particularly since it is unclear to them just what the added channels will deliver.[26] Meanwhile, billions of dollars, as well as the future shape of large parts of the American media industry, will be at stake as consumers vote with their pocketbooks on the new flood of information and entertainment that will become available in their living rooms.[27]

Full-scale installation of fiber-optic networks to homes may be delayed, or even short-circuited, by another technology, which is more immediately available. It involves the upgrading of cable television networks that use coaxial cable—the standard means of piping programs into homes for over 40 years. "Coax" has considerably less transmission capability than a fiber-optic circuit. However, its capacity can be upgraded to hundreds of channels through digital compression, a computer-driven process that squeezes more transmission capacity into existing circuits. Digitally compressed coaxial cables are being installed by many cable system operators to expand their conventional video channels and to add new services such as interactive video, stereo music, and videotext data.[28] In 1993, Tele-Communications Inc., the country's largest cable system owner, began construction of a network that will ultimately provide its 9 million customers with as many as 500 channels of information and entertainment programming.

The telephone and cable TV industries are competing to determine which will be the primary deliverer of advanced information and entertainment services directly to homes. Both industries also face competition from entrepreneurs who want to use communications satellites to deliver these services. Each group claims superior competence to do the job. These claims form the basis for one of the most intense debates in American business history, currently being waged in corporate board rooms, in the courts, and in the halls of Congress.[29]

Meanwhile, the media industries have been drawn into the debate. Broadcasters, publishers, and filmmakers see their future strongly affected by decisions on how, and when, the new high-capacity consumer networks will be built. Their concerns are well founded. Fiber-optic and advanced coaxial cable circuits represent a giant step toward creation of the national information utility, a sophisticated network delivering a wide range of voice, video, and print products, transmitted on a common channel to homes and other consumer locations. It is quite probable that the utility itself will be a hybrid mix of technologies: fiber optics, satellites, and cable TV, which will allow the telephone companies and their rivals to compete on more or less equal terms, using different networks, for the consumer information market.[30] (See Figure 3.1.)

This network of networks will, collectively, form a high-tech link into American homes. It will displace many of the circuits that now provide telephone, cable TV, broadcast television, radio, and computer services. Ultimately, all information and

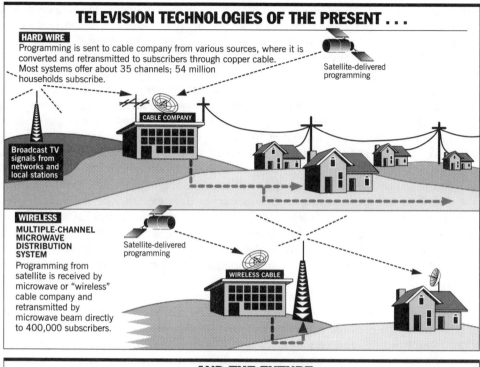

TELEVISION TECHNOLOGIES OF THE PRESENT . . .

HARD WIRE
Programming is sent to cable company from various sources, where it is converted and retransmitted to subscribers through copper cable. Most systems offer about 35 channels; 54 million households subscribe.

Satellite-delivered programming

CABLE COMPANY

Broadcast TV signals from networks and local stations

WIRELESS
MULTIPLE-CHANNEL MICROWAVE DISTRIBUTION SYSTEM
Programming from satellite is received by microwave or "wireless" cable company and retransmitted by microwave beam directly to 400,000 subscribers.

Satellite-delivered programming

WIRELESS CABLE

. . . AND THE FUTURE

HIGH-POWERED DBS
DIRECT BROADCAST SATELLITE
Programming is transmitted via high-frequency electronic signals directly to homes with a low-cost receiving dish or plate 12" to 18" across. Channel capacity uncertain.

VIDEO DIAL-TONE
Programming is sent to homes via phone company's fiber-optic telephone lines, which also carry telephone calls and other data such as computer transmissions. Households would be connected like current telephone networks, allowing individuals to send video images to one another. Could transmit hundreds of channels, but it is not yet clear who would provide programming under this proposed system.

PHONE COMPANY

BY MICHAEL DREW—THE WASHINGTON POST

FIGURE 3.1 Advanced Information Delivery Technologies

SOURCE: The *Washington Post*, January 14, 1992, p. 14. © 1992, The *Washington Post*. Reprinted with permission.

entertainment services could be brought into homes on one common high-tech channel.

This all-purpose channel will be, in the engineer's phrase, an *information pipe*.[31] The debate on how to set a common global technical standard for this pipe has been going on for 20 years, mostly within obscure technical committees at the International Telecommunications Union, a United Nations agency in Geneva. By the early 1990s, the broad outlines of a common standard had been codified. The result is an international agreement on the kinds of computer-based software needed to operate what is called an **integrated services digital network** (ISDN). Its purpose is to allow access to any kind of information—data, video, or sound—through all telecommunications networks, many of which are now technically incompatible with one another. The new ISDN technical standards may appear arcane to a layman but they are the necessary foundation for building the new universal information utility.

The implementation of ISDN standards will profoundly affect the media industries. ISDN will vastly expand the quality and variety of information and entertainment services available to consumers. For example, the broadcasting and film industries have an important stake in HDTV services transmitted at the ISDN standard.[32] The print industries—newspapers, magazines, and books—will have an equal interest in ISDN delivery of advanced electronic messaging and high-resolution facsimile.

The new standards will encourage the entry of new kinds of competition in media markets. For example, ISDN-based communications make it more practical to expand electronic home shopping services well beyond the simple versions now provided by cable TV channels. Using a channel based on ISDN standards, consumers can shop via multimedia electronic catalogs, which provide video, voice, and print descriptions of the merchandise. They will page through video descriptions of the products, ask questions either by voice or through a personal computer, and then take an order directly to the vendor's computer. Marketing goods and services in this manner provides an option for consumers that could have a direct competitive effect on newspaper, magazine, and broadcasting advertising—the primary revenue sources for these media. In 1993, Nordstrom, one of the largest U.S. retail chains, announced plans for an interactive video shopping service available on home TV sets. The company plans to have 1 million TV customers by 1996.

ISDN networking is a present reality in many parts of the U.S. communications system, and it is expanding steadily. Its evolution, however, has been somewhat slower than its more enthusiastic supporters had hoped. The delay has less to do with technology than with economics. Shifting to ISDN standards constitutes an expensive move for telephone companies, which bear much of the cost. The main users of current ISDN networks are large corporations and government agencies. These are important customers, but they often do not need the full range of ISDN capabilities. As a result, phone companies are reluctant to make the investment needed for complete transition to ISDN capabilities.

The transition will depend on the prospects for expansion into mass consumer markets. It will happen when there is pressure from millions of consumers interested in buying advanced information and entertainment services. In short, if ISDN is to become the standard for a multimedia information utility, it will have to reach beyond corporate and government applications to a wider consumer market.

This expanded utility will put the media industries into competition with the telephone companies as information service providers. The phone companies claim they must be allowed to increase their consumer information services to justify the expense of building and operating ISDN-standard facilities. They have been traditionally shut out of these activities due to government regulations, except for such services as weather and time-of-day information, Dial-a-Prayer, and Dial-a-Joke. This barrier was breached in 1991, after intense legal maneuvering, which led to federal court cancellation of many of the information-provider restrictions.[33] Since then, the telephone companies have been active in projects to expand into the consumer information services market. In 1993, New Jersey Bell announced plans to install a major fiber-optic network that will supply a broad range of information and entertainment channels to its customers. Other phone companies have similar projects. In effect, they are positioning themselves (despite pious protestations to the contrary) to use their enormous economic and technological clout to compete directly with newspapers, broadcasting, and other media. The media industries, in turn, have mounted a major lobbying campaign, aimed at limiting what they regard as phone company intrusion onto their turf.

Whatever the outcome of this confrontation, the media industries will supply a large share of the video, sound, and print products that will move through the new ISDN networks. A common feature of the networks will be their ability to deliver two-way services to consumers, who will be able to interact with information and entertainment sources through two-way communications. Currently, the most familiar form of interactive service is the way computer owners use their keyboards to search a remote database until they reach and retrieve the material they want. There is a steady growth in such videotext services. One example is IBM's Prodigy, the consumer-oriented data network described in the previous chapter. Fiber optics and the other advanced consumer circuits will vastly expand these capabilities, particularly for identifying and retrieving video materials such as Hollywood films.

Interactive connection to homes and other consumer locations is a promising field for the television, cable TV, and film industries, as they seek new markets for their present and future products. The cable industry, in particular, has been trying for years to tailor its products to fit the individual tastes of subscribers, a service usually known as pay per view (PPV). The format used is addressability, a technique that permits the consumer to order up a special program at a specific time. Until recently, addressability meant that the home viewer made a telephone call to the cable system office to request a particular program. In most cases, the pay-per-view menu has offered movies and sports events, although special entertainment programs, such as live rock concerts, are becoming more available. More sophisticated pay-per-view technologies, involving an attachment to television sets, which permits the customer to order a program by keypad, have been developed but are not yet widely used. Fewer than 25 percent of the country's 9,400 cable systems had fully addressable services by 1993. That ratio could increase with the introduction of advanced interactive information and entertainment networks similar to one being built by Time Warner's cable TV division in Orlando, Florida.

The most extensive experiment in interactive cable TV was conducted in Columbus, Ohio, from 1977 to 1985. Known as *Qube,* the service was, for most of its brief history, a joint venture of Warner Amex, owned by Hollywood-based Warner Communications and Amex Cable, an affiliate of American Express. Qube offered 30 channels, divided equally between regular cable TV offerings, local community programs, and pay-per-view channels.

The pay-per-view channels allowed viewers a choice of special entertainment programs, selected by pressing a remote-controlled keypad, which sent a signal to Qube's computerized program delivery center. Customers were billed monthly. Qube was an important test, if only because it was a preview of the opportunities and problems that will arise when, inevitably, interactive information and entertainment programming becomes more common in U.S. homes. Qube's managers were intent on using the system's interactive channels to offer innovative services. The best of these was Pinwheel, a children's channel that provided noncommercial, nonviolent programs. For five hours daily, Pinwheel presented a lively schedule of entertainment and instruction, winning praise from educators and parents.

The Qube network also tried, with mixed results, an experiment in what its managers called electronic democracy. This involved polling Qube subscribers electronically on national and local issues of the day. Subscriber opinions were transmitted instantaneously to city council meetings. The experiment was hailed by its supporters as a way to receive direct reaction from citizens on important municipal issues. Critics of the project pointed out, however, that most of Qube's customers were a high-income minority and that the polling results were reported as a percentage of an unspecified number of responses from an unspecified number of sets in use in Qube households.

Other Qube projects were less concerned with electronic democracy and more with the system's capabilities as a marketing tool. Questions were raised about customer privacy when Qube set up a computerized data bank of detailed information on customer viewing habits. The system's computer monitored home television terminals every two minutes, recording which channels were in use and the last response button touched. Although Warner Amex assured customers it would protect their privacy, it reserved the right to sell aggregated information collected from its computer sweeps. Viewers continued to object, pointing out that they were paying for the "privilege" of being solicited by sellers of goods and services.[34]

Qube also conducted the first experiment in *infomercials*—long advertising segments presented as informational programming. The infomercial format has since become a standard part of many cable network offerings. It is a lucrative business for cable operators, although infomercials often irritate viewers who do not want commercials disguised as legitimate programs. The Qube service folded in 1985, the victim of poor viewer response. Its demise put a chill on similar pay-per-view schemes for years. By the early 1990s, however, enthusiasm for interactive services quickened again among cable system operators looking for new revenues.

Pay-per-view and other interactive programming will be standard consumer offerings before the end of the decade, as fiber-optic cable and other high-capacity circuits reach into U.S. homes. Telecomputers, described in the previous chapter, will be the home terminal for these services. Consumers will then have full two-way remote control over the services they want, signaling directly from special decoder/transmitters in their telecomputers to television studios or cable TV offices.

They will be able to choose the format and content of special programs. A new program could be formatted to individual interests. Viewers may signal that they do not want to look at sports but would like some national news and a full menu of local events. Another innovation put forward by the industry's interactive enthusiasts would allow viewers to choose between alternative endings for soap operas and other video dramas while they are in progress.

Skeptics may doubt whether the public will be interested in such gimmicks. The broadcasting, film, and cable TV industries, however, see interactive programming as a potentially lucrative revenue source, attracting advertisers as well as new customers. In addition to its interactive attributes, the system can generate a great deal of commercially useful information about individual viewers' life-styles and interests by tracking the programs they have chosen—a subject of great interest to advertisers and other marketers.

Meanwhile, until full-scale video interactivity comes on the scene, broadcasters and cable TV managers are experimenting with limited forms of the art. Typically these efforts focus on getting viewers to vote their preferences on some controversial issue or event, usually by calling a 900 number. One such early experiment in real time viewer polling was conducted by NBC's "Saturday Night Live" show. The issue was the fate of an actor dressed as Larry the Lobster: should he be tossed into the pot for dinner or saved? (Larry was saved by a slim margin.) Viewer balloting may fall somewhat short of full electronic democracy, but media managers see it as a useful attention-getter, hoping to curb viewer tendencies to change channels.

Most high-capacity circuits delivering interactive services into homes will use wire technology—either fiber optic or coaxial cable. The alternative is advanced wireless systems, which transmit signals over the airwaves. The most familiar of these are mobile telephone networks. Although used primarily for voice telephony, advanced mobile phone instruments can also receive and transmit data information. In 1992, IBM joined with nine major cellular telephone companies to develop plans for a nationwide data service over cellular networks. The data would be transmitted in packets during idle time on cellular systems. Engineering studies have shown that about 40 percent of cellular channels are not in use at any given time.

Another proposal for wireless media delivery concerns data broadcasting services, potentially capable of transmitting vast amounts of digitized information to personal computer users at low cost. These transmissions piggyback on existing radio signals. Plans for an experimental data broadcasting service were announced in May 1992 by McCaw Cellular Inc., the biggest U.S. cellular phone operator, and Oracle Corp., a major supplier of database software. The service can broadcast a wide variety of digitized information, including electronic newspapers, books and manuals, computer video, and electronic mail. Transmitted at 1.5 million bits per second, the service's transmission facility would be fast enough to send the equivalent of an average-sized novel to millions of receiving points every five seconds. The special computer attachment needed to receive the transmission could be made in quantity for less than a hundred dollars, according to McCaw engineers.[35] The other wireless technologies for transmitting media services to homes are wireless cable on the ground and broadcasting satellites in space. Both promise to be active competitors in the marketing of media services to homes.[36]

Wireless cable is a consumer-oriented version of the microwave networks that crisscross the country, carrying telephone and data traffic. Known technically as **multichannel microwave distribution service** (MMDS), wireless cable arrived on the scene 20 years ago in cities and suburban areas that did not have conventional cable TV systems. MMDS systems use microwave bands to transmit television programming to small receiving antennas on houses and apartment buildings. During the 1980s, the FCC issued MMDS licenses in many large and medium-sized cities.

Wireless cable was originally seen as a stopgap arrangement, providing a limited service until full-scale coaxial cable networks were installed. But that did not happen. Wireless cable has made a comeback in the 1990s for two reasons. First, it can provide program services for the estimated 10–15 million homes in small towns and rural areas that are still beyond the reach of cable TV systems. Second, it is one answer to the political pressure on the FCC to encourage diversity in delivery of entertainment and information programming. Wireless-cable networks can provide an alternative service, competing with cable TV systems, which are seen as taking undue advantage of their locally granted monopoly franchise. In 1990 and 1991, the FCC processed over 15,000 license applications for wireless cable systems.[37]

Despite their current proliferation, MMDS systems will probably play a minor role in the delivery of advanced media services to homes over the long term. This is due in part to technical limitations. Wireless systems transmit fewer channels than conventional coaxial-cable networks. Moreover, their owners do not have the financial and marketing clout of the established cable TV systems, now dominated by national conglomerates that own or have access to the most popular sports and entertainment services. Small, wireless systems cannot attract the large audiences enjoyed by these well-endowed firms.

The other microwave delivery technology to challenge broadcasting and cable delivery of advanced media services to homes is represented by communications satellites. Satellites have been used by media organizations for news and entertainment transmissions since the first "birds" were orbited in the mid-1960s. Media-related traffic has expanded as satellites have become more sophisticated and as transmission costs have come down. By the early 1990s, network television and cable TV firms were the largest customers of the 18 satellites serving the U.S. market.[38]

The big change in recent years has been in the more extensive use of satellite facilities by *local* television stations. A 1990 National Association of Broadcasters survey reported that local stations have an average of four satellite earth stations on their premises. One usually receives national network programs. The others are used for local or regional services, including news "remotes"—events covered by station reporters operating from satellite news-gathering vehicles.[39] Satellite news-gathering will gain greater technical flexibility by the mid-1990s when a mobile satellite system, capable of providing remote coverage from any point in North America, is expected to go into operation.[40]

A small but profitable satellite delivery service is being exploited by FM radio stations that use part of their frequency assignment (known as a subcarrier) to market paging messages, stock quotations, and other consumer information. These messages are delivered to the FM station by satellite, then retransmitted to local subscribers by telephone lines for a fee.[41] Satellites may also play an important role in the radio broadcasting industry's newest technological advance, called **digital audio broadcasting,** which provides a level of sound quality that is a distinct improvement over current FM transmissions. The industry expects that satellites will deliver a significant amount of such digital programming to local radio stations. Meanwhile, a number of cable TV systems already offer videotext delivery by satellite. One service, Tempo, is a video version of the conventional stock market ticker, supplying current quotations on over 8,000 stocks to cable subscribers. Each listing is color coded to give a quick indication of whether the price of any particular stock is rising, falling, or unchanged.

Despite the current heavy use of satellites for program delivery by the cable and broadcasting industries, many media observers believe use of satellites will decline by the end of the decade as cable networks expand to reach most of the locations currently dependent on satellites. Satellites may, however, get a new lease on life in the next few years. The prospect depends on the introduction of the direct broadcasting satellite (DBS), which beams television, cable TV, and radio programs from space into homes and other consumer locations. DBS transmissions could take up much of the slack in communications satellite use in the United States caused by the competition from fiber-optic networks.

Direct broadcasting from space has been a technological possibility for over 20 years, ever since the development of satellites powerful enough to send a video signal to small earth terminals. Its introduction as a direct-to-home media service has been repeatedly postponed, however, primarily because no one, including the managers of some of the nation's most prestigious media firms, has been successful in putting together a financial and marketing package that would exploit the technology. In the early 1980s, a dozen national DBS networks were proposed in response to an FCC decision to issue satellite broadcasting licenses. All of these projects failed, due to a combination of inadequate technology, weak financing, and poor marketing strategies.

More recently, a new generation of advanced broadcasting satellites has set the stage for a DBS comeback. Originally, DBS technology was seen as a means for reaching the 15 million American homes in rural areas not adequately served by conventional television and cable systems.[42] This will continue to be a potentially important market, as indicated by the 2 million earth stations already dotting the rural landscape. Most of these dishes pick up entertainment and sports programs that are being transmitted to local cable systems by HBO and other national program distributors.

The new DBS entrepreneurs see a wider market, involving direct broadcast transmissions to urban and suburban homes. Programs will be delivered to very small terminals, each less than two feet in diameter. Instead of the familiar round dishes, many of the new terminals will be square in shape. Known as **squarials,** they can be attached unobtrusively to roofs or to the sides of houses and apartment buildings. Squarials are one of the many varieties of very small aperture terminals—little earth stations that send and receive an increasingly large proportion of U.S. communications satellite traffic.

The growth rate of DBS networks in the next few years will depend on the parallel development of HDTV, discussed in the last chapter. HDTV can be transmitted to homes in several ways. These include over fiber-optic telephone lines, through advanced cable TV circuits, on standard broadcast channels, or by microwave on the ground or from space satellites. The new DBS networks are based on the economic premise that broadcasting satellites will capture a significant share of the HDTV delivery market. Satellites have some significant advantages over other technologies in this market. Not only can they be configured to provide the extra power and spectrum bandwidth needed for HDTV, but they can, unlike any other delivery system, send a signal directly to every home in the country. The current debate on HDTV service centers largely on the question of how the market will be split up among satellites, cable systems, and other technologies.[43] Because satellites have built-in advantages for HDTV service, there will probably be two, and possibly three, national DBS satellite networks, each equipped to deliver HDTV programming, by the late 1990s.[44]

Direct satellite broadcasting has been primarily the concern of the broadcast television and cable TV industries, but it has also attracted Hollywood's attention. The film industry expects to be the major supplier of the HDTV entertainment programs that are broadcast from satellites, much as it will be for terrestrial television and cable. Hollywood studios are also looking at ways they can use satellites for delivering films from a central point to theaters for direct projection. Such a distribution system would eliminate projection booths as well as unionized projectionists. It would also do away with the need for hundreds of copies of films in cans and would eliminate shipping costs. The prospects for such a shift in film distribution methods increased in 1991 when a group of U.S. and Japanese entrepreneurs announced a plan for sending HDTV productions by satellites to movie theaters throughout East Asia.[45]

How will the media industries restructure themselves and their products in the face of broadcasting satellites, HDTV, and other technological prospects? There is no all-purpose formula for this. History demonstrates the unintended effects, both positive and otherwise, that accompany any major technological innovations in the media. A classic example can be found in historian Elizabeth Eisenstein's study of the introduction of the printing press in the fifteenth century. She notes that the early presses were intended primarily to copy treasured old volumes, mostly religious writings. Soon, however, printers found lucrative markets for other types of publications. Those additional products, covering a wide range of subjects, had a profound effect on the Renaissance and the Reformation.[46]

A generation ago, Canadian communications scholar Marshall McLuhan suggested that the dominant medium technology in any age is a powerful force in shaping the social structure by its imposition of a particular mental regime, which enables people to process the information encoded in the technology. In other words, McLuhan argued, the media teach us how to think.[47] Another scholar, Carolyn Marvin, advances the view that the impact of each new technology depends less on the innovative aspects of the technology itself than on the convergence of economic and social forces favoring its adoption.[48]

Other scholars have studied the time lag that usually occurs between the invention of useful technologies and their widespread adoption. Stanford University economist Paul David sees this claim reflected in what he regards as the relatively slow pace of computerization in the past 40 years. According to Professor David, only 10 percent of the world's 50 million business enterprises use computers, and only 2 percent of all business information has been digitized.[49] Professor David's findings parallel those of a survey of Fortune 1000 companies in the late 1980s, which indicated that only 6 percent of those companies' business transactions involved computers and other electronic resources, while 79 percent remained on paper. Reliance on electronic transactions has increased at a faster pace since then, but such transactions are still a relatively minor factor in most American businesses.[50]

These observations are relevant to our study of the electronic future of the media industries. There is, in the economist's phrase, a diffusion lag that has more to do with administrative, economic, and social factors than with the capabilities of the new technologies. The videocassette boom in the 1980s is a prime example of the quick success that can occur when technology, economics, and consumer preferences converge. A small handful of media technologies will share a similarly happy fate in the coming years. Many others will fail, laid to rest in the same technological graveyard as Sony Betamax, Atari computer games, and 3-D movies.

A recent example of a useful but largely unsuccessful media technology is **low-powered television** (LPT). Hailed as a breakthrough in the 1980s, LPT uses special broadcast frequencies that permit low-cost television stations to operate within a limited range of 10–15 miles. The idea was to allocate these short-range video channels to minority groups and public service organizations for local programming purposes. Technically, thousands of such stations could operate throughout the United States. In fact, only a few hundred are operating, and most of them are struggling to survive. Their problems stem from the fact that such specialized programming cannot compete with the glitzy program offerings of commercial broadcasting and cable TV for the time and attention of most people.[51]

LPT is a minor example of both the failure of a useful technology and the difficulty of modifying people's media habits. There is psychic resistance to giving up such media standbys as the daily newspaper, couch potato television, and the weekend trip to the movies complete with a cardboard barrel of popcorn. Nevertheless, the electronic transformation of U.S. media will continue. Popular tastes and comfortable habits will change. In a postindustrial society, people will simply need more information to function in their job and in their private life. The dimensions of the so-called information age are already clear. Sixty percent of the work force are employed in information-related activities, including the mass media. All these activities share one characteristic: they depend on the fusion of information and telecommunications technologies. The mass media are increasingly a part of this evolving electronic national information utility. The distinctions that formerly separated one mass medium from another are blurring as all media become more dependent on shared, computer-driven delivery systems.

This transformation is more than a matter of restructuring the media industries. The long-term health of the U.S. economy, as well as our political and social future, depends on how information resources are integrated into a national electronic utility. For the present, the United States is the global leader in setting the pace and direction of such a resource. The development of similar resources by European and Japanese industries is a significant element in their efforts to match the U.S. economy.[52]

America leads in this field, but we cannot take much comfort from this. There are disturbing signs of slippage, particularly in the failure to clear many of the political and economic hurdles that stand in the way of maintaining a strong position in the telecommunications and information sectors. Politically, there is no strong consensus to develop an advanced information utility as the underpinning for a vital post-industrial democratic society in the new century, despite efforts of the Clinton White House to promote this theme. Economically, there are doubts about U.S. industry's ability to provide the goods and services for the new consumer-based information structure. Thirty years ago, the answer would have been clear. Consumer electronic products were largely a U.S. monopoly. The director of MIT's computer lab, Michael Dertouzos, points out that over 90 percent of all consumer electronics worldwide were U.S. produced in the early 1960s. That U.S. share has since dropped to 5 percent. The largest share now is supplied by Japan and other East Asian countries.[53]

This decline in U.S. produced consumer electronics was not accidental. We need only look at the pattern of change over the past three decades in the television receiver industry. Thirty years ago, the United States was the world's largest producer of TV sets. Within a few years, a series of corporate decisions resulted in effectively closing down most production lines in this country. In 1991, the last domestic producer of TV receivers, the Zenith Corporation, transferred its facilities to Mexico. Retailers have become totally dependent on imports (many of them bearing U.S. labels) from Asia and Latin America.

This is industrial suicide, according to Professor Dertouzos. With U.S. producers opting out, Japan soon dominated global consumer markets. By the early 1990s, 70 percent of Sony's orders came from outside Japan.[54] More important, that production and marketing lead gave Japan the economic clout and technological skill to pursue advanced research in the area of television and in other consumer electronics areas. Japan currently enjoys a commanding lead in the race to supply the consumer products needed to take advantage of new technologies in the media industries. Research in HDTV equipment, for example, has been pioneered by Japanese companies, encouraged by their government. As a result, those firms will probably have the edge in marketing HDTV equipment around the world. Japanese industry is making similar research gains in such advanced media machines as laser-based videocassettes and digital audio equipment.

Not surprisingly, the ability of U.S. companies to cope with Japanese and other foreign competition in this area has become a political issue. One side argues for economic protectionism, calling for a retreat to an electronic Fortress America. This, however, is a self-defeating strategy. A better case can be made for recognizing the critical importance of the electronics sector and for developing an aggressive strategy to meet foreign competition with more technologically advanced products.[55]

There have been some encouraging signs in recent years that the U.S. consumer electronics sector is rebounding at home and abroad. This is happening particularly in the burgeoning new markets for multimedia equipment. One factor in the shift is the success U.S. companies have had in developing the special microchips and the advanced software needed for multimedia products (The United States produces 60 percent of all computer software worldwide.) As a result, an industry leader such as Apple Computer saw its annual sales in Japan jump from $20 million in 1987 to $400 million by 1992. In large part, the reason has been Apple's ability to stay technologically ahead of other global competitors, including Japan. None of these competitors have matched the company's Quicktime software, which lets a Macintosh computer synchronize up to 24 different channels of information—voice, video, data, fax, or whatever—into a single recording or message.[56]

The other major development favoring the rebuilding of U.S. electronic competitiveness is the new willingness of American firms to develop strategic partnerships with innovative foreign companies. A leading example is Apple's linkup with Sony, the Japanese electronics giant. After failing to make a dent in the computer business on its own, Sony now makes components for Apple, including a Macintosh laptop— the Powerbook 100. Even IBM, traditionally a lone player, has developed a network of working partnerships with European and Japanese firms.

There are still pitfalls on the road to rebuilding U.S. leadership in consumer electronics. Industry observers recall that the most recent hot seller in that market— videocassette recorders—was invented in California by the Ampex Corporation in 1961. But then Hitachi, Sony, Sharp, and a half dozen other Japanese companies outdeveloped, outproduced, and outmarketed Ampex and other American firms. The moral is that it could happen again with the new wave of advanced multimedia products that will dominate the market in the coming years.

The media industries have a critical stake in how the U.S. economy deals with these changes. The transition to a new mass communications pattern involves more than technological innovation. The new media technologies have to be fitted into the larger realities of an evolving postindustrial society.

In the next chapter, we take a closer look at the ways in which political and economic forces are affecting that transition.

NOTES

1. Norman Macrae, "The Next Ages of Man," special section of *Economist* (London), 24 December 1988, p. 10.
2. For discussions of the information utility concept, see "Communications, Computers and Networks," a special issue of *Scientific American* 265, no. 3 (September 1991): Michael Dertouzos, "Building the Information Marketplace," *Technology Review* 94, no. 28 (30 January 1991): pp. 29–40; "Netting the Future: A Survey of Telecommunications," *Economist* (London), 10 March 1990; and Karen Wright, "The Road to the Global Village," *Scientific American* 262, no. 1 (March 1990): 83–94.
3. Robert W. Crandall, *After the Breakup: U.S. Telecommunications in a More Competitive Era* (Washington, D.C.: Brookings Institution, 1991).
4. "Motorola Plans Sale of a New Small Phone," *New York Times,* 7 August 1991, p. D-4.
5. "Phones Getting Smarter with Built-in Computer," *New York Times,* 17 April 1991, p. D-1.
6. "Your New Computer: The Telephone," *Business Week,* 3 June 1991, pp. 126–131.
7. "Telemedia: A Concept Whose Time Has Come," *Infotext* (June 1990): 43–44.
8. "Let Your 800 Number Do the Talking," *Los Angeles Times,* 13 September 1992, p. D-1.
9. "Defending Canada with an 800 Number," *Washington Post,* 15 July 1991, p. A-13.
10. "900 Services Reach $975 Million in Billings," *Infotext* (December 1991): 50.
11. "IBM and NBC will Market a News Service to PC Users," *New York Times,* 12 November 1992, p. D-21.
12. "Extra! Extra! Hot off the Faxes," *Business Week,* 23 December 1991, p. 84-E.

13. Maryrose Wood, "Just the Fax, Please," *PC Publishing and Presentation* (July 1991): 35–44; Peggy Campbell, "Fax-on-Demand," *Infotext* (July 1991): 38–48.
14. "Syscom Campaigns for the Right to Help Candidates Communicate," *Washington Post* business supplement, 2 November 1992, p. 5.
15. "First Way to Get News That's Hot off the Fax," *New York Times,* 3 July 1989, p. D-10.
16. "Gannett Plans Japanese Issues," *New York Times,* 4 November 1991, p. D-8.
17. "Small Fax Newspapers See a Way to Big Profits," *New York Times,* 3 July 1991, p. D-8.
18. "Extra! Extra! Hot off the Faxes."
19. "Papers Finding New Ways to Make Faxes a Business," *New York Times,* 6 July 1992, p. D-6.
20. "A Media Pioneer's Quest: Portable Electronic Newspaper," *New York Times,* 28 June 1992, p. F-11.
21. "The Optical Enlightenment," *Economist* (London), 8 July 1991, pp. 87–88.
22. "The New Boy Tightens His Grip," *Economist* (London), 10 August 1991, p. 63.
23. "Fiber Optics at Home: Wrong Number?" *New York Times,* 17 November 1991, p. E-18.
24. "Cable's Secret Weapon," *Forbes,* 13 April 1992, pp. 80–84.
25. "Fiber Optics at Home: Wrong Number?" See also Leland Johnson, *Common Carrier Video Delivery by Telephone Companies,* Report R-4166-MF-RL (Santa Monica, Calif.: Rand Corporation, 1992).
26. Consumer confusion over choices of advanced information services is documented in *Fiber Optics to the Home: What Does the Public Want and Need?* Donald McGannon Communication Research Center, Fordham University, May 1989.
27. "There's Fiber in Cable's Future and Telco's Too," *Broadcasting,* 17 October 1988, pp. 42–44. See also Karen Wright, "The Road to the Global Village," *Scientific American* 262, no. 1 (March 1990): 83–94.
28. "What Cable Could Be in 2000: 500 Channels," *Broadcasting,* 1 April 1991, pp. 27–28.
29. "Cable TV Battling Phone Companies," *New York Times,* 29 March 1992, p. 1.
30. For a useful discussion of the issues involved, see Leland Johnson and David Reed, *Residential Broadband Services by Telephone Companies? Technology, Economics and Public Policy,* Report No. R-3906-MF/RL (Santa Monica, Calif.: Rand Corporation, June 1990).
31. Stephen Weinstein and Paul Shumate, "Beyond the Telephone: New Ways to Communicate," *The Futurist* 23, no. 6 (November-December 1989): 12–16.
32. "Wire War: Putting America on the Line," *Washington Post,* 22 October 1989, p. C-3.
33. "Bells Win Right to Offer Information Services," *Communications Week,* 14 October 1991, p. 5.
34. For a comprehensive study of the Qube experiment and its implications, see Eileen Meehan, "Technical Capability Versus Corporate Imperatives: Towards a Political Economy of Cable Television," in Vincent Mosco and Janet Wasco, *The Political Economy of Information* (Madison, Wis.: University of Wisconsin Press, 1988) 167–187.
35. "Oracle and McCaw Tell of Radio Data Network," *New York Times,* 18 May 1992, p. D-3.
36. For a discussion of these changes, see G. A. Keyworth and Bruce Abell, *Competitiveness and Telecommunications: America's Economic Future—the House-to-House Digital Fiber-Optic Network* (Indianapolis, Ind.: Hudson Institute, 1990).
37. "Wireless Cable: The 'Will-Carry' Medium," *Broadcasting,* 15 July 1991, p. 17.
38. For an overview of communications satellite development in the 1990s, see "Satellites '91: Launching a Higher-Tech Future," *Broadcasting,* 29 July 1991, pp. 35–55. See also Joseph N. Pelton, "The Next 100 Years: Communications via Satellite," *Via Satellite* 6, no. 8 (September 1991): 61–64.
39. Marcia DeSonne, *Spectrum of New Broadcast/Media Technologies.* Publication of the research unit, National Association of Broadcasters, Washington, D.C., March 1990, p. 23.

40. Michael Major, "Revolution in the Newsroom," *Via Satellite* 6, no. 8 (September 1991): 74–75.
41. DeSonne, *Spectrum*, 21.
42. Early attempts to develop DBS services are described in David Owen, "Satellite Television," *Atlantic Monthly* 255, no. 6 (June 1985): 45–62.
43. Leland Johnson and Deborah Castleman, "Direct Broadcast Satellites: A Competitive Alternative to Cable Television," Report No. R-4047-MF/RL. (Santa Monica, Calif.: Rand Corporation, 1991).
44. "DBS: The Next Generation," *Broadcasting*, 26 February 1990, pp. 27–31; Michael Alpert, "High-Power DBS: The Long-Awaited Birth," *Via Satellite* 5, no. 7 (July 1990): 20–26.
45. "HDTV Cinema for the World," *Broadcasting*, 14 January 1991, p. 122.
46. Elizabeth Eisenstein's, *The Printing Press as an Agent of Change* (New York: Cambridge University Press, 1980).
47. Marshall McLuhan was a prolific writer on media subjects. His media views are summarized in *Understanding Media* (New York: New American Library, 1964). For information on the evolution of research on the effects of technology on the media, see "Mass Media Effects," in *International Encyclopaedia of Communications* Vol. 2 (New York: Oxford University Press, 1989), 495.
48. Carolyn Marvin, *When Old Technologies Were New* (New York: Oxford University Press, 1988).
49. Paul David, "The Dynamo and the Computer: An Historical Perspective on the Modern Productivity Paradox," *American Economic Review* 80, no. 2 (May 1990): 355–361.
50. "Paper Still Leads Electronics in Corporate Communications," *Washington Post*, 29 December 1988, p. E-1.
51. DeSonne, *Spectrum*, 67–69.
52. Kiyoto Uehara and Hirotoshi Nishida, "The International Market for Multimedia Communications: Looking Beyond the Fax Machine"; also Dennis Gilhooley, "Rewiring Europe: New Politics, New Networks"; both reports are in Gregory Staple (ed.), *The Global Telecommunications Traffic Report—1991*, International Institute of Communications (London), August 1991, pp. 13–34.
53. "Fast Forward—a Survey of Consumer Electronics," *Economist* (London), 13 April 1991, p. 18.
54. Ibid., p. 17.
55. These alternatives are discussed in *Telecommunications in the Age of Information*, National Telecommunications and Information Administration, U.S. Department of Commerce, August 1991.
56. "America's Empire Strikes Back," *Economist* (London), 22 February 1992, pp. 61–62.

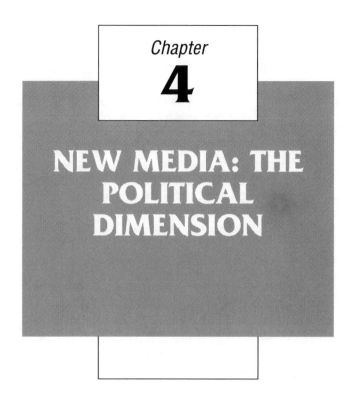

Chapter

4

NEW MEDIA: THE POLITICAL DIMENSION

America is the country which is inventing the future." These words were written a generation ago by French sociologist Michel Crozier. American influence may have since diminished in many areas, but Crozier's observation applies with particular force to the sectors we are examining here—the old and new media in mass communications. Most of the new technologies that are setting the pace for global media changes have indeed come out of American laboratories and are being applied here first. These innovations are not happening in a vacuum. They are nurtured by a political and cultural environment that encourages them.

It is useful therefore to look at the political and social factors that are shaping the transition from old to new media patterns in postindustrial America. The event that has had the most influence in stimulating new media developments in the past dozen years took place *outside* the media sector. It was the lifting of regulatory restraints on the U.S. telephone industry, culminating in the 1984 breakup of the AT&T monopoly. The competitive telecommunications structure that has emerged since then has given the media industry a powerful incentive to develop new electronic services and modify older ones. The shift is still in its early stages; the coming decade will see its full flowering, with more far-reaching changes than in any other period in the history of U.S. mass media. In the process, the United States has become the test case for a new media environment that is taking us beyond old industrial era patterns into a postindustrial society.

This trend was first documented two decades ago ago by Harvard sociologist Daniel Bell in *The Coming of Post-Industrial Society.*[1] Professor Bell forecast an America in which the production, storage, and distribution of information would be the dominant social and economic activity. His ideological thesis was given economic underpinning in the research done by Fritz Machlup and Marc Porat, who documented the growth of information-based activities in the U.S. economy.[2] Most recent research has confirmed their findings, although not without challenges to some of their conclusions.[3]

The future of American media is directly tied to this evolving postindustrial pattern and its emphasis on information activities. It is a pattern with many strands — economic, ideological, demographic, and political. As the dominant force in mass communications, the media play a dual role, both influencing these developments and being influenced by them.

The most identifiable force acting on the media is the economy. The United States is the largest and most successful free-trade area in the world, involving a quarter billion people. A critical part of that economic commonwealth consists of an information and communications infrastructure, the resource that binds the commonwealth together and makes it work. No other society is more dependent on these resources in its day-to-day activities. Americans make a billion and a half telephone calls a day — six for every man, woman, and child in the country. The economy would be immobilized if there were a serious national disruption of telephone and computer networks. The media industries are particularly vulnerable given their increasing dependence on electronic resources for producing and distributing their products.

Beyond economics, the mass media in the new information-based environment are sustained by a national ideology. It is embodied in the First Amendment and the cat's cradle of laws, regulations, and practices that the amendment has fostered over the course of more than two centuries. The decision of the writers of the Constitution that government should not license or otherwise control the press was revolutionary in an era when such controls were taken for granted. Today it is still a unique proposition in most parts of the world. Despite setbacks, the First Amendment is a remarkable force, now expanded to include all forms of public information resources, from television to computerized data banks. Its power is complemented and energized by another U.S. belief, that of salvation through technology. The idea that technology and democratic ideals can combine to form a new kind of society has been a continuing theme, from the time of Ben Franklin and his kite to the high-tech laboratories of today.[4]

Such is the tradition within which the mass media will seek a new role in postindustrial America. It involves the adaptation of a stunning array of technological prospects to social and economic conditions. New media technologies have always been disruptive, from the Gutenberg printing press to present-day electronics.[5] There is, however, a difference in the current transition. Previously, media innovations developed slowly, separated by decades. There was time to adjust the new entrants to existing social realities. In contrast, we are now witnessing the simultaneous convergence of a wide range of media technologies. The period allotted for sorting out their political and economic implications has been dramatically shortened.

Uncertainty has complicated the traditional pattern in which the existing media organizations try to preempt or slow down threatening new technology. These organizations do this to protect their entrenched interests, usually through a combination of political and economic pressures. In the early days of radio broadcasting, for instance, newspapers refused to run program schedules, in the hope of discouraging listenership. When television was new, the major Hollywood studios would not sell films to the networks. In these and similar instances, the boycotts ended only after the economic interests of the contending parties—the challengers and the defenders—were satisfactorily accommodated. That pattern of resistance and eventual accommodation is being repeated in the current wave of new media technologies. The outcome will shape the future pattern of the U.S. mass media industries. It is useful to examine the interplay of the economic and political elements that will influence the tone and direction of both the old and new media in the coming decade.

First, we consider the economic factors. The media are a $200-billion force in a society in which almost all information and entertainment products compete in the marketplace (Table 4.1). Commercialism has been the hallmark of the U.S. media industries almost from the beginning. In the early days of the republic, newspapers were often subsidized directly by political parties or other factions. That practice faded with the rise of the penny press and other publishing ventures that depended on mass circulation revenues rather than on direct patronage and subsidies.[6]

In the last century, the introduction of the new electricity-based technologies created tensions between the old and new media that are still with us. As media historian Erik Barnouw pointed out:

> Euphoric predictions greeted the advent of Morse's telegraph and the communication wonders that followed it—telephone, wireless, radio, television and the others. Each was seen to have a special significance for a democratic society: each seemed to promise wider dissemination of information and ideas. It can be argued that this has happened, as predicted. But other results, in a contrary direction, were not so readily foreseen. Each new medium offered new possibilities for the centralization of influence and control, and introduced monopoly possibilities.[7]

The managers of the new technologies did, in fact, attempt to establish monopolies in ways that threatened the existing media. The Western Union telegraph company, a monopoly in its early years, withdrew its services from newspapers that challenged its policies.[8] Decades later, the American Telephone and Telegraph Co. (AT&T) attempted to take over commercial radio broadcasting, until it was forced by the federal government to abandon its efforts. Similar actions were taken by the government in the late 1930s to modify the control that the big radio networks exercised over the programming aired on local stations.

These early federal government efforts to manage the introduction of new media technologies had, on balance, a beneficial effect. They led to the passage of the first

TABLE 4.1 Media Industries Growth

Industry Segment	1986 Gross Expenditures ($ Mil)	1986–91 Compound Annual Growth (%)	1991 Gross Expenditures ($ Mil)	1991–96 Compound Annual Growth (%)	1996* Gross Expenditures ($ Mil)
Television Broadcasting	21,427	2.4	24,110	6.3	32,800
TV Networks	8,342	2.5	9,435	6.2	12,750
TV Stations	13,085	2.3	14,675	6.4	20,050
Radio Broadcasting	6,949	4.0	8,450	6.4	11,500
Radio Networks	423	3.2	495	5.8	655
Radio Stations	6,526	4.0	7,955	6.4	10,845
Cable Television	9,405	13.6	17,780	8.6	26,920
Advertising	855	18.3	1,985	12.1	3,510
Subscriptions	8,550	13.1	15,795	8.2	23,410
Filmed Entertainment	15,483	9.9	24,773	7.5	35,580
Box Office	3,778	4.9	4,803	6.9	6,720
Home Video	5,015	17.0	10,995	8.1	16,230
Television Programs	6,090	4.8	7,700	6.7	10,650
Barter Syndication	600	16.3	1,275	9.2	1,980
Recorded Music	4,651	11.0	7,834	6.3	10,620
Newspaper Publishing	37,051	3.1	43,152	6.7	59,785
Daily Newspapers	34,352	2.9	39,612	6.7	54,820
Advertising	26,990	2.4	30,409	7.3	43,300
Circulation	7,362	4.6	9,203	4.6	11,520

Weekly Newspapers	2,699	5.6	3,540	7.0	4,965
Advertising	2,402	5.9	3,200	7.4	4,570
Circulation	297	2.7	340	3.0	395
Book Publishing	13,333	8.7	20,265	7.6	29,175
Consumer Books	7,921	10.0	12,735	8.1	18,785
Professional & Educational Books	5,412	6.8	7,530	6.7	10,390
Magazine Publishing	14,630	4.6	18,335	6.4	25,055
Consumer Magazines	10,070	4.9	12,780	6.6	17,570
Advertising	5,317	4.4	6,580	7.2	9,330
Circulation	4,753	5.5	6,200	5.9	8,240
Business Magazines	4,560	4.0	5,555	6.1	7,485
Advertising	3,200	4.8	4,055	6.8	5,625
Circulation	1,360	2.0	1,500	4.4	1,860
Business Information Services	15,680	9.1	24,206	7.6	34,860
Total Spending	138,609	6.4	188,905	7.1	266,295
Total Advertising	67,740	3.4	80,064	7.1	112,615
Total End-User	70,869	9.0	108,841	7.1	153,680
GDP	4,268,600	5.8	5,674,400	7.3	8,070,000
Communications as a % of GDP	3.2	—	3.3	—	3.3

*projected.

SOURCE: Veronis, Suhler & Associates. Reprinted by permission of Veronis, Suhler & Associates.

national law to deal with the electronic technologies—the Communications Act of 1934. To this day, the 1934 act is the only comprehensive legislation that defines the basic ground rules for telecommunications and the electronic media. Given the relatively primitive technology of the era, it dealt only with telephone and telegraph systems and radio broadcasting. The significance of the Communications Act is that it represented a social consensus between government and industry on the role of communications and information resources in U.S. life. The act set the goal of universal telephone service for the country—a bold move, considering how relatively few telephones there were at the time. It also created the FCC to regulate the telecommunications industry and radio. The commission's regulatory powers have since been expanded to include newer technologies: television, cable TV, satellite broadcasting, and the like.

In many ways, the provisions of the 1934 legislation have been overtaken by the current explosion of technologies and their economic and social consequences. The legislation can serve, however, as a general model for the new consensus we need to deal adequately with a more complex communications and information environment.[9]

The Communications Act ushered in a period of relative stability for the electronic media and other communications sectors, lasting more than 30 years. It was a time of expansion and general prosperity for the media industries. FCC regulation of broadcasting was generally benign, focused largely on protecting the industry from outside competition.[10] It was the heyday of the traditional mass media—newspapers, radio, film, and (after World War II) television.

The rumblings of change began in the 1960s. Radio declined as a nationally networked medium, retreating before the mass appeal of television. Cable TV expanded from its origins as a small-town retransmitter of broadcast television and began to develop its own programming resources. Its status as a major medium was confirmed in the mid-1970s when cable programmers began using satellites to distribute an expanded schedule of sports and entertainment products simultaneously across the country, similar to the broadcasting network pattern.

Another less visible development has had important consequences for the media industries. It is the new perception of the media as big business. Media communications, in aggregate, constitutes the ninth-largest industry in the American economy. If measured by compound-annual-growth standards, it ranks fourth.[11] With some exceptions, the annual growth rate in individual media sectors during the 1990s has so far been expanding steadily, in many cases doubling over a five-year period (Table 4.1).

Increasingly, the U.S. financial community saw the media as something more than a collection of separate, unrelated enterprises. Moreover, the industry has assets that have been, by Wall Street reckoning, generally undervalued. This has sparked an interest in mergers, buy outs, and other proposals for consolidating media operations into larger and potentially more lucrative combinations. The result is major changes in the ownership and operational patterns of many old-line media businesses. Such firms became hot properties in the Great Bull Market of the 1980s. Companies changed hands, often at inflated prices, which led to heavy debt loads. Many media organizations were adversely affected, and even wiped out, during the persistent economic recession of the early 1990s.

Another consequence of the new investment interest in mass communications was the emergence of a new breed of media managers. As a group, these entrepreneurs were intent on gaining control over a range of media services they could market in ways that would provide profitable synergies among their products. The result was a spate of mergers, buy outs, and takeovers by "information packagers." The most dramatic example was the merger of Time Inc. and Warner Communications in 1989. These two industry giants became the world's largest media conglomerate, with film, television, magazine, book, and musical record operations. Other information packagers included such relative newcomers such as Ted Turner, Australia's Rupert Murdoch, and Britain's Robert Maxwell, all three of whom expanded the information-packaging concept to international markets.[12]

The most significant change affecting the media industry took place, however, outside the industry's boundaries. It was the reorganization of the U.S. telecommunications sector to reflect new social and economic realities, a change brought about largely by federal government decisions designed to make the sector more competitive by removing or modifying regulatory restraints on its operations. The result was to end the virtual monopoly over national communications networks granted to AT&T in the Communications Act of 1934.

The deregulatory process began in 1968 when the FCC ruled against AT&T claims that only equipment made by its manufacturing subsidiary, Western Electric, could be used in its network. (The company's imperious attitude was reflected in its characterization of non–Western Electric equipment as "foreign devices.") A year later, MCI, then a struggling young firm, was given permission by the FCC to operate the first interstate long-distance network in competition with AT&T. Over the next dozen years, the AT&T monopoly was steadily eroded in a series of decisions by the FCC and the courts. Finally, in 1982, AT&T agreed to divest itself of its local telephone operations in order to settle a long-standing U.S. Justice Department antitrust case against the company. As part of the settlement, the company was given permission to compete in other kinds of communications and information businesses previously denied to it.[13]

The media industries have been a major beneficiary of this sweeping reorganization of the national telecommunications structure. AT&T is still the major player in U.S. telecommunications but it now competes with thousands of firms, each offering new services or improving on old ones. A more diverse mix of technologies, entrepreneurs, and audiences has resulted, reshaping U.S. mass communications for a new era.[14]

By the 1990s, the media industries were in a state of splendid disarray. The traditional firms were positioning themselves, with some hesitation, for life and profitability in the new environment. New entrants into the field were sharing with older firms the pressures of tight money in the economic recession that followed the giddy expansion of the 1980s. They also faced demographic challenges as the post-war baby boomers—the media targets of the 1980s—settled into two-paycheck families, with responsibilities that left less time for such activities as reading and TV viewing.[15] Another demographic challenge, critical to the media industry's long-term strategy, is that over two-thirds of population growth in the next 15 years will be accounted for by minority groups—African Americans, Hispanics, and Asians.

The federal government's decisions to deregulate the national communications structure have had, as noted earlier, a major economic impact on mass communications. The decisions have also subtly changed the political balance between government and media, particularly in the sensitive area of media freedoms. The First Amendment's prohibitions against political interference with media remain a formidable barrier against direct government intervention. It is, however, by no means a guarantor against more indirect kinds of interference.

The First Amendment is an absolute prohibition: "Congress shall make no law . . . abridging the freedom of speech, or of the press." This is more easily understood in its original eighteenth-century context than in today's more complex communications environment. On one hand, the media industries continue to seek First Amendment independence while pressing for political advantages in their relations with government at all levels. Those advantages show up in such privileges as lower postal rates, favorable radio spectrum allocations, exemptions from wage-and-hour laws for newspaper deliverers, and antitrust relief for newspapers. Special privileges for the media, granted by government, are a long-standing tradition, almost always justified by a somewhat tenuous appeal to the First Amendment.

On the other hand, federal, state, and local governments have their own agendas in dealing with the media. In large part, this reflects official sensitivities to the media's self-appointed role as a watchdog over public policies and actions.[16] Occasionally, that sensitivity boils up into active political pressure on the media. The classic example in recent times was the attempt by the Nixon Administration in the early 1970s to intimidate the television industry with regulatory threats because of the industry's alleged opposition to Nixon policies. The administration's campaign was led by an otherwise forgettable politician, Vice President Spiro Agnew, who attacked the New York networks as "a concentration of power over American public opinion unknown in history."[17] More recent official attempts to put pressure on the media have usually been more subtle.

This chronicling is important because the government will continue to play an intrusive role in media affairs—in its role as lawmaker, regulator, and supplier of public services. And that role is expanding as U.S. society becomes more dependent on information resources, including the media, to survive and thrive in a postindustrial era. A recent study, sponsored by Harvard University's Institute of Politics, describes the development as the transition to an electronic commonwealth. The study claims the new communications technologies are a critical factor in determining whether democratic government in the United States can adapt to the complexities of a postindustrial society.[18]

The political issues involved in the transition go well beyond protecting First Amendment rights of expression, however important that may be. Federal and state governments regulate public telecommunications systems and other areas of the economy that affect the media. Washington bureaucracies also finance, directly or indirectly, the development of most of the new information technologies on which the media depend. Government at all levels sets standards affecting the media in such areas as environmental controls, tax regulations, workplace safety rules, and data privacy protection. New electronic services have placed increasing pressures on the radio spectrum, a natural resource that is managed by the federal government and that is critical to broadcasting and other media operations.[19]

The media industries have become, in recent years, an important element in U.S. trade policy. Information and entertainment products and services represent one of the largest net export earners in U.S. international trade. This lead will probably be maintained in the coming years, although it may be eroded by the enlarging stake of foreign companies in U.S. media operations. The most publicized, and controversial, example of this is the takeover of several large Hollywood studios by Japanese firms in recent years.[20]

The government's involvement in these media-related issues, both direct and indirect, is becoming more pervasive. There are fundamental public policy issues involved in the decisions now being made about the shape and direction of information resources, including the mass media. The litmus test for judging these policies is whether they help or hinder the prospects for greater access to the information we need to thrive, individually and collectively, in a more complex democratic society. In the United States, this test has usually been resolved in the marketplace, which sets a cost for information, whether it is the price of a daily newspaper or data on a compact disk.

The marketplace will continue to drive the development of media resources in the new information environment. There are no longer any serious barriers to the creation of a full-scale information utility in which the mass media will play an important role. The technologies needed for the venture are tested and available. We are now crossing the economic divide, as witnessed by the extraordinary expansion of competitive new information resources in recent years. The major unresolved issues are political and social, involving public decisions on the form and purpose of the new information structure.

These political decisions are sensitive, constrained as they must be by First Amendment limits on government involvement. They go against the powerful impetus to let the marketplace decide, based on past successes in generating the most extensive information resources any society has yet developed. The marketplace is, however, powered by its own internal dynamics, dealing with particular outcomes based on bottom line standards governing economic success.

Is reliance on market economics enough to ensure the information resources we need for a postindustrial democracy? The basic issue is power, and particularly power to control information. That issue takes on greater force these days given the tendency of many new technologies to foster centralization and manipulation of a wider range of information resources whether by government or by private entities. This fact argues against our present inclination to assign most decisions in the communications and information fields to the marketplace. The point was stressed by former AT&T board chairman John DeButts, when he said: "It is not technology that will shape the future of telecommunications in this country. Nor is it the market. It is policy."[21]

But what policy? Hands-off by government, or more involvement? The First Amendment is an important standard, but it is an inadequate guide to defining specific solutions. As communications scholar Ithiel de Sola Pool has pointed out, the writers of the Constitution did not take an absolutist approach to government's role in information. Their constitutional injunctions were

> somewhat contradictory, though in fact their goals were quite consistent. In one clause the government was told to keep its legislative hands off of speech and press, while in two others it was told to promote the conveyance of knowledge by means of copyright and postal service. But both injunctions have the common goal of facilitating autonomous communication by private individuals.[22]

Professor Pool's point is an important one as we move deeper into decisions about the future form and direction of information resources, including the mass media. Ensuring a workable outcome is not a zero-sum game, a legalistic choice between rights and wrongs. It calls for a broadened policy debate that includes both the public and private sectors. The goal should be a national consensus that goes beyond particularistic interests. The essential issue concerns preserving and expanding the legacy of two centuries of information freedoms in the postindustrial environment.[23]

The mass media constitute an important part of this consensus, both as active participants defending their own interests and as public recorders and analyzers of the debate. This is, in fact, familiar ground for the media industries given their continuing and often confrontational relations with political authorities on issues involving laws, regulations, and other controls affecting the media.

The government has seldom resorted to the kind of cynical, direct efforts at intimidation and control exhibited by the Nixon Administration in its attack on television broadcasters. Media relations with government are not always confrontational. More often, media firms have sought the government's help and protection against other media. A recent example is the attempt by over-the-air broadcasters to curb, through congressional legislation, what they regard as unfair competition by the cable television and telephone industries in providing advanced information services.[24] This is a classic case of government's being asked to serve as referee in settling competing claims between an older medium and newer ones. In such cases, both sides loftily claim First Amendment rights even when their proposals involve, directly or indirectly, imposition of controls on the media operations of their opponents.

The cable TV industry has been particularly adept at lobbying its interests in this way. During the 1980s, it was the beneficiary of congressional legislation that almost totally deregulated its activities. By 1992, the industry's free-wheeling practices, including excessive charges for its services, resulted in the reimposition of regulations contained in congressional legislation that was pointedly titled the Cable Television Consumer Protection and Competition Act.[25] This action was followed in 1993 by settlement of a massive antitrust dispute in which federal and state attorneys general extracted concessions from the major cable TV companies, designed to help open to other forms of competition the industry's virtual monopoly over TV subscribers.

Appeals for government intervention are likely to become more strident as new forms of high-tech information products challenge powerful existing media. The trend will be complicated, as it is now, by the fact that there is no central agency, no "Department of Communications," in the United States with overall policy or regulatory authority in this area. Decision making is scattered among a dozen major Washington agencies, the Congress, state and local agencies, and, ultimately, the courts. The resultant confusion has the valuable attribute of diffusing political power in this sensitive area.[26]

This fragmentation of responsibilities is compounded by the lack of up-to-date legislative guidelines defining the government's relationship to the electronic media. The problem with the 1934 Communications Act is that it is over a half-century old. The act laid out a useful framework for national communications policy, but it belongs to a simpler period. The congressional framers of the 1934 legislation could not have anticipated the massive changes that were to take place in media and telecommunications, particularly after World War II, such as television, cable systems, satellites, and data networks. In the 1970s, a concerted attempt was made to bring the Communications Act up to date. The project failed after hundreds of hours of congressional committee hearings over a period of five years. The communications structure had become so complex that a consensus could not be reached among all the public and private interests, including the media industries that have a stake in setting new directions in national communications policy.[27] As a result, the 1934 legislation has been modified in small pieces over the years, primarily to establish some ground rules for integrating new technologies into the communications structure.

When legislators fail, the courts have often had to step in to mandate changes in the media industries. The courts' role in breaking up centralized radio monopolies in the 1930s has already been mentioned. More recently, in 1976, the Justice Department successfully challenged the television networks' vertical integration in a case involving the National Broadcasting Company. Between 1938 and 1946, the courts were involved in settling a massive legal case in which eight major film studios were charged by the Justice Department with being in restraint of trade. The outcome was a major reorganization of the industry, a move that strengthened the ability of independent film companies to produce and market their products.

In summary, the U.S. communications landscape is littered with a multitude of laws, court decisions, and administrative rulings. That very confusion itself serves to reinforce First Amendment protection against domination of the media by any one group. Nevertheless, the fragmentation of responsibilities makes it difficult to identify, much less implement, the policies and actions needed to ensure a successful transition to a new mass communications environment. As a result, the transition is proceeding at varying speeds and at different levels. The critical change in recent years is that the protected, monopolistic telephone network, dominated by AT&T, has given way to a deregulated telecommunications utility, which makes possible an expanded range of electronic services for media organizations.[28]

This high-tech national grid is already being used imaginatively in many ways, particularly for serving business and government needs.[29] The next step is to make it a truly universal utility. Simply put, what has to happen is the full consumerization of the grid. More than a technological challenge or an economic opportunity, this is a political concept—the full realization of democratic communications in postindustrial America. To achieve this, most of the present telecommunications infrastructure will have to be upgraded or replaced. This will be a massive exercise in the "creative destruction" economist Joseph Schumpeter described as the hallmark of creative capitalism. The new utility involves a fundamental change in the means of delivering mass communications.

The overall prospects for completing the new information utility are good. The basic technology is available, and the entrepreneurial urge to exploit its potential is strong. But the major levers of media power are still in the hands of relatively few organizations, who have the resources to dictate the pace and direction of media growth. They will be key players in determining the political and economic adjustments needed to bring the mass media into the new universal information utility. In true U.S. tradition, they will make a deal, or rather a series of ongoing deals, in which the economic interests of all the participants will be accommodated.[30]

The new utility will not lead us to an electronic Utopia, nor will it be a monolithic monster, wielding information mastery over society. It will be something in-between, a more coherent but still competitive arrangement of networks that can provide a wider range of information services for more people than any society has ever achieved. Everyone stands to win if this goal is met. It can happen, however, only if we develop a clearer consensus on our information needs in a democratic post-industrial era. This need for consensus is too important and too immediate to be treated with benign neglect or to be left to the Micawberish hope that something will turn up.

Technology alone cannot dictate a universal communications utility, but it can facilitate one. Consider, for example, the potential social impact of fiber-optic cable technology. Advanced versions of fiber cable have more than 10,000 times the capacity of telephone copper wire. Because of this staggering capacity, a fiber cable can transmit any combination of video, sound, and data communications simultaneously. Until now, the mass media industries have operated as separate entities, each with its own production and distribution systems. In the coming years, fiber cable and other delivery technologies will give them a common link into consumer markets as part of the information utility.

Michael Dertouzos, head of MIT's Laboratory for Computer Science, has projected some of these implications for what he calls the National Information Infrastructure (NII). It would be

> a common resource of computer-communication services, as easy to use and as important as the telephone network, the electric power grid, and the interstate highways. . . . The NII would make possible a United States where business mail would routinely reach its destination in five seconds instead of five days; where advertising could be done in reverse with consumers broadcasting needs to suppliers; where goods could be ordered and paid for electronically; where a retired engineer in Florida could teach high-school algebra to a bunch of students in New York; . . . where you might enjoy from your easy chair your choice of a high-definition video movie from the millions produced; where national treasures like the National Gallery could be explored at your own pace and with your interests in mind—and on the list goes, limited only by our imagination.[31]

In summary, the stage is set for the most far-reaching changes in the history of U.S. media, involving a unique convergence of technological, economic, and political issues. The debate on resolving these issues has already begun. Many of the key decisions must be made within the next few years if the transition to a universal mass communications utility is to get under way in earnest.

We examine the impact of this development as it affects individual media sectors—broadcasting, publishing, and film—in the chapters that follow. Two basic issues have to be resolved before a full-service advanced network can become a reality. The first is: who will build the new utility? The second is: how will it be organized to ensure equitable access by consumers? The two issues are, of course, related. For the present, the question of access has been overshadowed in the fierce debate over who will build the network.

The chief opponents in the debate are two powerful industries—the cable television systems and the telephone companies. But there is a third party in the wings—the direct broadcast satellite (DBS) industry. The last group is made up of companies that want to build satellite networks that would transmit advanced information and entertainment services directly into small earth stations mounted on houses and apartment buildings. DBS networks have one distinct advantage over telephone and cable TV systems: they can transmit a signal directly into every U.S. home. Beaming programs from 22,000 miles away in space, the satellites have a "footprint"—their coverage area—which includes the entire country, as well as parts of Canada and Mexico.

The problem with DBS services is that they are still undeveloped, in large part because no one has figured out a successful economic formula for making them work. The technology has been available for over 20 years, but a full-service DBS network will not be fully operational in the United States until the mid-1990s. DBS networks will play a role in the evolution of the new information utility, but it is doubtful that they will overtake the lead currently enjoyed by telephone and cable TV networks in the race to provide a high-capacity information channel in U.S. homes.[32]

The telephone and cable TV industries each bring special strengths to this project. Over 11,000 cable systems directly serve 60 percent of U.S. homes; cable lines pass by another 30 percent of homes that are not cable subscribers. Most cable systems provide 40 or more channels of information and entertainment programming; that capacity can be readily doubled or tripled within a few years, using the same cables, through the digital compression techniques described in Chapter 2. Many cable systems are currently being upgraded so that they can provide any form of interactive video, sound, or data services. The cable TV industry is thus a formidable player in the political and economic competition to determine who will supply advanced electronic services to U.S. homes.

The telephone companies have equally formidable qualifications, including more than a century of experience in wiring U.S. homes: over 95 percent of U.S. residences subscribe to phone services. The companies also have a long history of providing specialized information services, ranging from weather reports to Dial-a-Prayer. Their laboratories have pioneered most of the technologies needed for a high-capacity consumer information utility. AT&T's Bell Laboratories have been, for instance, a pioneer in fiber-optics research. Along with other phone companies, AT&T has installed millions of miles of fiber cables throughout the country, gradually replacing the 200 million miles of copper wire in the national phone system.[33] The phone companies also have the financial resources to undertake what will be the largest single construction project ever built by any U.S. industry. Equally important, consumer information channels and services will be a primary area of U.S. economic growth in the 1990s and into the next century.[34]

The phone companies are still experiencing barriers to full participation in this project. They continue to be limited by the many restrictions placed on their information service activities by Congress and by federal and state regulatory agencies. Both AT&T and the seven regional telephone companies that emerged from the 1984 AT&T breakup were prohibited from expanding into electronic information services, as well as into certain other business areas.[35] The original intention of the restrictions was to prevent phone companies from using the profits from their regulated telephone business to cross-subsidize nontelephone operations. Although the seven regional companies are known as the "Baby Bells," they are neither small nor helpless. They control more than half of U.S. telecommunications assets, and they have combined annual revenues of over $80 billion.[36]

From the time the information restrictions were imposed on them in 1984, the Baby Bells lobbied hard to have them removed.[37] Their primary target was U.S. Circuit Court judge Harold C. Greene, who had been assigned to monitor their performance in implementing the agreement. Judge Greene proved to be a tough overseer. He maintained that the companies should concentrate on their traditional product—local phone service—and he resisted their appeals to be allowed to become information providers on their own.

The turnaround for the Baby Bells came suddenly, all within a few weeks during the fall of 1991. Years of judicial appeals against Judge Greene's information services restrictions paid off when a U.S. Court of Appeals panel ruled that the regional phone companies could develop and market any information services they wished. The ruling in effect overturned Judge Greene's restrictions and gave a new thrust to the evolution of a full-service national information utility. The court's decision confirmed that, from now on, the telephone industry would be actively involved as both a producer and a transmitter of information services.[38] By 1993, all seven regional Bell companies were implementing plans for marketing consumer data information to home subscribers.

The court's decision did not, however, put the final seal on the Baby Bells' plans to move into the information business. It merely shifted the debate to the political arena, where the U.S. Congress and the FCC faced pressures to maintain restrictions on the phone industry's information plans. Those pressures came largely from the media industries, particularly cable TV, broadcasting, and newspaper publishing, each sector fearing that the phone companies, with their economic clout and their access to almost every U.S. home, would unfairly dominate the electronic information field.[39] For their part, the phone companies argue that lifting all the information restrictions imposed on them would boost the overall economy, providing (by their estimates) a million and a half new jobs and an additional $100 billion in gross domestic product by the end of the decade.[40]

The telephone industry won a significant advantage just two weeks after the favorable circuit court decision in the fall of 1991. The occasion was an FCC ruling that outlined its ideas on regulating a national information utility. The FCC proposed that telephone companies be permitted to build and operate high-capacity networks capable of delivering data, voice, and video services to homes and other locations. The FCC's ruling quickly became known as the "video-dial-tone" decision. The commission proposed that phone companies could supplement their familiar dial tone for regular voice service with one that would connect customers to television entertainment and other video services. In effect, the companies would provide any subscriber nondiscriminatory access to these services at government-regulated rates, in the same way that they now offer ordinary phone services.[41] The first video-dial-tone tests were begun by New York Telephone in three Manhattan apartment buildings in early 1993.

The FCC's video-dial-tone proposal avoided one sticky issue. It concerned whether there should be a relaxation of FCC rules limiting telephone companies from becoming information and entertainment program providers. The commission did, however, suggest that the companies could provide "video gateways"—on-screen program menus and searching features to help viewers find the services they want. This did not satisfy phone industry representatives, who wanted permission for their companies to become multimedia program providers.[42] The resolution of this issue over the next several years will be an important test of phone company plans for expanding services in this area.[43] Bell Atlantic, one of the largest regional phone companies, took active steps in 1993 to compete directly with cable TV companies in Alexandria, Virginia, and Toms River, New Jersey, proposing a full range of video-dial-tone services.

The cable TV industry reacted strongly against the FCC ruling and its premise that phone companies could become competitors to cable systems and start to provide information and entertainment services for homes. The ruling was "obviously unfair," declared James Mooney, cable TV's chief Washington lobbyist. Mooney and his colleagues objected particularly to the FCC proposal that telephone companies and video programmers would not need to obtain cable franchises from local municipalities. Most such franchises require cable systems to pay a hefty annual fee and to assume other costly obligations. In late 1992, the National Cable Television Association, the industry's lobbying group, petitioned the FCC to halt phone company plans for video-dial-tone services, basing its case on the danger of anticompetitive behavior.

The cable industry was joined by other media groups in opposing the FCC's proposals. Among the protesters was the influential American Newspaper Publishers Association, whose members fear the erosion of both readership and revenues if the phone companies establish electronic classified ads and yellow pages as one of the services they will offer.[44] The publishers' fears are probably justified: classified advertising is a critical revenue source for most newspapers. In 1992, NYNEX became the first regional phone company to market electronic yellow pages services, offering 1.7 million listings that can be accessed by PC users.

The FCC ruling, together with the circuit court decision on telephone information services, set the tone and direction for the evolution of a full-scale national information utility within the next 15 or 20 years. In the near term, it pits the powerful resources of the telephone companies against those of cable TV and other media industries in a struggle to determine how the future market for home-delivered information and entertainment services will be shared.

Inevitably, the legislative and regulatory decisions will be challenged in the courts, a process that could stretch out over many years. In the meantime, the contending parties continue to lobby their interests in Washington, which has resulted in a flurry of congressional bills, some supporting and some opposing telephone company competition in electronic information services.[45] In the early days of the debate, the Clinton administration took a cautious view of the issue given the difficult political consequences of choosing between the powerful forces involved. The Clinton White House has generally supported the idea of open competition among all information suppliers. These views were reflected in a Department of Commerce report that proposed allowing regional telephone companies to own, control, and distribute television programs, in effect permitting them to expand their operations to include ownership of cable systems.[46] The Clinton administration has generally followed the lead of the Democratic leadership in Congress in stressing consumer protection needs over a strongly marketplace-oriented resolution of the issues involved.

Meanwhile, the main contenders for the mass information services market—the cable TV systems and the telephone companies—are positioning themselves to operate in each other's business. Telecommunications Inc. (TCI), the largest U.S. cable TV conglomerate, has active plans to offer telephone service over its facilities. Bell Atlantic, a regional phone company, is implementing a $1.5-billion project to offer video services in competition with cable systems in New Jersey. In 1993, Southwestern Bell, another regional phone company, announced plans to buy two major Washington, DC, area cable systems.

These moves are merely the early skirmishes in an ongoing political and economic struggle to decide the form and direction of a national information utility. Although the telephone and cable TV industries are the leading contenders, the mass media and other information producers cannot be dismissed as future challengers. Old-line media firms in television, films, and publishing are beginning to assess the long-term impact of a high-capacity integrated information network. Even more intriguing is the potential role of new media entrepreneurs, particularly database providers. A preview of what could happen is offered by Prodigy, the IBM/Sears Roebuck consumer data network, which already has over 2 million consumer users. For the time being, Prodigy service is limited to videotext, with some graphics. When a full-scale information utility is developed, Prodigy and its competitors will expand their offerings to include a wide range of video programming and other services.

This full-scale utility will probably not emerge until after the turn of the century. Even when the legal and political issues are sorted out, the problem of assembling the capital investment needed for the project will be formidable. Two hundred billion dollars is an optimistic estimate for completing a fiber-optic network reaching into most U.S. homes. A more realistic estimate, according to many experts, is a half trillion dollars.[47]

Both the telephone companies and the cable TV operators have begun to install fiber cable for household services, but neither can afford to rush blindly into large-scale projects. They may be sobered by the Japanese experience with fiber-optic networks. Nippon Telephone and Telegraph, the dominant phone company in Japan, has been installing fiber cable in homes on a limited basis for 20 years. Its schedule for completing the system, which is roughly half the size of any comparable U.S. effort, has a target date of the year 2015.[48]

In the United States, the information utility project raises a familiar management dilemma. Which should come first: market demand or a fully functioning system? The conventional answer is market demand. Both the telephone and the cable industries face the fact that there is no loud consumer outcry for the kinds of new or expanded information services that can be delivered by high-tech networking into homes. Almost all marketing surveys find that most consumers think they have all the information and entertainment facilities they need. These attitudes also worry mass media firms as they try to measure the potential demand for new information and entertainment products on the network. It is small comfort to them to suggest that, eventually, consumers will want the new services. The immediate question facing the industry is whether to spend large sums of money now to develop high-tech products for a market that will then take a long time to mature.[49]

How will the new network evolve? A reasonable guess is that its evolution will take place in two phases—a limited network by the end of the century and a completed one by the year 2015. That probability rests on the premise that there will be, within the next few years, resolution of the current political debate on the telephone companies' role in the new utility. The eventual compromise will most likely allow phone companies to participate, but with some restrictions on their activities in order to protect the interests of the cable TV industry and other mass media firms.

The interim system, until the end of the century, will be built by telephone firms and cable TV companies. Cable TV firms are already investing in fiber-to-the-home networks. In 1992, an estimated 20 percent of U.S. cable TV systems were upgraded with fiber-optic circuits.[50] The remaining systems may rely on less high tech solutions to increase their channel capacity. In most cases, that involves digital compression of their present coaxial cables, permitting a doubling or tripling of channel capacity.[51]

The telephone companies have not matched the cable TV industry's rush to provide large amounts of fiber-optic facilities reaching down to households. In part, this reflects the companies' reluctance to invest heavily in fiber to the home until legislative and regulatory ambiguities about their role are resolved. Their interim strategy is to upgrade present phone circuits, enabling them to provide limited video services before they begin large-scale fiber-to-the-home networking.

Bellcore, the research arm of the Baby Bells, has developed a system, known in engineer-speak as an asymmetrical digital subscriber loop (ADSL), which transmits one-way, VCR-quality video over existing copper wires. ADSL installations are relatively cheap (about $500 per home), and they can be used to connect subscribers to thousands of information and entertainment sources. A disadvantage noted by many experts is that ADSL's VCR-quality signal is relatively poor compared to that of cable signals and to HDTV. Nevertheless, it allows phone companies to move into video-on-demand services (e.g., movies) at relatively low installation costs, positioning the companies in the potential market for more sophisticated fiber network services down the road. In 1993, AT&T announced development of an improved telephone attachment, which allows customers to receive movies and other television programs over ordinary telephone lines. Alternatively, phone companies can pursue the strategy of simply investing in existing cable operations, a practice permitted under present government regulations provided that the investment involves cable systems outside the company's normal service area. As previously noted, Southwestern Bell became the first regional phone company to take advantage of this provision when it bought several cable TV systems in the Washington, D.C., suburbs in 1993.

This scenario would put a limited information utility in place by the turn of the century. It will be a network of competitive networks—telephone, cable, and DBS transmissions—each seeking a stake in an expanded electronic information and entertainment market. Such an interim arrangement of networks would establish a base for building a more advanced information utility, with a wider range of services. How will this full-scale utility evolve? Will it evolve at all? Might not consumers be satisfied with the limited expansion of services promised in the next few years? These are practical questions, which must wait for marketplace answers. The answers will determine the shape and direction of the mass media industries well into the next century.

The technology of choice for the full network will be fiber-optic cable, barring another major (and unanticipated) technological breakthrough in information delivery. Fiber cable services to the home will require a massive expansion of the fiber networks that currently serve business and government needs. The economics and technical capabilities of this basic backbone system are proven. The focus now is on ways to extend the network efficiently to over 90 million homes.

Which industry will eventually gain the upper hand in providing a full-service network? Separate fiber-optic links to homes by the phone and cable TV companies would be an unnecessarily expensive, and wasteful, solution. Simple efficiency argues for a single high-capacity wire, which suggests that the telephone industry may become the dominant provider of fiber cable for homes. The phone companies not only have more technical experience with fiber systems but also have greater financial resources, with annual revenues five times those of the cable TV industry. Another possibility is that the fiber-optic utility will be developed jointly by cable TV and telephone companies, each providing different services that share a single line. This option has already been tested in several U.S. cities.[52] Such a partnership could hasten construction of the network, particularly if the phone companies are given financial incentives (in the form of accelerated depreciation of their investment) to build the network.[53]

The eventual resolution of the issue may turn on an important constitutional principle. For the first time, we are dealing with what may be called a multimedia First Amendment issue—information rights in a technological system in which all kinds of communications resources will be squeezed into a two-way information pipe (e.g., fiber cable) for delivery to U.S. living rooms and other consumer locations. This involves a massive extension of First Amendment prospects, well beyond the limited challenges to information access we have experienced over the past two centuries. The modern reformulation of the First Amendment is known as the Associated Press principle, after a 1943 antitrust action brought by the U.S. Justice Department against the Associated Press (AP) news agency. In deciding against AP, the court asserted that the First Amendment's underlying premise is to foster "the widest possible dissemination of information from diverse and antagonistic sources."

In his opinion in the AP case, Judge Learned Hand said that

> this principle presupposes that right conclusions are more likely to be gathered out of a multitude of tongues, than any kind of authoritative selection. To many, this is, and always will be, folly; but we have staked our all on it.[54]

The new information utility makes possible an unprecedented expansion of Judge Hand's multitude of tongues—thousands of channels of information in voice, video, and print formats. The First Amendment challenge is to guarantee full access to the utility by both the providers and the users of its information. There are few direct precedents for determining the information utility's role in maintaining First Amendment rights in the coming years.

For the immediate future, that role will be defined by political decisions on how the new utility is to be organized. As noted earlier, the utility will be a competitive network of networks in its early years, involving telephone, cable, and satellite circuits. Such diversity gives useful assurance of competitive information channels. However, it does not in itself guarantee First Amendment rights. That will happen only if the utility is eventually organized as some form of common carrier, the regulators' term for a system that provides nondiscriminatory access for all users. The classic example, of course, is the telephone network, open to all who pay their phone bill at the end of the month.

In summary, some variation of the common carrier telephone system will be the best model for ensuring First Amendment freedoms in any future information utility. This fact strengthens the case for strong phone company participation in building and operating the new utility. There seems little prospect at present that cable TV networks can be reorganized as common carrier enterprises. Unlike the phone companies, they operate on a variety of technical standards; they are franchised individually by thousands of municipalities; and, most important, they are free to refuse access to information providers. This has happened consistently, most notably in 1985 when major cable companies effectively prevented NBC from setting up a cable TV news service that would compete with the existing Cable News Network (CNN), a channel in which the cable companies had a financial interest.[55]

The cable industry's answer to such criticism has been to support, somewhat reluctantly, the practice of leased access, which requires cable systems to open a certain number of channels for use by independent video programmers. This would, in principle, modify the tight control that cable TV operators have over their systems' programs. By allowing access to programs not under their direct control, leased access would put local cable networks on a sounder, First Amendment footing.

The leased access option to diversifying cable programming has been around for a long time. In a modified form, it was mandated in congressional legislation, by way of the Cable Communications Policy Act of 1984. Despite this legislative imprimatur, leased access arrangements have languished. The reason, according to a 1991 Northwestern University study, is that "the bargaining leverage is entirely with the monopoly cable operator."[56] Not all cable TV observers see First Amendment virtues in the leased access approach. Indiana University law professor Fred H. Cate argues that government-enforced right-of-access is contrary to First Amendment principles.[57]

In the inevitable compromise that will emerge, both the telephone companies and the cable TV operators will have some restrictions placed on their programming patterns. The 1992 Cable Television Consumer Protection and Competition Act forbids cable conglomerates from withholding their programs from competitors such as DBS operators and from setting prices for the programs so high that competitors are at a disadvantage to a cable company.[58] The phone companies, in turn, face the prospect of limitations on the number of information and entertainment services they own or lease. The result, overall, will be an imperfect formula for ensuring a wide variety of information resources available to consumers. Economist Leland L. Johnson argues that any limitations placed on the two industries should be roughly comparable, in the interests of providing competitive symmetry and encouraging diversity of services.[59]

The eventual pattern of a full-scale information utility is difficult to predict. It will be the result of a series of political compromises that satisfy primarily the interests of the industries involved. Nevertheless, government intervention in the process will always be flawed, given the inability of the political process to match the pace of communication changes. As the London *Economist* noted:

> Technology will change faster than the government's ability to regulate it. . . . The right communications policy for America is one that maximizes revenues for the government and lays out an open field for competition.[60]

The ultimate test of the new information utility will be its power to strengthen First Amendment freedoms. Will the media and other information providers be free to supply a full range of competitive information resources? Is there reasonable and affordable access by all Americans to these services? This latter test will be critical. Americans are accustomed to cheap (or even free) access to consumer information services, from public libraries to inexpensive newspapers. The new electronic services, involving expensive equipment, may erode that tradition. We may be moving toward what communications researcher Vincent Mosco calls the "pay-per society," involving higher prices for access to electronic information.[61] The end result could be to isolate large segments of Americans from the benefits of the new technologies.

In the next four chapters, we examine this and other issues that are emerging in the electronic transformation of the U.S. media environment.

NOTES

1. Daniel Bell, *The Coming of Post-Industrial Society* (New York: Basic Books, 1973).
2. Fritz Machlup, *The Production and Distribution of Knowledge in the United States* (Princeton N.J.: Princeton University Press, 1962); Marc Porat, *The Information Economy*, 9 vols., Office of Telecommunications Special Publication 77-12, U.S. Department of Commerce, Washington, D.C., 1977.

3. See Stephen S. Cohen and John Zysman, *Manufacturing Matters: The Myth of the Post-Industrial Economy* (New York: Basic Books, 1987). Also James Beniger, *The Control Revolution* (Cambridge: Harvard University Press, 1986); Michael Traber, *The Myth of the Information Revolution: Social and Ethical Implications of Communications Technology* (Newbury Park, Calif.: Sage, 1988); and Michael R. Rubin and Mary T. Huber, *The Knowledge Industry in the United States, 1960–1980* (Princeton, N.J.: Princeton University Press, 1986).

4. The idea of salvation-through-technology is analyzed in Leo Marx, *The Machine in the Garden* (New York: Oxford University Press, 1964).

5. This pattern is documented in Carolyn Marvin, *When Old Technologies Were New* (New York: Oxford University Press, 1988).

6. Richard D. Brown, *Knowledge Is Power: The Diffusion of Information in Early America, 1700–1865* (New York: Oxford University Press, 1989).

7. Erik Barnouw, "Historical Survey of Communication Breakthroughs," in Gerald Benjamin (ed.), *The Communications Revolution in Politics,* Proceedings of the Academy of Political Science, 34, no. 4 (1982): p. 13.

8. Alvin F. Harlow, *Old Wires and New Waves* (New York: Appleton-Century, 1936), 337.

9. For a useful summary of the policy issues involved in creating a new consensus, see *Telecom 2000,* National Telecommunications and Information Administration, U.S. Department of Commerce. Washington, D.C., 1989.

10. The FCC's performance is documented in Stanley Besen, *Misregulating Television: Network Dominance and the FCC* (Chicago: University of Chicago Press, 1984).

11. *Communications Industry Forecast: Industry Spending Projections 1992–1996,* 6th annual ed. (New York: Veronis, Suhler & Associates, June 1992), 17.

12. The rise of the new international information packagers is documented in Greg MacDonald, *The Emergence of Multi-Media Conglomerates,* Working Paper No. 70, Multimedia Enterprises Program (Geneva, Switzerland: International Labour Organization, 1990. See also Anthony Smith, *The Age of the Behemoths: The Globalization of Mass Media Firms,* Twentieth Century Fund Paper (New York: Priority Press, 1991).

13. The AT&T divestiture and its implications are discussed in Robert W. Crandall, *After the Breakup: U.S. Telecommunications in a More Competitive Era* (Washington, D.C.: Brookings Institution, 1991), and George H. Bolling, *AT&T—Aftermath of Antitrust* (Washington, D.C.: National Defense University Press, 1983). For critiques of the decision to divest AT&T of its local phone operations, see Alan Stone, *Wrong Number: The Breakup of AT&T* (Boston: Basic Books, 1989), and Vincent Mosco, "The Mythology of Telecommunications Deregulation," *Journal of Communication* 40, no. 1 (Winter 1990): 36–49.

14. For a useful summary of the changes, see Jeffrey B. Abramson, Christopher Arterton, and Garry R. Orren, *The Electronic Commonwealth: The Impact of New Media Technologies on Democratic Politics* (New York: Basic Books, 1988), 32–65.

15. Jib Fowles, "The Upheavals in the Media," *New York Times,* 6 January 1991, p. D-13.

16. In recent years, the subtleties of government-media relationships have been extensively explored. See, for example, Gerald Benjamin, *The Communications Revolution in Politics,* Proceedings of the Academy of Political Science, 34, no. 4 (1982); Montague Kern, *Thirty Second Politics: Political Advertising in the Eighties* (New York: Praeger, 1989); W. Lance Bennett, *The Governing Crisis: Media, Money and Marketing in American Elections* (New York: St. Martin's, 1992); and Jarol B. Manheim, *All the People, All the Time* (Armonk, N.Y.: M. E. Sharpe, 1991).

17. Morton Mintz and Jerry S. Cohen, *America Inc.: Who Owns and Operates the United States* (New York: Dell, 1972), 156–157.

18. Abramson et al., *The Electronic Commonwealth,* 274–280.

19. "The Elbowing Is Becoming Fierce for Space on the Radio Spectrum," *New York Times,* 25 June 1990, p. 1.

20. Trade in information services has become such an important issue for the United States that it lobbied, successfully, to include such trade for the first time in the most recent round of trade liberalization negotiations conducted under the General Agreement on Trade and Tariffs. U.S. media organizations helped to develop the U.S. proposals designed to reduce the foreign barriers that limited access to their products and services. The extent of these barriers was first documented in a CBS Inc. survey entitled Trade Barriers to U.S. Motion Picture and Television, Prerecorded Entertainment, Publishing and Advertising Industries, issued in 1984. The survey identified hundreds of tariff and nontariff barriers to U.S. media products in over 60 countries.

21. John DeButts, "Policy, Not Technology, Will Shape the Future of Communications," *Communications News,* June 1975, p. 47.

22. Ithiel de Sola Pool, *The Technologies of Freedom* (Cambridge: Harvard University Press, 1984), 18. See also T. Carter, M. Franklin, and J. Wright, *The First Amendment and the Fifth Estate: Regulation of Electronic Mass Media,* 2d ed. (Mineola N.Y.: Foundation Press, 1988).

23. For a useful summary of current public policy issues affecting the mass media and other communications industries, see *Critical Connections,* Publication No. OTA-CIT-407, Office of Telecommunications Policy, U.S. Congress, Washington D.C., 1990.

24. "Cable TV Battling Phone Companies," *New York Times,* 29 March 1992, p. 1.

25. "The Act's Aftermath: On to the FCC," *Broadcasting,* 12 October 1992, p. 32.

26. There have been a number of attempts to centralize government control over information policy, notably during the First and Second World Wars. More recently, the Nixon administration set up a White House Office of Telecommunications Policy in 1969, designed to advise the president on communications matters. It quickly became politicized, playing a major role in administration attacks on the media. It was abolished by the Carter administration in 1977 and replaced by a more research-oriented agency, the National Telecommunications and Information Administration in the Department of Commerce.

27. One beneficial outcome of the attempt to revise and update the Communications Act in the 1970s was an upsurge in public policy research dealing with communications on both the public- and private-sector levels. The congressional committee in charge of the legislative hearings produced one of the more impressive studies. See U.S. Congress, *Options Papers,* Subcommittee on Communications of the Committee on Interstate and Foreign Commerce, U.S. House of Representatives, 95th Congress, 1st Sess, Committee Print 95-13, May 1977.

28. An authoritative description of changes taking place in the telecommunications structure can be found in *The Geodesic Network: Report on Competition in the Telephone Industry,* Antitrust Division, U.S. Department of Justice, Washington, D.C., January 1987. Written by Peter W. Huber and known popularly as the Huber Report, the document traces the transition of the telecommunications network from a rigid pyramid to a flexible geodesic structure, capable of a wider range of services.

29. For a description of the high-tech network and its future, see Al Gore, "Infrastructure for the Global Village," *Scientific American,* special issue on communications, computers, and networks 265, no. 3 (September 1991): 150–164.

30. Elie Noam, *The Rivalry Between the Traditional Media: Books, Film and the Electronic Media,* Center for Telecommunications and Information Studies, Columbia University Graduate School of Business, November 1985.

31. Michael Dertouzos, "Building the Information Marketplace," *Technology Review* 94, no. 28 (January 1991): 30.

32. Scott Chase, "The U.S. Satellite Services Industry: No Consensus on the Future," *Via Satellite* 6, no. 9 (September 1991): 54–60. See also "Satellites '91: Launching a Higher-Tech Future," *Broadcasting*, 29 July 1991, pp. 33–55.
33. "Fiber Optics at Home: Wrong Number?" *New York Times*, 17 November 1991, p. E-18.
34. "How Do You Build an Information Highway?" *Business Week*, 16 September 1991, pp. 108–112. For a survey of the technological, economic, and policy issues involved in phone company entry into advanced information services for homes, see Leland L. Johnson and David P. Reed, *Residential Broadband Services by Telephone Companies?* Report R-3906-MF/RL (Santa Monica, Calif.: Rand Corporation, June 1990).
35. Crandall, *After the Breakup,* 5–6, 157, 161.
36. Walter S. Baer and Martin Greenberger, "Consumer Electronic Publishing in the Competitive Environment," *Journal of Communication* 37, no. 1 (Winter 1987): 49–63.
37. "Everyone Has Taken Lumps in This Lobbying War," *Business Week*, 21 October 1991, pp. 89–92.
38. "Baby Bells' Right to Enter Data Market Is Affirmed," *Washington Post*, 9 October 1991, p. D-1. See also "Growing Babies' Ring of Confidence," *Financial Times* (London), 9 October 1991, p. 9.
39. For descriptions of the reactions of mass media firms to telephone company entry into the field, see "Newspapers Prepare for Competition with RBOCs," *Presstime*, American Newspaper Publishers Association (September 1991): 16–21; "Why Cable Companies Are Playing Rough," *Business Week*, 12 August 1991, pp. 66–67.
40. "RBOCs Say Telco Entry Will Boost Economy," *Broadcasting*, 15 June 1992, pp. 31–32.
41. "Video Dial Tone Advances at FCC," *Broadcasting*, 28 October 1991, p. 26.
42. "Telcos to Go for Half a Loaf on Cable Entry," *Broadcasting*, 2 December 1991, p. 51.
43. "Will Telcos Dial TV's Signals?" *Broadcasting*, 21 September 1992, p. 36.
44. "Newspapers Prepare for Competition with RBOCs," *Presstime*, American Newspaper Publishers Association (September 1991): 16–21.
45. "Senate Adds New Wrinkle to Information Services Debate," *Broadcasting*, 2 December 1991, p. 10.
46. "Telecommunications in the Age of Information," Report by the National Telecommunications and Information Administration, U.S. Department of Commerce, August 1991.
47. The cost of fiber wiring of individual homes is discussed in Leland L. Johnson and David Reed, *Residential Broadband Services by Telephone Companies: Technology, Economics and Public Policy,* Report R-3906-MF/RL (Santa Monica, Calif.: Rand Corporation, June 1990), 13–16.
48. "Fiber Optics at Home: Wrong Number?"
49. "Fiber Optics at Home: Wrong Number?"
50. "Selling Information Services Is Hard Test for 'Baby Bells,'" *New York Times*, 5 August 1991, p. D-1.
51. "What Cable Could Be in 2000: 500 Channels," *Broadcasting*, 1 April 1991, pp. 27–28.
52. "The Condo Approach to Telco Entry," *Broadcasting*, 3 February 1992, pp. 26–28.
53. This case is made forcefully in Henry Geller, "Fiber Optics: An Opportunity for a New Policy?" Annenberg Washington Program, Washington, D.C., November 1991, pp. 31–39.
54. *United States v. Associated Press.* 52 F. Supp. 362, 372 (S.D.N.Y. 1943).
55. The incident is described in Geller, "Fiber Optics," 19–20.
56. *Cable Television Leased Access,* Annenberg Washington Program on Communications Studies, Northwestern University, Washington D.C., 1991, p. 4.
57. Fred H. Cate, "The First Amendment and Compulsory Access to Cable Television," in *Cable Television Leased Access,* pp. 41–45.
58. "Bill Covers a Wide Range of Practices," *Washington Post*, 4 October 1992, p. D-2.

59. Leland L. Johnson, *Common Carrier Video Delivery by Telephone Companies,* Report R-4166 MF/RL (Santa Monica, Calif.: Rand Corporation, 1992).

60. "Re-Regulation Frenzy," *Economist* (London), 15 February 1992, pp. 25-26.

61. Vincent Mosco, "Information in the Pay-per Society," in Vincent Mosco and Janet Wasco (eds.), *The Political Economy of Information* (Madison, Wis.: University of Wisconsin Press, 1988), 3-26.

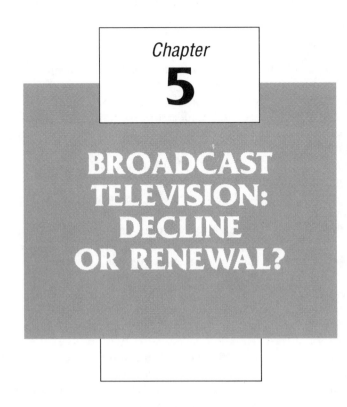

Chapter

5

BROADCAST TELEVISION: DECLINE OR RENEWAL?

Nowhere is the impact of the new media on the old more visible than in television broadcasting. Over-the-air television is under siege these days, largely because its audiences (and its revenues) are being increasingly preempted by cable television and home videocassette recorders. That trend will accelerate as newer technologies such as DBS and fiber-optic delivery of information and entertainment services to homes continue to compete for consumer attention.

Television is, nevertheless, still the most powerful and pervasive U.S. mass medium. None other can match the hold it has on the tens of millions of viewers who spend many hours daily in front of the tube. "Television is our common cultural ground," said media critic Charles Paul Freund. "It is the only thing most Americans know and experience more or less together, and whatever is next on the list is small beer compared to it."[1]

Television has evoked strong reactions, pro and con, from its earliest days. In the 1950s, radio satirist Fred Allen saw its creating a race of people "with eyes as big as grapefruit and no brains, no brains at all." Architect Frank Lloyd Wright called it chewing gum for the eyes. Historian Daniel J. Boorstin noted, "We can no longer say, with Oscar Wilde, that life imitates art, for now life imitates television."[2] According to communications researcher George Gerbner, "If you can write a nation's stories, you needn't worry about who makes its laws. Today, television tells most of the stories to most of the people most of the time."[3]

The most famous critique of the medium came from former chairman of the FCC Newton Minow, in a 1961 speech to broadcasting executives. He characterized television as "a procession of game shows, violence . . . sadism, murder, western bad men, western good men, private eyes, gangsters, more violence and cartoons." Television was, he concluded, a vast wasteland—a phrase that has since become the standard shorthand criticism of the medium and its ways.[4]

These comments give a rough measure of television's impact on life in the United States. Each contains, in varying degrees, hard truths about the medium. Too often, the television industry has frittered away its social and cultural potential. But television has also had a positive impact in the recording and shaping of critical events since World War II such as the civil rights movement, the Kennedy assassination, Watergate, Vietnam and the Persian Gulf wars, and the collapse of Soviet communism. Each was defined for Americans largely through television images.

In short, broadcast television is still immensely influential despite the challenges posed by the new technologies. With almost 3,000 outlets of all kinds reaching into American homes, broadcast television is second only to radio as the most available mass medium (Table 5.1). The decline in its viewing audiences is leveling off from the precipitous drops of recent years. According to a 1992 viewing habits survey, television watching increased by 3.1 percent in 1991.[5] (The survey attributed the jump to a decrease in out-of-home activities resulting from the economic recession at the time.) In the latter half of the 1990s, TV-viewing households will actually increase in number to about 100 million, up 10 million from the late 1980s.[6] The industry overall is very much alive and thriving, with revenues for the big three networks totaling $11 billion in 1991.[7]

Broadcast television is, however, an industry in long-term decline. The erosion in network viewing is probably irreversible. Despite the increase in television-viewing households, previously described, the number of viewers watching prime-time programs declined from 36.9 million in 1975 to 32.7 million in 1990, according to an FCC study.[8] Commenting on the study at the time, the commission's chairman, Alfred Sikes, noted, "The transmission medium that has been dominant is now secondary. . . . Broadcasting has been eclipsed by cable."[9]

The debate on assigning the causes for television's decline is already in full swing. In an influential 1991 book, *Three Blind Mice*, investigative reporter Ken Auletta focused on corporate mismanagement and greed.[10] Demographers emphasize the decline in numbers of the networks' most sought-after audience segment—the postwar baby boomers now moving into middle age. Economists cite rising program costs at a time of audience declines. Others point to the magic moment, sometime in the late 1970s, when cable TV changed from being primarily a delivery system retransmitting local television stations to an entertainment service in its own right, supplying programs not found on over-the-air TV. With dozens of cable channels available, the networks' presence on the tube was diminished, a problem magnified by the widespread introduction of remote control devices ("zappers"), which allow viewers to graze through program offerings, creating havoc among program-listening surveys in the process.[11] Viewer loyalty to individual programs has also dropped

TABLE 5.1 Summary of Broadcasting and Cable

Broadcasting			
Service	*On Air*	*CP's*[1]	*Total**
Commerical AM	4,956	181	5,137
Commercial FM	4,836	910	5,746
Educational FM	1,605	309	1,914
Total Radio	11,397	1,400	12,797
Commercial VHF TV	558	12	570
Commercial UHF TV	592	142	734
Educational VHF TV	124	4	128
Educational UHF TV	240	9	249
Total TV	1,541	167	1,708
VHF LPTV	471	137	608
UHF LPTV	871	988	1,859
Total LPTV	1,342	1,125	2,467
FM Translators	1,967	413	2,380
VHF Translators	2,472	84	2,556
UHF Translators	2,439	388	2,827
Cable			
Total Subscribers		55,786,390	
Homes Passed		89,400,000	
Total Systems		11,254	
Household Penetration†		60.6%	
Pay Cable Penetration/Basic		79%	

*Includes off-air licenses.
[1]Construction permit.
†Penetration percentages are of TV household universe of 92.1 million.
SOURCE: Nielsen, NCTA, and Broadcasting&Cable's own research. Reprinted with permission of Broadcasting&Cable, May 10, 1993 © 1993 by Cahners Publishing Company.

sharply. A 1992 study by the J. Walter Thompson advertising agency found that over 70 percent of viewers watched only one or two of their favorite shows in a month.[12]

Each of these factors has contributed to television's woes in recent years. The industry's critics tend to simplify a complex situation by focusing on the Big Three networks, thus slighting other important players such as independent local stations, public broadcasting, expanding Spanish-language networks, religious broadcasters, and Fox Broadcasting—the upstart "fourth network"—which has enjoyed healthy profits, unlike its three larger competitors.[13] The Fox network began in the late 1980s as a weekend operation. By the 1992–1993 season, it had expanded to seven nights of programming.

The national networks are still, however, the most important single factor in U.S. television. A majority of local stations are beholden to them for their most popular programs. The big three provide stability for the whole system by supplying large audiences for big-spending national advertisers. Overall viewing of network TV may have dropped to 60 percent, but it is still substantially greater than viewership of cable channels, none of which average more than 3 percent of the cable network audience.

More than any other medium, broadcast television depends on advertising (Table 5.2). The networks have thrived on rating formulas that put them in competition with each other for programming that attracts audiences the advertisers want to reach. Independent program producer Norman Lear underscored their goal: "Commercial television's moral north star, from which nearly all bearings are set, is quite simply: 'How do I win Tuesday night at eight o'clock?' That is the name of the game, the only thing that matters."[14]

It has been a spectacularly successful formula for over 40 years, but it is in trouble. The networks' share of television advertising revenue dropped from 45 percent to 36 percent in the 1980s. The difference represents gains for independent stations and for local network affiliates. At the same time, the networks and the local stations both are losing advertisers to cable television. Meanwhile, the advertising

TABLE 5.2 Television and Cable TV Advertising Patterns

	1975	1980	1985	1990
Video Ad Volume ($ Million)				
National	3,929	8,494	15,178	20,153
Broadcast Network	2,306	5,130	8,060	9,383
National Spot	1,623	3,269	6,004	7,788
National Syndication	—	50	520	1,589
Cable Network	—	45	594	1,393
Local	1,334	2,975	5,844	8,252
Local Spot	1,334	2,967	5,714	7,856
Cable (Nonnetwork)	—	8	130	396
Total	5,263	11,469	21,022	28,405
Percent of Total				
National	74.7	74.1	72.2	70.9
Broadcast Network	43.8	44.7	38.3	33.0
National Spot	30.8	28.5	28.6	27.4
National Syndication	—	0.4	2.5	5.6
Cable Network	—	0.4	2.8	4.9
Local	25.3	25.9	27.8	29.1
Local Spot	25.3	25.9	27.2	27.7
Cable (Nonnetwork)	—	0.1	0.6	1.4

SOURCE: Federal Communications Commission (p. 116, FCC/OPP Report).

industry has been going through its own shake-up, shifting its dollars from television and other mass media to campaigns that target consumers more directly, such as supermarket coupons, telephone marketing, and mail order catalogs.

In summary, the Big Three networks are experiencing a domino-style falling off of audiences, advertising revenues, and overall influence. One result is that they have been losing control over their affiliated stations, the ones committed to take network programming. Most network managers failed to see these changes coming, out of either myopia, inertia, or self-delusion. It was a case of corporate whistling past the graveyard. As early as 1987, for instance, total audience viewing of programs broadcast by network affiliates had dropped below 60 percent during some weeks, well under the happy projections made by the networks at the time.[15]

Network managers tended to dismiss such figures as temporary aberrations, to be corrected in the next cycle of program ratings. They persisted in regarding their business as a closed competition among the Big Three networks for viewers. This attitude masked the steady shift in viewer attention to cable networks and to home videocasettes. Warnings from executive suite Cassandras went unheeded. But the Cassandras were right. Media historians may someday identify more precisely when the forces leading to an irreversible downturn in network fortunes came together. A symbolic crossing point may have occurred in October 1991 when comedian Bill Cosby, star of the highest-rated program of the 1980s, decided to desert the networks and market his new show, "You Bet Your Life," directly to local stations.[16] As it turned out, the show was not a success and was canceled in 1993.

The key event that changed the culture of network broadcasting, however, took place in the mid-1980s. It was the simultaneous takeover of the Big Three networks by outside corporate interests. This shift in ownership transformed the shape and direction of the networks, with particular implications for their role in the new media environment.[17] The network takeovers all took place within a year, in 1984 and 1985. Each was unique, in terms of who took over and why.

ABC was bought by Capital Cities Communications ("Cap Cities"), the largest nonnetwork owner of television stations in the country. Cap Cities was the only one of the new network owners that brought a range of direct media experience to its new acquisition. In addition to its ABC television holdings, Cap Cities owned nine AM and eight FM stations, a videocassette production company, and interests in cable programming services. The last included the ESPN sports network, one of the largest (44 million subscribers) in the cable industry.

NBC became a division of General Electric as part of a takeover of RCA, the electronics firm that owned NBC. The CBS takeover came about through the acquisition of a controlling interest in its stock by Laurence Tisch, head of Loews Corporation, a conglomerate best known for its chain of hotels and control of Lorillard, the tobacco company. Unlike Cap Cities, the new owners of NBC and CBS did not have any significant holdings in other electronic media beyond their over-the-air TV operations.

The three firms involved in the takeovers represented a curious mélange of corporate cultures. Their motivations were mixed but they shared a belief that network television was a profitable business that would strengthen their overall balance sheets. They were right. In the mid-1980s, ABC, CBS, and NBC were all big money-makers both in their network operations and in the small group of local stations that each owned.

Those local stations, whose individual profits ran as high as 40 percent of their revenues, were of particular interest to the takeover groups. At the time, the FCC limited network ownership to seven stations apiece. For years, the networks had lobbied for a loosening of this restriction. In the pro-business, deregulatory spirit of the Reagan era, the commission relaxed the rule so as to permit ownership of up to a dozen stations. That decision opened possibilities for greater profits for the networks. What the networks had not adequately foreseen was that the new potential for profit would also make them a more attractive investment, and therefore more vulnerable to corporate takeover. And that, of course, is what happened. Ironically, none of the takeover groups exploited the opportunity to expand network ownership of local stations at the time. The reason was that they quickly found themselves enmeshed in fiscal problems at the network level that precluded any thoughts of buying more stations, particularly at the inflated prices then current. More recently, however, the three networks have been acquiring local stations.[18]

Although network profits were high in the first years of the takeovers, the new owners found themselves dealing with the dilemma of rising costs at a time when their audience base was being eroded by the expansion of cable television channels and home videocassette players.

NBC was particularly hard hit. In 1988, it was the top network, enjoying 69 straight weeks as the Neilson audience survey winner. At the end of that year, it had posted $500 million in profits. Three years later, the company's profits had disappeared, and it had sustained the largest viewer decline among the networks. To add to these corporate woes, two television personalities, Johnny Carson and Bill Cosby, who had added so much to NBC's luster (and revenues) left the network in 1992.[19]

The new management at all three networks reacted to harsh fiscal realities by instituting tough cost-cutting programs. ABC laid off 2,000 employees soon after the Cap Cities takeover. NBC's personnel dropped from 8,000 to 5,700 in five years. Cutbacks at CBS were equally severe. The old management teams were decimated. The executives who remained were made grimly aware of the new importance of bottom line economics. GE sent NBC managers to its in-house Management Development Institute, where the curriculum included three days of survival training on an isolated Maine island.[20]

The personnel cuts saved money but they did not directly address the networks' primary problem: the combination of viewer decline and rising program costs. That combination changed the rules for network television. Gone were the days of simple three-way competition among the networks for audiences, advertising dollars, and profits. Now they faced uncomfortable outside competition, including the successful fourth network, Fox Television. Audiences for cable television and for home videocassettes continued to expand. Direct broadcasting from satellites would be a reality by mid-decade. Meanwhile, another competitive threat loomed in the form of the telephone companies and their plans not only to transmit information and entertainment programs into homes but also to be the originators of some of the programs.[21]

The more immediate challenge to broadcast TV, however, came from cable television. The networks were at a structural disadvantage in their attempts to match cable's appeal. They had only one channel with which to reach the home audiences that advertisers wanted. They were, in effect, delivering a single mass audience, a large segment of which was not attractive to individual advertisers. Cable systems, however, with 50 or 60 channels, could do a better job of supplying the smaller target audiences sought by advertisers.

Meanwhile, network program costs were rising as advertising revenues fell. This was especially true of the more popular programs the networks needed in order to keep what was left of their competitive prime-time edge. "Cheers," the Boston saloon saga, was a critical element in NBC's efforts to stanch further audience losses. However, the show's costs escalated wildly in the early 1990s. By the time the series ended in 1993, Ted Danson, one of its stars, was reportedly earning a half million dollars for each episode.[22] The producer of the series, Paramount Television, received about $2 million in license fees per program in its 1991 negotiations with the network, according to trade sources. In reporting this, *Broadcasting,* the industry's trade magazine, noted that the average deficit incurred initially by the networks for each prime-time show at the time was $250,000, or an average of $6.5 million annually, for each half-hour production.[23]

Even in the topsy-turvy world of television financing, this was not a formula for success. Furthermore, the networks' hopes for recouping the costs of these programs, through reruns and other means, were further blighted by the persistent economic recession of the early 1990s, which deepened their losses from advertising revenues.[24] As the networks' economic fortunes were declining in the 1990s, they began to look like an endangered species, or at least one that needed a new identity. By 1993, there were persistent rumors that the Big Three were "in play"—a Wall Street term for companies ripe for takeover. The rumors were particularly insistent about NBC and CBS, both of which had reportedly been put on the block at various times by their owners.[25] The most logical new bidders would be the Hollywood studios, assuming that FCC restrictions on mergers between television and film companies were lifted. Hollywood clearly has an interest in maintaining the viability of the networks, since they are major buyers of its productions.[26]

The networks' fiscal problems also led to serious talk, for the first time, about the possibility of foreign investment in their operations. Such investment has been restricted over the years by provisions of the Communications Act of 1934. The purpose of the restrictions was to prevent undue foreign influence over U.S. broadcasting. The law allows, however, for a waiver of these restrictions if the FCC decides that foreign investment is in a vaguely defined public interest. The loophole was seized upon by the Bush administration in 1991 to signal its willingness to open up the broadcasting industry to international investment, under the rubric of stimulating the domestic economy. A 1993 policy report issued in the last weeks of the Bush administration by the U.S. Department of Commerce recommended relaxation of the restrictions on foreign investment.[27] The future prospects for such investment will depend on a Clinton administration reevaluation of the benefits, and obstacles, in greater foreign control of U.S. broadcasting.

Barring an infusion of new funds by way of a takeover or other investment, the networks will have to work out their corporate destiny on their own. They are still, collectively, the keystone of U.S. TV broadcasting, albeit somewhat chipped and battered. Their future is hostage to trends that are largely irreversible—smaller audiences, higher costs, and lower revenues. A 1991 FCC study on the future of broadcasting estimated that the New York networks might find themselves with an audience share as low as 15 percent by the end of the decade.[28]

How do the networks deal with this harsh new economic environment? One network watcher suggests that the continuing financial squeeze is "forcing network executives into a schizophrenic dance of mixed messages."[29] What is clear is that most of the old formulas for network success no longer apply. Quick-fix projects by the corporate conglomerates that now own the networks won't work anymore. Their early cost-cutting campaigns were useful, signaling the end of the fat-and-happy era of network management. But any deeper cuts, particularly in personnel, are probably counterproductive.

At one point in the late 1980s, the networks tried an attack-the-enemy approach. It was an advertising campaign aimed at the cable TV industry, with the theme "the cable fable." The idea was to convince advertisers and others that cable was no match for television's marketing impact. It was a rearguard strategy, which was unsuccessful in the face of cable's rapid audience growth. Having failed to turn back the alleged enemy, the networks shifted their strategies. Their plans took them beyond the comfortable old ways of doing business and the recognition that innovative approaches—some of them radical—are needed. Each network has adopted a different approach but they share an interest in the possibilities opened by advanced media technologies.

Network plans for investing in new-media technologies are necessarily long range in nature, constrained by the squeeze on their financial resources. In the meantime, the networks are addressing more immediate problems in maintaining their traditional operations. Not the least of these problems is keeping their networks intact. For ABC, CBS, and NBC, the network means primarily the hundreds of affiliated local stations who contract to transmit their national programming. Despite competition from cable TV, these affiliates are very profitable operations, taking in the lion's share of the $15.8 billion in advertising earned by all local stations in 1990.[30] In addition, the affiliates are paid compensation by the New York networks to carry their programs.

By 1993, network-affiliate relations were on rocky ground. The networks clearly need the affiliates. The question is whether the affiliates need the networks in quite the same way. The overall decline in network audiences has obviously hurt the local stations.[31] More and more, the affiliates see that they can make more money (via advertising they control) with popular syndicated shows, such as the "Oprah Winfrey Show" and "Wheel of Fortune," rather than sharing ad revenues from network programs. Despite this shift, about one-third of local stations showed a pretax loss in 1991.[32]

The local affiliates are also reevaluating their traditional reliance on network news programs. Local news is usually their biggest money spinner, often accounting for a third of station revenues and an even higher share of profits. Increasingly, the affiliates are moving into nonnetwork regional and national news coverage, through cooperative agreements with independent news organizations. By the early 1990s, hundreds of local stations had agreements to broadcast CNN programming, lessening their dependence on network news from New York.[33]

Although relatively few local stations have cut off their network affiliations, the network-affiliate relationship is eroding. As part of their cost-cutting operations, ABC, CBS, and NBC all have reduced the compensation they pay out to local affiliates to run network shows. They have also cut back the number of network programs local stations are required to carry, a move made in response to affiliate pressures to control prime-time programming because they, and not the networks, will get the advertising revenues.[34] The high-stakes competition among the networks to keep their traditional hold over evening programs reached a climax of sorts in 1993 when CBS lured talk-show host David Letterman from NBC, reportedly offering him an annual salary of $14 million.

The networks' difficulties with their affiliates are part of the much larger problem in their primary business—national programming that will attract big audiences. The Big Three networks operate virtually around the clock, from the morning wake-up shows to the late-night talk programs. The formulas for success have always been elusive, and they are more so these days. Introducing new programs can be particularly perilous. There was a 46 percent turnover in programs among all the networks between the 1990 and 1991 seasons.[35] A new show's fate is usually sealed, for better or for worse, within a month after it is introduced. Most of them are eventually canceled, resulting in heavy losses.

The networks' programming problems are compounded by the fact that they do not control most of their prime-time shows. They have to share the losses when a program fails, but they are cut out of a large part of the profits if it is successful. This is due to a long-standing FCC regulation known in the industry as "fin-syn," for financial interest and syndication rules. Fin-syn is intended to prevent the networks from having monopoly control over the production and distribution of their programs. The idea was to ensure a competitive program-production market in which Hollywood studios and independent producers, not just the networks, could be players. Originally, fin-syn rules prohibited a network from producing more than five hours of weekly prime-time entertainment programming. More important was the prohibition against their sharing in profits from programs sold for second-run syndication either to cable networks and local stations in this country or to television stations abroad. The profits went to the program producers, usually the Hollywood studios.

The FCC's fin-syn regulations probably made sense at the time they were promulgated back in the 1970s. The networks were riding high then and could dominate outside program producers. As the networks' financial troubles mounted in recent years, however, the case for changing the rules became stronger, especially since the film studios and independent producers exercised virtually monopolistic control over TV program reruns worth billions of dollars.

In 1990, the networks launched a full-scale campaign to get rid of the fin-syn restrictions. They were met with an equally determined campaign by the Hollywood studios to maintain the status quo. The result, a year later, was an FCC ruling that, in effect, eased the fin-syn regulations. Under the revised rules, the networks were allowed to produce more of their prime-time programs and to syndicate those shows both at home and abroad. They could also acquire a financial interest in and syndication rights to programs produced by other companies, subject to certain restrictions. Most of the original fin-syn rules barring networks from the international marketplace were thus removed.[36]

These changes gave only marginal relief to the networks, however. They successfully challenged the revised ruling in the courts, and the FCC was ordered to reconsider its fin-syn rules. In 1993, a compromise-minded FCC voted to allow the networks to own a financial interest in the production of all their prime-time shows. Although the new ruling continued the prohibition against domestic syndication of programs by the networks, it did allow them to share in revenues from the resale of those programs in which they hold a financial interest.[37]

The networks also sought relaxation of regulatory restrictions in other areas. At the FCC, they argued successfully for modification of restrictions on network ownership of cable systems. Under new rules, the networks can generally acquire cable systems serving up to 10 percent of homes nationwide with access to cable TV facilities, and up to half of such homes in any local market. They lobbied for congressional legislation that would require cable systems to negotiate payment to television stations for retransmitting their programs—a change incorporated in certain 1992 legislation that strengthened federal government regulation of the cable industry. The networks also supported regulatory controls on telephone company plans to produce information and entertainment programs.

The television industry has been only partly successful in its efforts to get what it describes as a level playing field on which to meet the new competition from cable systems, telephone companies, and others. The partial relaxation of government regulations has permitted the networks and the local stations to diversify their operations in recent years. This has not, however, solved their major problem, which is the restructuring of their programs in ways that will check the erosion of their audience base.

The industry's operating cliché is "quality television," a phrase that has been difficult to translate into successful programs. The problem was defined succinctly in 1991 by Warren Littlefield, head of NBC's entertainment division:

> You have to be clear about what your goals are. We're in a rebuilding era and we have to invest in new product. It's hard to predict what the audience will like. But we figured if we were at the crap table, why not gamble on high quality shows?[38]

Littlefield's comments were a hopeful sign that broadcast television may take the high road, in terms of program quality, to attract audiences. The industry's strategy for higher-quality programs has had, however, mixed results. There have been some attempts by the networks to invest more money in shows that rise above the usual lowest-common-denominator standard. More often than not, these programs have failed to attract the larger audiences needed to justify their higher costs. Meanwhile, the networks rely increasingly on low-cost talk shows to bolster their revenues. A series like the "Oprah Winfrey Show," which costs about $20 million a year to produce, generated $157 million in revenues in 1991.[39] When King World Productions, owners of "Wheel of Fortune" and "Jeopardy," negotiated an extra 30 seconds of advertising time in 1992, the change added an estimated $30 million in annual revenues from the two shows.[40] In addition, the networks and the local stations are turning to sleazier shows in an effort to turn a profit. The programs, known euphemistically as tabloid TV, include "A Current Affair," "Inside Edition," and "Geraldo"—all big money-makers that are, by any standard, mindless and exploitative.[41] The sleaze prize may belong to the syndicated show that ended up with combative married couples engaging in a food fight.

The networks have occasionally turned to a tried-and-true formula: the blockbuster program. This approach reached its apogee in 1991 when CBS joined in an $8-million deal for the television rights to *Scarlett,* the potboiler sequel to *Gone with the Wind.* Production costs for the miniseries based on the book were set at $30 million.[42] In a more innovative effort, Cap Cities/ABC has been experimenting with the possibility of charging viewers for individual quality programs, an increasingly common practice among cable TV networks. (In industry jargon, this is known as pay per view.) In pursuit of pay-per-view (PPV) program material in the early 1990s, ABC became the third-largest investor in Broadway musicals, with major stakes in such hits as *Miss Saigon, Phantom of the Opera,* and *Les Misérables.*

Most of these expensive programming projects have focused on attracting prime-time viewing. Meanwhile, the networks have had trouble keeping audiences in three other traditionally successful program areas—soap operas, news, and sports. The afternoon soap operas have suffered steady audience declines, primarily because large segments of their traditional audience, stay-at-home housewives, are now out of the house and in the work force. News program viewing is also down, a factor some media critics attribute to the budget cutbacks imposed on news operations in recent years by the networks' new corporate owners. By 1991, network newscasts were attracting only 54 percent of viewers, a loss of nearly one out of every three viewers in less than 10 years.[43]

Another factor contributing to audience losses for network news is competition from CNN. At a time when the networks were cutting back their news budgets, CNN was aggressively expanding its operations. Its worldwide staff of 1,700 people gives it a news-gathering advantage, compared with the 1,000 or so employees who were left at each of the networks after the budget cuts in the late 1980s. CNN's round-the-clock coverage has adversely affected network news viewing, particularly when important news is breaking. CNN also has challenged the networks by negotiating agreements with network affiliates and other local stations to feed and receive news footage that duplicates, and often improves on, the networks' news offerings. By mid-1992, CNN's television affiliate was supplying news services to 268 local stations nationwide.[44]

The networks have also taken a big hit in sports programming, traditionally a certified money-maker. Their longtime control of baseball and football broadcasting has been eroded by competition from cable TV sports channels. Another factor has been the astronomical rise in prices for broadcast rights demanded by sports organizations. CBS paid $1.6 billion in 1988 in a four-year contract deal for major-league-baseball programs. One industry analyst estimated that, given the depressed advertising market since then, CBS may have overpaid by as much as $400 million.[45] The two other networks, NBC and ABC, have also suffered steady losses in their sports programming.

The long-range threat for the networks is the eventual shift of major sports events to cable systems, using a PPV formula. The three networks have an ally, however, in the U.S. Congress, whose members are mindful of the fact that sports-loving voters resist the idea of paying for what they now get free. In 1991, a congressional committee extracted a promise from the National Football League that the league would not seek PPV arrangements for several years.[46] No one, including congressional legislators, doubts that such a move will come eventually. Billions of dollars will accrue to the baseball and football leagues in any PPV contract. The PPV trend may be accelerated by deals being made by local stations in cities with major-league-baseball and -hockey teams. By 1993, at least a dozen such arrangements were actively in operation or being negotiated.[47] Eventually, the Big Three television networks could become minor players in sports programming. To counter this threat, ABC Sports signed up with three major college-football conferences to broadcast PPV games during the 1992 season, with the expectation that the arrangement would continue in future seasons.[48]

Faced with the combination of audience and revenue losses from programs that were once gilt-edged winners, the networks are considering alternative business opportunities, a major recommendation in the 1991 FCC research report that examined the future of over-the-air television broadcasting.[49] The report implied strongly that the networks had lagged in seeking out new opportunities throughout the 1980s, focusing too narrowly instead on cutting back their operations, a strategy that could result in hastening their decline as national over-the-air program providers.

Audience decline is forcing the big three networks to take a hard look at their options in a new media environment. This has led occasionally to fanciful schemes for investing in nonbroadcast operations. At one time, NBC was considering going into the theme-park business.[50] Such schemes reminded industry observers of disastrous projects in the past, notably the CBS decision to buy the New York Yankees baseball team in the 1960s, a move that proved to be a management and financial failure.

The networks have several options in deciding how their production and marketing know-how could be applied to new projects. First, they could expand their international operations through investment, coproduction deals, and other arrangements with foreign broadcasters. Second, they could move into other domestic media fields, particularly cable TV, through mergers, buy outs, and production arrangements. A third, longer-range, option would be to restructure their over-the-air broadcasting operations by adding new technologies such as DBS services or fiber-optic transmission of data, sound, and video products for home consumption.

Expanding into international operations would revive a strategy that all of the networks actively pursued in the 1960s. Their overseas activities at that time centered on program sales, in an era when foreign stations were forced to rely heavily on U.S. products to fill their schedules. It was a very profitable business for the networks. One survey indicated that, by the early 1980s, U.S. programs accounted for 77 percent of program offerings in Latin America, 70 percent in Canada, and 44 percent in Western Europe.[51]

In addition to program sales, the networks and other broadcasters also invested in foreign broadcasting operations. ABC sponsored a Central American network, in part to support its program sales. By 1965, NBC had made minority investments in 13 overseas stations in eight countries. CBS was a stockholder in a major Argentine network. Time Inc. (now Time Warner) invested in stations in Latin America and Asia. These and similar deals at the time pointed to the possibility of a major U.S. stake in global television.[52] But this did not happen. One serious barrier was the difficulty of managing overseas investments at a time when international communications were considerably less efficient than they are today. And many of the investments turned out to be poor bets. There was also a chauvinistic backlash in many countries against the sheer volume of U.S. programs on local television. This manifested itself as attacks on "U.S. cultural imperialism," which culminated in efforts within the United Nations to place international restrictions on television exports. Although the effort failed, many countries reacted by imposing quotas on U.S. program imports and by prohibiting or limiting foreign investment in local television.

Despite those barriers, sales of U.S. television productions continue to be an important source of export revenue, totaling over a billion dollars annually, even though U.S. programs are generally less prominent on overseas television schedules than they once were. In a 1987 survey of the top 20 prime-time programs in France, Germany, and Great Britain, only one U.S. show made the list—"Dynasty" ("Der Denver Clan Dynastie")—which was number 19 in Germany. Nevertheless, U.S. production companies have found useful niches in European TV schedules. One company, Fremantle Corp., produces about 80 percent of all game shows in Europe, including "What's My Line," "I've Got a Secret," and "Call My Bluff."[53]

The primary beneficiaries of these export sales have been the Hollywood studios and the independent program syndicators, not the networks. The reason is the fin-syn regulations, described previously, which effectively cut the networks out of foreign-sales profits after 1976. Although the rule was changed in 1993 by the FCC, export sales by the networks are still limited because of continuing fin-syn restrictions on the number of entertainment programs they can own.

The television industry's overseas prospects are similar to those now faced by other U.S. industries in increasingly competitive global markets. The advantage that the networks and other program sellers have is the increase in the number of privately operated television stations abroad. (Until recent years, most overseas stations were controlled by governments.) These new stations tend to favor U.S. programs and advertisements featuring globally available products. Tony the Tiger—Kellogg Co.'s Frosted Flakes salesman—makes his television pitch in more than 20 countries abroad and in just about as many languages. Procter & Gamble advertises Ivory soap and Pampers baby diapers in 54 countries.[54]

Competition in the program-sales market is, nevertheless, more intense abroad as foreign broadcasters and overseas production firms move into the market. U.S. program exporters also face political and economic barriers to program sales abroad. One example is a 1989 European Economic Community (EEC) directive that imposes a 50 percent quota on foreign (i.e., U.S.) entertainment programs. The aim of the directive is to promote program production in EEC countries.[55]

U.S. program exporters have sought new market opportunities in Russia and Eastern Europe following the collapse of Communist regimes there. One of the most popular programs on Polish television has been a dubbed version of the "Oprah Winfrey Show." In 1992, tens of millions of viewers in the former Soviet Union got their first glimpse of American prime-time shows, from "Murphy Brown" to "Perfect Strangers." The shows, dubbed in Russian, were part of a festival of U.S. programs organized by U.S. exporters eager to crack the Russian market. U.S. programs are also a regular feature on television stations in the People's Republic of China. They include "Night Court," "Falcon Crest," and "Hunter," all dubbed in Mandarin.[56]

Despite quotas and other barriers, television program exports will continue to be an important revenue source for the networks and other program producers. A new element has been added in recent years, however, by the increasing activities of foreign media investors in the U.S. market. For the time being, U.S. television and radio broadcasters are protected from takeovers by overseas investors, thanks to FCC prohibitions against foreign ownership. Nevertheless, foreign competitors are increasingly evident. The prime example is the Fox Television Network, owned by Rupert Murdoch's News Corporation, a company with strong British connections. The Japanese takeover of two major Hollywood studios, MCA and Columbia Pictures, also affects the television industry because both firms are major producers and syndicators of TV programs. The British Broadcasting Corporation is one of a number of European program producers that have entered the U.S. market to sell their own programs and to develop coproduction deals with U.S. firms.[57]

U.S. television firms are responding to the new competition by stepping up their own international investment activities. The leader to date has been Cap Cities, owner of the ABC network, which had invested over $100 million in its European operations by the early 1990s. The company holds minority stakes in a number of French, Spanish, and German production firms, as well as a half interest in the satellite-based European Sports Network. These investments provide ABC with a series of local bases in Europe from which to explore further business relationships in the rapidly developing program production market there. In 1992, ABC expanded distribution of its "ABC World News Tonight," "Nightline," and "Good Morning America" shows to Europe via satellite, where the programs are retransmitted by television stations in Britain, Germany, Spain, and Denmark.[58]

NBC has been less successful in recent foreign projects. Small ventures in Australian and New Zealand TV stations failed, as did an attempt to create a commercial station in the Netherlands. The company has invested in a small coproduction venture, Tango Productions, in Britain, which gives it a foothold in that important market. The most successful of NBC's overseas investments has been its partnership with the British Broadcasting Corporation and the Reuters news agency in Visnews, an international newsfilm distributor. In 1992, however, Reuters bought out its other two partners. CBS has been the least aggressive network on the international scene, limiting itself to several news-exchange and coproduction arrangements in Europe and Japan.[59]

American interest in overseas television ventures has been sparked by a set of new players. The best known is Ted Turner, who has made his Cable News Network an international force in both television and cable TV, with program agreements in over 90 countries. In 1992, Turner extended his international reach further when he signed an agreement with Russian entrepreneurs to build a privately operated television station in Moscow.[60]

Time Warner, the media conglomerate, has also placed heavy emphasis on what it calls "strategic partnerships" with foreign firms. The company has made a series of overseas deals in recent years, from constructing movie theaters in Russia to investing in a new Scandinavian commercial television network. Time Warner's biggest strategic-partnership deal came in 1992, when two Japanese firms, Toshiba and C. Itoh, each invested $500 million in Time Warner Entertainment, to be used in part to expand the firm's international operations.[61] In summary, the U.S. networks and other broadcasting firms can expect to find increasing opportunities in overseas markets. With some exceptions, however, international business will represent a relatively minor part of their operations. By and large, broadcasters will give priority to developing alliances with other domestic media firms, both in and outside the television business, in order to improve their financial prospects.

This possibility was very much on the minds of the corporate conglomerates that took over the Big Three networks in the mid-1980s. As it turned out, the new owners found themselves too bogged down in the more immediate problems of audience and revenue erosion to spend time considering outside ventures. A partial exception was Cap Cities/ABC, which developed strong ties with the cable industry, notably its majority investment in ESPN, the country's largest cable TV network, and a minority stake in two other cable services—Arts & Entertainment and Lifetime. These diversified investments helped make Cap Cities/ABC the most financially successful of the big three television companies in the early 1990s.[62]

More recently, the networks have taken a greater interest in developing new corporate alliances. Logically, the first place to look for partners is Hollywood, the source of most prime-time network programming. However, the networks' attempts to link up with the film studios have been largely unsuccessful. The next network target for deal-making is the cable TV industry. The problem here is the love-hate attitudes that have characterized relations between the two industries for many years. The networks had a cozy relationship with cable TV until the 1970s, when cable networks were small-town operations, retransmitting over-the-air television programs from distant cities. The networks were happy with the extended coverage, and the new audiences, that cable systems supplied.

Those attitudes changed, however, when the cable industry developed satellite-based national channels such as HBO, Showtime, and ESPN. Cable was no longer a local mom-and-pop industry. It is now dominated by large conglomerates, which control most of the larger local cable systems, as well as the more popular entertainment, news, and sports channels. This vertical integration of production and distribution resources gives the major cable firms (known as MSOs—multiple-system operators) both a strategic and a highly profitable advantage over their broadcast network competitors. And they have been less burdened by the kinds of regulatory restrictions imposed on the networks. There is no limit to the number of local cable networks they can own. Nor do the FCC's fin-syn rules limiting profits on television program sales apply to the cable companies.

The cable industry's ability to control program and distribution resources has been a powerful stimulus to its growth. In seeking alliances with cable, the broadcast networks are supplicants, asking to break into a powerful national industry that a decade or so ago, was merely a collection of small-town businesses. Moreover, they are dealing with an industry that is a labyrinth of interlocking interests. As one TV executive involved in cable negotiations noted, "Working with cable is like dealing with the Mob."[63]

Like it or not, the New York networks have had little choice but to deal. Cable programming is one of the few areas where they can exploit their programming and management skills. Only CBS has held back, generally attributed to a combination of money problems and inept leadership. ABC took an early lead in 1987, with the purchase of a major stake in the ESPN sports channel. The network was betting on the eventual transfer to cable of big-time football and baseball games. In February 1987, the National Football League signaled its willingness to begin the process by negotiating a five-year, $1.4-billion contract with ESPN to show 13 games annually.

The 1987 NFL-ESPN contract was a major psychological turning point for both the cable and broadcasting industries. Cable's maverick, Ted Turner, underscored its significance in a speech to cable TV advertisers at the time. The NFL contract was, he declared, a milestone, involving

> the continuing migration of the most important programming to cable. . . . I consider the networks kind of like the Germans were in late 1942: they held a lot of territory very thinly. Two out of three of them are unprofitable now. . . . There has been a basic financial power shift.[64]

It was a crude analysis, but it has proved to be a realistic one. As a result, NBC and ABC in recent years have been more aggressive in developing strategies for becoming more directly involved in the cable industry. In addition to its investment in the ESPN sports channel, ABC has set up an in-house production unit to supply programs both to cable channels and to international markets, a venture that has proved profitable.[65] In 1991, its corporate owner, Cap Cities, entered a joint venture with Paramount Communications, specializing in PPV musical events for cable systems. NBC was less successful in its initial forays into the cable business. Its woes began with a decision to develop an all-news cable channel, building on its longtime news expertise. In 1987, NBC tried to buy a controlling interest in Ted Turner's CNN, which was then in serious financial trouble. The deal foundered on Turner's refusal to cede editorial control to NBC.

NBC's next step was to proceed with an all-news cable channel on its own. It proposed to compete directly with CNN, a reasonable decision given the fact that the Turner channel was a fairly amateurish operation at the time. On the way, however, NBC bumped into the Byzantine realities of the cable business. Not only did a small group of cable conglomerates control most of the cable TV systems where NBC hoped to place its new news channel, but they also owned a significant share of the stock in Ted Turner's far-flung operations, including CNN. It soon became clear that they were not interested in competition from another cable news channel, particularly one run by a television network that would bring superior resources to cable newscasting.

NBC had to give up its plans for a general cable-news channel in favor of a more specialized operation, namely CNBC, the Consumer News and Business Channel, which concentrates on financial news and personal-living features. The cable conglomerates showed their power by setting conditions for CNBC's entry into their local systems, specifying that CNBC could not become a news service in direct competition with CNN, the channel in which they had a financial interest. The cable industry's willingness to sacrifice the principle of program diversity to bottom-line profits was affirmed.[66]

Despite this setback, NBC has expanded its cable interests. By the early 1990s, it had become a co-owner of several cable program services, in addition to investments in the Sportchannel America, Bravo, Court Television, and American Movie Classics channels. In 1993, it moved more deeply into cable operations when it became a production partner in two new all-sports channels—the Prime SportsChannel Networks, with an audience of over 40 million cable subscribers.[67] The network also announced plans for a joint venture with NYNEX, the regional phone company in the Northeast, to develop a nationwide closed-circuit network supplying entertainment and advertising programs to shoppers in supermarkets.[68]

By 1993, the New York networks were adjusting their ambivalent attitudes toward cable TV competition, moving from uneasy confrontation to wary cooperation. The change was spurred by their realization that a major expansion in the number of cable channels will take place in the next few years, thanks to digital compression technology, which can double or even triple the capacity of current 60-channel systems.

This expansion will be a mixed blessing for the networks. Although it means a further erosion of their traditional audience base, it also opens up important opportunities to produce programs for the new channels. As noted earlier, ABC and NBC are already actively producing programs for cable systems. NBC's strategy for the 1992 summer Olympics, for example, depended heavily on transmitting part of its coverage on cable channels as a PPV feature. The most direct move into cable programming, however, was made by the Fox Television Network. In 1991, it announced plans for a second production facility, Foxplex, to deliver programs directly to cable systems.[69]

In addition to their current cable-programming ventures, the Big Three networks want to own cable systems. This option was opened in 1992 when the FCC partially lifted its ban on such ownership. The commission's action was part of what it called an attic-to-basement review of broadcast regulations. Although the networks can now invest in cable systems, they face opposition from within the broadcasting industry. Most local television stations, including the network affiliates, have opposed the idea, fearing that it will lead to greater competition between themselves and local network-owned cable systems for the same advertisers.[70]

On another front, the networks lobbied for greater restrictions on cable systems, this time supported by their local affiliates. The networks focused on the issue of "retransmission consent," a device to extract payments from cable systems for transmitting over-the-air broadcasts from local stations. Retransmission consent gives broadcasters the right to deny cable operators permission to carry their signals, in effect giving network affiliates leverage to demand payment or other compensation for their broadcasts. It was a long jump from the situation that existed only a few years previously, when television stations competed to offer their transmissions freely to cable systems in order to expand the stations' audience base.

In 1992, Congress passed a cable regulation bill, which included a retransmission-consent provision. In the debate preceding the bill's passage, the cable television lobby argued that retransmission payments would impose a 20 percent "tax" on cable subscribers, totalling $3 billion a year. The television industry countered with newspaper ads about the cable monopoly and its alleged conspiracy against "free television."[71] The charges and countercharges highlighted the uneasy relationship that continues to exist between the cable TV and network television industries, even as the networks seek to invest in local cable operations.

The two media have, however, found common ground in their mutual opposition to telephone industry plans to expand into information and entertainment services for home consumers. Although their respective positions differ in some details, both the cable TV and network television industries want regulatory restraints placed on telephone company activities in this area. Specifically, they seek assurances that the phone companies will not use their technological and economic power to dominate the information and entertainment services sent electronically into homes. The phone companies have made it clear that they intend to provide such services. But through legal and regulatory restraints, the television and cable TV industries are equally intent on limiting the phone companies' power to do so.[72]

The telephone industry's and cable TV industries' proposals to install high-capacity fiber cables has forced the television industry into a serious discussion of its technological future. For the present, the networks and their affiliated stations are each limited to a single channel. Fifteen years ago, they were confronted with competition from 60-channel cable systems. Eventually their single-channel outlets will be swamped by the hundreds of channels that will become available to consumers as phone companies and cable TV firms upgrade their circuits.

This change is already under way, and it will be in full motion in the late 1990s.[73] The prospect of the new interactive multimedia services' further eroding present television viewing patterns is a serious one for broadcasters. It is no longer a distant threat. In 1992, Radio Shack introduced a "video information system" device, which enables users to play games, read electronic books, and perform other tasks on an ordinary television set.[74]

Where will the television broadcasters fit in this new pattern? Their present strategy is mainly a defensive one, aimed at limiting the phone companies' role as information and entertainment suppliers. This strategy serves the public interest in that it aims to ensure supplier diversity among the expanded home networks. It does not, however, address the specific question of where, and how, the television industry adjusts to the new media environment.

The broadcasters' expertise in program production and network management is a valuable resource, which can be put to good use in expanding information and entertainment services for advanced networks that serve homes as well as schools and other institutions. The opportunity could be a transforming one for an industry whose present mode of doing business is in long-term decline. ABC/Cap Cities has shown strong initiative in developing new products that draw on the firm's management and production expertise. One of its affiliates, ABC News InterActive, produces educational videodiscs, primarily for school classroom use. NBC teamed up with IBM in 1993 to produce an experimental multimedia news service, called NBC Desktop

News. Delivered directly to PCs, the service combines text, graphics, video, and sound in a format designed to look like a TV newscast.

In the meantime, the networks and their local affiliates have some pressing decisions to make about HDTV, the first major change in broadcast technology since the introduction of color TV 35 years ago. HDTV is a breakthrough toward the computerization of home television sets, leading to their eventual use as multimedia telecomputers. Even before that transformation occurs, HDTV offers the advantage of an improved picture, with roughly twice the clarity and detail of present screens. The screen itself is in a different shape, more rectangular in ways that give a wide-screen effect. Eventually every television set in the country will be replaced by receivers with HDTV capabilities, involving a shift from analog to digital standards.[75]

Broadcast television will be only one source of HDTV transmissions, and it may well play a minor role. HDTV can be transmitted by cable TV, telephone fiber-optic circuits, or communications satellites. Present television broadcasting frequencies are technologically inadequate for high-definition transmissions. However, broadcasting engineers are developing digital compression techniques to squeeze HDTV into over-the-air frequencies.[76]

The problem is spectrum bandwidth. An HDTV signal requires a lot of space in the frequency spectrum. And because of the current national expansion of all electronic communications, spectrum is a high-demand commodity, particularly in the bands where broadcast television operates. By using digital compression techniques (described in Chapter 3), television broadcasters can be active players in the competition to offer HDTV programs to mass audiences. However, broadcast TV will probably not be able to match the overall technical capabilities of cable TV, fiber-optic wires, or satellites in terms of carrying HDTV signals. The cable industry, in particular, has been working with equipment manufacturers to develop compression technologies that will enhance the industry's ability to deliver HDTV programs on its present coaxial cable lines.[77]

The television industry does not want to be left out of HDTV developments given the high financial stakes involved. The broadcasters' ability to compete depends heavily on decisions by the FCC, which has been wrestling for years with the problems of regulating HDTV. The commission's basic position is that there should be a level playing field for all potential HDTV providers, including the broadcasters. The commission has also ruled that any HDTV technical standards it approves must allow broadcasters to transmit conventional and HDTV signals simultaneously during the transition period to full adoption of the new technology. This was a key requirement in the HDTV standards being developed by a consortium of leading electronics firms that was formed in 1993.

The FCC guidelines have assured the TV broadcasters that they will not be elbowed out of the HDTV sweepstakes. However, the commission has also put pressure on the broadcasters to invest in HDTV operations soon or risk losing their chance for getting additional spectrum to transmit the new technology.[78] The commission has proposed that stations should continue broadcasting conventional signals on their current channels but at the same time begin to transmit HDTV on the new simulcast frequencies that it will make available to broadcasters. Once these frequencies are available, after the middle of the decade, stations would have six years to begin constructing full-scale HDTV transmitters. If they should delay beyond the time allowed, they will risk losing their licenses for HDTV radio-spectrum frequencies.[79]

In the complex world of HDTV technology, this is a tight deadline. It comes at a time when the networks are strapped for the large amounts of cash needed for HDTV development. The cost to broadcasters of switching over to HDTV has been estimated at $10 billion. There are, moreover, persistent doubts about whether HDTV is, in fact, television's wave of the future. Although HDTV supplies a better picture, there has been no great consumer ground swell for its adoption.[80] HDTV receivers will be expensive. When the Japanese inaugurated the world's first regular HDTV network in 1991, their sets cost over $30,000 apiece.[81] By 1992, Sharp, the Japanese electronics company, had produced a 36-inch set, which went on the market in Japan for $8,000. The price will come down further when extensive high-definition programming begins in the United States. HDTV will, nevertheless, be a consumer luxury item for some time.

The television industry knows that HDTV can be a critical factor in its future. It is both encouraged by and apprehensive about a 1992 survey suggesting that over 50 percent of U.S. households will own a high-definition receiver early in the next century.[82] Nevertheless, the industry remains ambivalent about how to cope with the technology. Its attitude has been summarized by television executive Joel Chaseman who headed the FCC's industry research group on high-definition prospects: "Part of what I'm hearing . . . is that there is a gun-shy generation of broadcasters so up to its ears in alligators that it can't see an opportunity that is chancy."[83]

Television's problem in adapting to HDTV is matched in radio broadcasting, which faces a similar technological revolution. Forty years ago, radio broadcasting was transformed by television's ability to attract audiences and revenues. Radio made a comeback, for two reasons. One was the popularity of new FM stations, with their superior musical sound. The second was radio's shift from mass audience to specialized programming. Today, over 12,000 radio stations use dozens of different formats, from hard rock to classical music. Each format is designed to attract relatively small audiences. Particular attention is given to two audience groups beloved of advertisers—teenagers and commuting automobile drivers. Commuters are the ultimate captive audience, whose listening and buying habits have been studied in exquisite detail by the radio industry. Teenagers are compulsive radio listeners, who also represent a $100-billion consumer market. A 1991 survey found that 94 percent of all teens aged 12–19 listen to radio regularly.[84]

Despite the outsized radio habits of commuters and teenagers, the radio business overall is in trouble. In recent years, over 250 radio stations have failed, half of them in 1991. Big-city stations, which represent less than 1 percent of the nation's stations, accounted for 11 percent of the industry's revenues and 50 percent of its profits in 1991, according to the FCC. Stations with less than a million dollars in annual revenues—75 percent of all stations—lost money that year.[85]

Radio broadcasters face a technological shift that promises to make their AM and FM operations increasingly obsolete. It is digital audio broadcasting (DAB), involving the same shift to digital transmission that eventually will be adopted by television broadcasters. In 1992, the FCC allocated frequencies that permit DAB programs to be broadcast either from satellites or from ground transmitters.[86] Despite the industry's hesitations about DAB's viability, at least one firm, Washington-based Satellite CD-RADIO Inc., has applied for permission to begin digital audio service from a communications satellite in 1996.

DAB technology is well advanced, but its full-scale application may be delayed for several reasons. One is sharp disagreements within the radio industry on how and when it should be introduced. The industry is, understandably, not keen on the idea of having to spend billions of dollars to replace its AM and FM facilities. Moreover, there is a question about acceptance of DAB by radio listeners. The technology requires replacement of present receivers with more expensive sets. Finally, DAB has competition from other developing forms of consumer digital audio services: cable, microwave, compact disks, and digital audio tape. As a result, it may be a decade or more before DAB becomes a significant force in U.S. radio broadcasting.[87] Its growth may depend on its capability to permit listeners to make crisp CD-like high-quality sound recordings at home on minidisks or digital cassette tapes. The result, according to media consultant Michael Tyler, could be an "armchair record store" with thousands of titles available on demand for home recording.[88]

Meanwhile, the television broadcasting industry is scheduled for a bumpy transition in the coming years. Its major competition, cable TV, is consolidating an already strong position by increasing its channel capacities. In addition to cable TV competition, TV broadcasters and their affiliated stations may also have to share audiences and revenues with direct-to-home satellite broadcasters and eventually with telephone companies.

There are tentative signs that the Big Three networks' 10-year slide in prime-time audience viewing has slowed down. This has led to renewed optimism throughout the industry about a turnaround and a new cycle of growth performance. Despite its troubles, broadcast television is still the most prosperous U.S. media sector. Its 1992 revenues totaled $22.77 billion, a 6 percent increase over the previous year. However, most industry observers see little prospect for a long-term improvement in the networks' prospects if they continue in their present pattern. As the *Washington Post*'s Paul Farhi pointed out:

> No one believes the networks will ever relive their glory days, when they were the nation's "electronic hearth," around which more than 90 per cent of the TV audience gathered on a given night. With dozens of existing viewing alternatives, and the prospect of perhaps hundreds of new TV channels through technological advances, even the most bullish analysts concede the networks will continue to lose audience share.[89]

The inevitable trend is toward alliances between the TV networks and the cable industry. As Michael Fuchs, chairman of HBO, noted, "At the end of this decade, it's not going to be cable and broadcast anymore, it's going to be *television*. It is not even inconceivable that a cable company might own a network."[90] In the panicky rush to redefine themselves in this new environment, the worst thing the TV networks could do is to weaken their most durable stock-in-trade, namely, good entertainment programs and solid news operations, which are the services they can deliver, when they choose to, better than other medium.

Their model might conceivably be a media competitor whose relevance to their problems would have been dismissed out-of-hand a few years ago. It is public television, which itself needs to be reshaped to the new realities. The Public Broadcasting System (PBS) network is no small enterprise, with 300 stations and annual revenues of over $1.3 billion. For decades, it operated in what media historian Erik Barnouw has called safely splendid isolation, wavering between a desire to be popular and a hard-to-shake elitist image. Mike Barnicle, a *Boston Globe* columnist, once satirized a typical PBS program as "How to Prepare Quiche While Wearing a Bow Tie."

Despite its occasional preciousness, PBS has, with relatively limited resources, demonstrated the audience appeal of good programming. After years of hesitation, it has also taken some important steps to expand into the cable TV, videotape, and educational program markets.[91] More important, public television has kept its commitment to high-quality productions, from "Sesame Street" to "American Playhouse," which cumulatively draw large audiences. It is difficult to imagine a mass conversion of born-again New York television executives to the public-broadcasting program pattern. Nevertheless, a variation of this pattern is one of their choices—greater commitment to high-quality programming aimed at stabilizing their diminishing audience base.

The decline of the networks and their local stations is something less than an apocolyptic event. As *Washington Post* television critic Tom Shales reminds us, God has not declared that there be three networks, as He did with the Ten Commandments. But what we are losing, he suggests, is more than just three highly visible business enterprises:

> Everything is ending. Nothing is beginning. Television as we have known it is unraveling, and when the strands and threads are put back together, it may be all but unrecognizable. . . . For forty years we were one nation indivisible, under television. That's what's ending. Television is turning into something else, and so are we. We're different. We're splintered. We're not as much "we" as the "we" we were. We're divisible.[92]

NOTES

1. Charles Paul Freund, "Save the Networks!" *Washington Post,* 28 July 1991, p. C-1.
2. Quoted in "And the Tube Shall Make Us Free," *Washington Post,* 24 April 1977, p. H-1.
3. Quoted in "What TV Drama Is Teaching Our Children," *New York Times,* 28 July 1991, p. C-1.
4. Minow's speech was delivered at the annual convention of the National Association of Broadcasters in May 1961. For the text of the speech, and Minow's latter-day reflections on it after 30 years, see *How Vast the Wasteland Now?* Freedom Forum Media Studies Center, Columbia University, August 1991.
5. *Communications Industry Forecast: Industry Spending Projections 1992–1996,* 6th annual ed. (New York, Veronis, Suhler & Associates, June 1992), 58.

6. "CBS Study Shows Slight Decline in Three-Network Viewing through 1995," *Broadcasting,* 12 December 1988, p. 49.
7. "Big Three's Financial Results Advertise a Bad Year," *Broadcasting,* 13 April 1992, p. 4.
8. The estimate is from Florence Setzer and Jonathan Levy, *Broadcast Television in a Multi-channel Marketplace,* OPP Working Paper No. 26, Federal Communications Commission, Washington, D.C., June 1991, p. 19.
9. "Sikes Looks to Strengthen Broadcasters' Hand," *Broadcasting,* 8 July 1991, p. 23.
10. Ken Auletta, *Three Blind Mice* (New York: Simon & Schuster, 1991).
11. James R. Walker and Robert V. Bellamy Jr., "Gratifications of Grazing: An Exploratory Study of Remote Control Use," *Journalism Quarterly* 68, no. 3 (Fall 1991): 422–431.
12. "TV Viewing's No Dating Game," *Variety,* 24 August 1992, p. 15.
13. "Has Fox Made the Grade?" *Television Broadcasting International* (May 1992): 32–40.
14. Quoted in Les Brown, "Reading TV's Balance Sheet," *Media & Values* no. 40 (Summer/Fall 1987): 13.
15. "TV's Shifting Balance of Power," *Broadcasting,* 12 October 1987, p. 40.
16. "Cosby Sidesteps Networks in Big TV Deal," *New York Times,* 28 October 1991, p. D-1.
17. The corporate takeover of the three networks has been extensively documented, most particularly in Ken Auletta, *Three Blind Mice.* See also Sally Bedell Smith, *In All His Glory* (New York: Simon & Schuster, 1990) (a study of CBS founder William Paley), and J. Fred MacDonald, *One Nation Under Television: The Rise and Decline of Network TV* (New York: Pantheon Books, 1990).
18. "Networks Still Tops in TV Group Ownership," *Broadcasting,* 30 March 1992, p. 47.
19. "A 180 Degree Turn of the Wheel of Fortune Befalls NBC," *New York Times,* 14 October 1991, p. D-6.
20. For a summary of the networks' cost-cutting activities, see "One of TV's Best Secrets: How ABC, CBS and NBC Have Taken the Bite out of Program Costs," *Broadcasting,* 9 December 1991, pp. 3–4.
21. "There's No Bigness Like Show Bigness," *Economist* (London), 25 March 1989, pp. 77–78.
22. "Fear Stalks the Small Screen," *Economist* (London), 25 April 1992, p. 81.
23. "The Rise and Rise of Program Prices," *Broadcasting,* 23 September 1991, pp. 44–45.
24. "Television in Recession," *Television Business International* (March 1991): pp. 34–40.
25. "The Networks in Play," *Broadcasting,* 11 November 1991, pp. 3–5.
26. "Big Shifts in Network-Studio Relationships," *New York Times,* 27 April 1992, p. C-8.
27. *The Globalization of Mass Media Firms,* National Telecommunications and Information Administration, U.S. Department of Commerce, January 1993.
28. Setzer and Levy, *Broadcast Television in a Multichannel Marketplace,* p. 15.
29. Bill Carter, "TV Networks, in a Crisis, Talk of Sweeping Changes," *New York Times,* 29 July 1991, p. D-1.
30. "A $16 Billion Advertising Market," *Television Business International* (February 1991): p. 30.
31. "Endangered Species," *Forbes,* 3 February 1992, pp. 43–44.
32. "TV Station Profitability: Half Full or Half in the Red?" *Broadcasting,* 10 August 1992, p. 32.
33. "The Sky's the Limit," *Time,* 27 November 1989, p. 73.
34. "The Networks and Affiliates May Be Falling out of Love," *Business Week,* 15 June 1992, p. 41.
35. "Countdown to '91: The Shape of Things to Come," *Broadcasting,* 2 September 1990, p. 19.
36. "FCC Defends New Fin-Syn Rules in Court," *Broadcasting,* 22 June 1992, p. 40.
37. "Ruling Eases Hollywood's Grip on TV Syndication," *Washington Post,* 2 April 1993, p. F-1.
38. "Quality TV: Hollywood's Elusive Illusion," *Broadcasting,* 18 November 1991, p. 17.

39. "Talk Is Cheap, But Profitable, on TV," *New York Times,* 22 June 1992, p. D-1.

40. "King Tags 30 to 'Wheel,' 'Jeopardy,'" *Broadcasting,* 3 August 1992, p. 16.

41. "Now It Can Be Told: Tabloid TV Is Booming," *New York Times,* 23 December 1991, p. D-10.

42. "CBS Group Buying 'Scarlett' as If There Is no Tomorrow," *New York Times,* 4 November 1991, p. 1.

43. Auletta, *Three Blind Mice,* p. 563.

44. "All the News That Can Be Had on the Cheap," *Business Week,* 6 May 1991, p. 87. See also "CNN TV News Service Grows," *Variety,* 15 June 1992, p. 29.

45. "World Series Is a Hit, But CBS Still Loses," *Washington Post,* 29 October 1991, p. D-1.

46. "No NFL PPV Until at Least 1994," *Broadcasting,* 2 September 1991, p. 17.

47. "Slow, But Sure, Local Sports Trying PPV," *Broadcasting,* 8 June 1992, p. 42.

48. "ABC Gives PPV Old College Try," *Variety,* 11 May 1992, p. 65.

49. Setzer and Levy, *Broadcast Television in a Multichannel Marketplace,* p. 15.

50. Auletta, *Three Blind Mice,* p. 575.

51. Tapio Varis, "The International Flow of Television Programs," *Journal of Communication* 34, no. 1 (Winter 1984): 143–152. See also "U.S. Programs Account for 75 Per Cent of International Marketplace," *Radio/Television Age,* 14 May 1984, p. 12.

52. For a description of U.S. investments in overseas television in the 1960s, see Wilson Dizard, *Television—a World View* (Syracuse, N.Y.: Syracuse University Press, 1966), 47–76.

53. "World Games: Growing U.S. Export Market," *Variety,* 3 February 1992, p. 60.

54. "Pitching the Global Village," *Washington Post,* 14 June 1992, p. H-5.

55. Fred H. Cate, "The European Broadcasting Directive," Communications Committee Monograph Series 1990/1, Section of International Law and Practice, American Bar Association, April 1990.

56. "Ready for Prime Time in Moscow," *New York Times,* 22 January 1992, p. D-1.

57. "BBC Seeks More Commercial Profile through Co-Productions," *Broadcasting,* 6 March 1989, p. 54.

58. "ABC Dishes It Out," *Broadcasting,* 5 October 1992, p. 18.

59. For an overall survey of current international television trends, see R. Negrine and S. Papathanassopoulos, "The Internationalization of Television," *European Journal of Communications* 6, no. 1 (March 1991): 5–32.

60. "TBS, Russo Co. Plan 1st Moscow Indie," *Variety,* 27 July 1992, p. 41.

61. "That's Not All, Folks," *Economist* (London), 2 November 1991, p. 64.

62. "Why the Losing Network Is Still a Winner," *Business Week,* 20 April 1992, pp. 98–99.

63. "NBC Walks into Cable Minefield," *New York Times,* 10 April 1989, p. D-1.

64. Quoted in Auletta, *Three Blind Mice,* p. 282.

65. "Cable, Overseas Program Markets Targeted by ABC," *Broadcasting,* 8 May 1989, p. 34.

66. For a discussion of the CNBC case and similar incidents, see Henry Geller, *Fiber Optics: An Opportunity for a New Policy?* Annenberg Washington Program, Washington, D.C., November 1991, pp. 19–20.

67. "More Sports Planned for Cable Television," *Washington Post,* 7 January 1993, p. D-2.

68. "Turner Puts McNetwork on the Front Burner," *Variety,* 18 November 1991, p. 1.

69. "Fox, Affiliates Aim for Dual Revenue Stream," *Broadcasting,* 25 November 1991, pp. 4–5.

70. "Networks, Affiliates Still at Odds over Cable Crossownership Ban," *Broadcasting,* 14 October 1991, p. 33.

71. "Broadcasters Counter Cable Ad Campaign," *Broadcasting,* 26 August 1991, pp. 15–16.

72. "Cable and Broadcasters Find Common Ground," *Broadcasting,* 10 June 1991, p. 39.

73. "Fiber Optics at Home: Wrong Number?" *New York Times,* p. E-18.

74. "New Device by Tandy," *New York Times,* 28 September 1992, p. D-3.

75. *The Big Picture: HDTV and High-Resolution Systems,* Background Paper OTA-BP-CIT-64, Office of Technology Assessment, U.S. Congress, Washington, D.C., June 1990, pp. 49–59.
76. "Compression: Changing the World of Television?" *Broadcasting,* 11 June 1990, pp. 68–71.
77. "HDTV/Compressed NTSC System in Works," *Broadcasting,* 9 December 1991, p. 29.
78. "HDTV Spectrum: 'Use It or Lose It,'" *Broadcasting,* 11 November 1991, p. 14.
79. "HDTV: Too Close for Comfort," *Broadcasting,* 13 April 1992, p. 4.
80. "HDTV Homes in on the Ultimate Test: The Market," *Business Week,* 27 April 1992, pp. 108–110.
81. "High Hopes for Japan's High-Priced High-Def TV," *Variety,* 18 November, 1991, p. 25.
82. "'Sets Up!' Says HDTV Study," *Broadcasting,* 1 June 1992, p. 16. The survey was sponsored by the Washington-based Advisory Committee on Advanced Television Services, an industry group that has worked closely with the FCC on HDTV planning.
83. "HDTV Spectrum: Use It or Lose It."
84. "Study Details Teens' Heavy Use of Radio," *Broadcasting,* 1 July 1991, p. 37.
85. "FCC Says Radio Is in 'Profound Financial Distress,'" *Broadcasting,* 2 February 1992, p. 4.
86. "FCC to Make Room for Satellite DAB," *Broadcasting,* 5 October 1992, p. 15.
87. "Broadcasters May Miss Digital Audio Bus," *Broadcasting,* 23 March 1992, p. 66.
88. "Digital Waves Clear the Air," *Financial Times* (London), 7 July 1992, p. 11.
89. "The Networks Stage a Comeback," *Washington Post,* 17 May 1992, p. H-1.
90. "Fuzzy Future of American TV," *Financial Times* (London), 27 January 1993, p. 16.
91. For a useful survey of recent public TV options, see *Strategies for Public Television in a Multi-Channel Environment,* Report by the Boston Consulting Group for the Corporation for Public Broadcasting, Washington, D.C., March 1991.
92. "TV's Sinking Net Worth," *Washington Post,* 31 July 1991, p. B-1.

Chapter

6

CABLE TELEVISION: THE PERILS OF SUCCESS

Cable television has redefined the U.S. media environment in the past two decades. From modest origins as a small-town service, it has expanded into national networks, each serving thousands of communities. Cable TV is the primary media link to the outside world in over 60 percent of U.S. households. More important, it has given Americans a preview of a future in which information and entertainment products will be delivered to their home by a single electronic utility.

Unfortunately for media historians, there is no defining moment for the beginnings of cable television—no Johannes Gutenberg looking at the first book from his multiple-copy printing machine, no Alexander Graham Bell, shouting, "Mr. Watson, come here" into his primitive telephone. If the cable industry decides one day to put up a monument to its founder, it should be dedicated to the Unknown Appliance Store Manager. Sometime around 1947, he (or perhaps she) had a clever idea for selling the store's supply of the newfangled black-and-white, 9-inch-screen television sets. The problem was that there was no television station in the community. Why not, the manager thought, put up a tall tower that would pick up TV programs from a nearby city, then charge a small fee for retransmitting the programs on cable wires to local households? The tower was built and the cable strung, and suddenly television had arrived in small-town America.

From these humble beginnings sprang the service known as Community Antenna Television (CATV), the origin of today's cable TV industry. CATV developed slowly; by 1950, only 14,000 households in 70 communities had cable television services. It was not until 1966 that CATV services had expanded sufficiently to warrant the first FCC regulations on its activities.[1] By 1970, cable TV was a fixture in most rural and suburban communities, and the first large networks were being installed in cities.

Today's cable industry is a $15-billion-a-year business, the most successful media enterprise of the past two decades. During the persistent economic recession of the early 1990s, most cable systems and their program suppliers continued to post increasing profits, unlike many other media businesses. A 1991 study by James Madison University researchers showed that U.S. consumers were willing to expand their media budget significantly in order to pay for cable TV.[2]

There are already signs that cable TV is entering the ranks of mature industries, with more and more of the aches and pains that institutional maturity brings. The early signs are recorded in the U.S. Department of Commerce's *Industrial Outlook,* the agency's annual survey of major U.S. industries. In the 1992 review, department analysts predicted a marked leveling off of cable TV growth. From the double-digit growth of earlier years (typically around 15 percent annually), single-digit cable TV growth is now projected for the rest of the 1990s. In part, this reflects the fact that cable TV is approaching a saturation point in the number of households it can effectively serve. Most industry analysts see the present 60 percent penetration rate topping off at 70 percent by the end of the decade.[3]

The cable TV business remains healthy, but the first bloom is off its rose. Among cable subscribers, there are grumblings of dissatisfaction with a system they had eagerly embraced only a few years ago. Their disappointment is reflected in a 1991 Consumers Union survey of 200,000 households on attitudes toward cable TV. Respondents gave a satisfaction index rating of 60 percent to cable, considerably lower than ratings recorded for other major services tracked by Consumers Union. The respondents' complaints were varied, but there was marked reaction against the upward creep of cable subscription fees. There was also criticism of cable programming, poor repair services, and system outages.[4] These and other consumer complaints were the driving force leading Congress to impose price controls and other regulatory restrictions on cable systems in 1992.

Consumer unhappiness also expresses itself in what the cable industry refers to as its "churn" problem—the continuing turnover in subscribers. Cable system circuits are available to 90 percent of all U.S. households, yet only two-thirds of those homes actually subscribe (Table 6.1). The increasing cost of cable subscriptions accounts for part of this; many householders simply cannot afford the service. Even more unsettling for the industry are those householders who do subscribe and then cancel all or part of their contracts because of disappointment with cable service and its rising costs. This turnover, or churn, is a persistent headache for local cable operators. The cancellations are offset, in part, by new subscriptions. But the loss of dissatisfied subscribers slows cable TV's overall growth. One industry source estimates that pay-cable channels experience a 50 percent turnover in their subscriber base every year.[5]

A longer-range problem for the industry is represented by the emergence of

TABLE 6.1 Homes Passed by Cable and Incidence of Subscription, 1986–1996

Year	TV Households (millions)	Homes Passed by Cable (millions)	Homes Passed as a % of TV Households (%)	Number of Cable Households (millions)	Cable Subscribers of a % of Homes Passed (%)	Cable Penetration of TV Households (%)
1986	86.8	68.0	78.3	39.6	58.2	45.6
1987	87.4	71.0	81.2	41.2	58.0	47.1
1988	88.6	74.3	83.9	44.2	59.5	49.9
1989	90.4	77.2	85.4	47.5	61.5	52.5
1990	92.1	83.6	90.8	50.5	60.4	54.8
1991	93.1	87.6	94.1	52.8	60.3	56.7
1992	92.1*	88.0*	95.5	54.9	61.5	59.6
1993	93.1	89.8	96.5	56.6	63.0	60.8
1994	94.4	91.6	97.0	58.6	64.0	62.1
1995	95.6	92.7	97.0	59.8	64.5	62.6
1996	96.8	93.9	97.0	61.0	65.0	63.0

*Revised downward based on 1990 Census.
SOURCE: Veronis, Suhler & Associates, Wilkofsky Gruen Associates. Reprinted by permission of Veronis, Suhler & Associates.

competition with alternative cable systems and with other technologies. From its beginnings, the cable TV industry has enjoyed monopoly status, through franchises granted by municipalities to its local networks. Now, however, pressure is forcing the renegotiation of many of these franchises so as to allow more competition. In 1992, only about 50 of the industry's 9,400 franchise areas had an alternative cable TV system. That competition will increase as more local franchises are modified to permit other systems. Even more formidable competition may emerge from newer technologies. These include information and entertainment programs supplied by microwave distribution systems ("wireless cable"), by fiber-optic circuits operated by telephone companies, and by transmissions from satellites broadcasting directly into homes.[6]

Although potentially competitive, these technologies are not an immediate threat to cable TV systems. The industry is still riding high, protected in most cases by local monopoly franchises and by its success in supplying a broad array of program services to subscribers. Cable TV has overcome its closest competition—broadcast television—by becoming the channel through which most people view local and network TV programs. All this is a long leap from cable's modest beginnings in the 1940s as a retransmitter of over-the-air television stations. By the 1960s, cable systems had begun providing other program services such as bulletin board announcements of community happenings, local high school football games, and an occasional transmission of city council meetings.

In the early 1970s, the age of modest innocence for the industry ended for two reasons—communications satellites and Ted Turner. By 1975, U.S. communications satellite networks had expanded to the point where they could transmit video signals anywhere in the country. Ted Turner, a Georgia advertising executive, saw what this could mean for a small local television station such as WTBS in Atlanta, which he happened to own. In late 1976, he leased a national satellite circuit and informed cable owners that they could retransmit WTBS programs without charge. Hundreds of cable owners installed small earth stations to pick up old sitcom programs, which were WTBS's stock-in-trade. Turner also bought the Atlanta Braves baseball team, adding their games to the station's schedule. In a short time, WTBS had a national audience of millions, and a new attraction for advertisers. Other "superstation" operations sprang up around the country, giving cable operators more programming choices as well as a merchandising tool for expanding their subscriber base.

Ted Turner's superstation gamble has taken on mythological stature in the cable industry over the years. Turner himself is not shy in claiming that his innovation revolutionized cable TV. In a 1989 interview, he declared, "On January 1, 1977, cable penetration was at 14 per cent. That's when we went on the satellite with WTBS, and now it's at 55 per cent. That's four times as much in only eleven years."[7]

In fact, Ted Turner has to share his cable revolution claim with a lesser-known figure, Gerald Levin. Levin was a vice president of Time Inc.'s video group in the mid-1970s when he proposed that HBO, the company's financially ailing pay-television service, deliver its programs to local cable systems by satellite. Levin's satellite proposal was a bigger gamble than Ted Turner's superstation venture, involving a heavier investment by both Time Inc. and the cable operators. Each operator had to invest $100,000 in an earth station to receive HBO programs. When HBO's satellite services began in 1975, there were only two such stations in place. HBO lost money for several years, but by 1980, over 1,700 local cable systems were receiving its satellite programming.[8]

In the process, the cable industry broke out of its small-town mold. A dozen other pay-television services adopted HBO's satellite delivery pattern with programming that brought tens of millions of new customers to local cable systems. The economics of the business changed dramatically. Previously, cable subscription rates had been calculated on a single monthly charge for all programs. With the arrival of satellite-delivered services, that billing pattern changed. A "basic service" charge was made for local television programs and other advertising-supported channels. HBO and other national pay-TV services became part of a "premium program" billing charge.

This multiple-billing practice, known as tiering in the industry, is the financial underpinning for cable systems and their program suppliers. In effect, it gives the industry a third revenue stream, adding lucrative pay-television fees to basic subscriber charges and to advertising revenues. A fourth revenue source, PPV programs, is now being phased in. These changes have fueled the expansion of satellite-delivered program offerings, which by 1993 numbered almost a hundred different services nationwide.

The national pay-TV services such as HBO, Showtime, The Movie Channel, and Disney Channel have the largest audience shares. There is, however, a smaller but still significant audience for the other channel offerings. MTV, the video-music channel owned by Viacom International, goes to over 50 million subscribers. Its programming is almost cost free to Viacom, since the record companies that produce the videos are paid only a nominal fee. Meanwhile, advertisers flock to the channel and its demographically desirable audiences of teenagers and young adults. MTV is also cable's international entertainment channel success, available in over 150 million homes abroad.[9] In 1991, MTV began a 24-hour service on an East Asian satellite, supplying programs to 30 countries in the region.

Other channels have settled for "narrowcasting" to smaller audiences. Bravo and Arts & Entertainment are consciously cultural, appealing to an upscale audience that is attractive to many advertisers. Lifetime makes a comfortable profit with women-oriented programming. The Nickelodeon channel is probably the biggest producer of children's programming in the world.[10] ESPN is the country's largest single entertainment network, with its macho collection of sports events, from baseball to truck-pull contests. Black Entertainment Television reaches an otherwise neglected segment of the national audience. Time Warner has been successful with a Courtroom Television Network, supplying armchair lawyers with sensational court trials. Other channels reach out to bingo players, sci-fi fans, weather watchers, Hispanics, and junk jewelry buyers.[11]

Not all new cable channels are successful. In January 1992, Ted Turner inaugurated Checkout Channel, a network of supermarket monitors that display snippets of news, fashion tips, and weather reports, along with advertisements, to shoppers waiting in line to pay for their groceries. However clever the idea may have sounded in the Turner organization's marketing department, it was unappealing to shoppers. The Checkout Channel was closed down in 1993.

Cable television has contributed two substantial media innovations. One is Ted Turner's CNN, whose 24-hour news service adds a new dimension to electronic news, especially for fast-breaking events.[12] CNN won its journalistic spurs with its around-the-clock live reportage and satellite-feed technology.[13] In 1992, CNN's impact as an international news channel was confirmed when 11 state-owned European television organizations announced that they would sponsor a regional satellite news channel, Euronews, that would pointedly compete with CNN's growing presence in Europe. Their purpose was less profit than cultural defense. "CNN is an American channel, an American point of view," Euronews executive Pierre Brunel-Lantena declared. "The point of Euronews is to give the viewer back his memories."[14] CNN also has competition in Asia where the BBC has a satellite-based television news service that is available to viewers in 38 countries.

CNN's techniques are imitated by a number of local cable channels in U.S. cities. In Honolulu, a Hawaiian-shirted announcer reports on daily surfing conditions, among other subjects. In Los Angeles, the cable news channel features "Dr. Drive," who monitors what he calls snafuskis on the local freeways. In 1992, a CNN-type regional news channel, New England Cable NewsChannel, was inaugurated, serving cable stations in six states.

Cable television's other important program innovation is C-SPAN, the public affairs channel. C-SPAN is the brainchild of Brian Lamb, a former federal government official, who saw in cable TV a means to document the political process for ordinary citizens. In the late 1970s, Lamb persuaded the U.S. Congress to allow coverage of its sessions. C-SPAN's schedule has since been extended to other public affairs forums, including state legislatures and the British and Canadian parliaments.

C-SPAN is one of the cable industry's more altruistic projects, since it is funded by local cable operators at a monthly cost of only several cents per subscriber. The importance of C-SPAN's service, however, was underscored in 1992 when the big three television networks slashed their presidential campaign coverage to a combined total of 100 hours. C-SPAN filled the gap with 1,200 hours of campaign programming.[15]

C-SPAN and other channel services have transformed cable TV into a national medium, more akin to the three old-line television networks than to a collection of separate small local systems. In the process, the cable industry has been restructured and redefined. Two decades ago, there was a clear distinction between local cable operators and the firms that supplied their programs. Today the industry is dominated by a handful of companies (known as multiple-system operators—MSOs), which are full or partial owners of the local cable systems that provide services for most U.S. household subscribers. These firms also own, wholly or in part, most of the popular national cable programming services supplied to local systems.[16]

The MSOs draw from a mixed bag of corporate styles. Some are "pure" cable companies, investing only in local cable systems and the program services supplied to them. Others are diversified communications conglomerates, whose interests often include publishing, broadcasting, filmmaking, and other media operations. The biggest of these conglomerates is Time Warner Inc., which is the second-largest local cable system operator as well as owner of HBO and a major shareholder in three Ted Turner cable channels—CNN, TNT, and TBS. Time Warner is also a leading publisher of magazines and books and a major producer of records and films. Even before its merger with Warner Communications in 1989, Time Inc. recognized the importance of cable TV in its multimedia operations. As Time Warner executive Gerald Levin noted, "Cable was a hardware business before. Now it is a video publishing business, something our company is more comfortable with."[17]

The executives of these megacompanies are the movers and shakers of a transforming change in U.S. media in recent years. They are also a faceless group, who would be among the unknowns in any name-recognition quiz about prominent Americans. The group includes HBO's Gerald Levin, Charles Dolan of Cablevision, Sumner Redstone of Viacom, and John Malone of Tele-Communications Inc. (TCI). The one name-recognition winner would be Ted Turner, who doesn't own any local cable systems but who promoted CNN against all the odds, was *Time* magazine's Man of the Year in 1991, and married Jane Fonda.

A less flamboyant, but more powerful, member of the new cable establishment is TCI's chief executive, John Malone. TCI owns or has financial interests in local cable systems with 13 million subscribers, nearly 25 percent of the nation's cabled homes. These holdings make TCI the biggest of the industry's multiple-system operators. A Yale graduate with a double major in economics and electronics engineering, Malone came to TCI headquarters in Denver in 1973. At the time, TCI was overextended financially, and unloved for its reputation for hard-nosed operations. At one point, in negotiating cable subscriber rates with municipal authorities in Vail, Colorado, TCI closed down its local cable programming for a weekend and transmitted only the names and home phone numbers of the mayor and city manager. The harried local officials quickly concluded the negotiations on terms favorable to TCI.[18] The firm's operating philosophy was summarized by John Malone in 1993 when he told an interviewer: "This is not touch football, this is tackle."

Malone expanded the company's cable holdings, but he made a notable change in direction when he cast the firm as a major player in national program services. His first large acquisition took place in 1987, when he led a consortium of cable conglomerates that invested $568 million in Turner Broadcasting. The Turner firm was in danger of going under as a consequence of Ted Turner's expensive purchase of a large part of the MGM studio's film library. (Characteristically, Turner's MGM gamble, which included such gems as *Gone with the Wind,* turned out to be a financial winner.) TCI holds a 22 percent interest in Turner Broadcasting, including its Cable News Network. TCI has also invested in other channels, including Black Entertainment Television, Discovery, and American Movie Classics.[19]

More recently, John Malone has been active in exploring opportunities in such areas as direct-to-home satellite broadcasting, fiber-cable installations, and PPV programming.[20] By 1993, over 500 of TCI's cable systems had been outfitted with addressable converters designed for PPV reception. Malone has also negotiated an arrangement with the Fox Television Network, which makes TCI the first formal broadcast network affiliate in the industry. He is also a leading advocate for the cable industry strategy of becoming an all-purpose provider of telecommunications and information services for homes, including telephone, data, and interactive multimedia circuits.[21] In 1992, he announced a $200-million project to upgrade TCI's capabilities to provide such services, using digital compression techniques, which promise to turn a 50-channel conventional system into a brawny 500-channel monster. TCI has also teamed up with a telephone company, U.S. West, in an international venture to explore cable and telephone investment opportunities in Europe. TCI's most ambitious venture, however, may be its 1992 linkup with IBM to develop a cable-based interactive network delivering information and entertainment services to homes across the country.[22]

TCI and other large multiple-system operators now dominate the cable television business. By 1993, the top 25 multiple-system operators controlled the circuits to 75 percent of all cable subscribers. This ratio probably will rise to 90 percent by 1996 as the MSO conglomerates compete to buy out smaller multiple-system operations as well as the remaining independent systems. According to some Wall Street analysts, these acquisitions will cost $18–$20 billion, financed mainly through debt.[23] The result will be an even tighter consolidation of cable TV transmission and programming resources in the hands of a very small group of companies, in effect an oligopoly of vertically integrated enterprises. These big conglomerates already exercise a greater degree of control over the cable industry than do their counterparts in any other U.S. media industry.

The cable industry's rationale for this development is that consolidation is necessary in order to finance and manage the planned expansion of each of its local systems to 150 channels or more in the coming years, together with the new programming that will be carried on those channels. What is generally left unsaid by cable executives is that they are positioning themselves to resist the anticipated incursion of telephone companies and other new competitors in the field of home entertainment and information services.

The threat of outside competition is only one of the cable industry's concerns. Another is that the industry will soon peak in terms of subscriber growth and the willingness of subscribers to spend more on new cable services. These are critical considerations at a time when cable systems are beginning their costly expansion of channel capacity and program services. Cable television will have to adapt its present pattern to these new realities if it is to maintain its profitable momentum.

The industry's hopes are currently pinned on the expansion of interactive PPV cable services. A cable subscriber can order on demand certain PPV programs such as Hollywood films, usually by sending a signal via a video keypad to the local cable office. The industry's aim is to capture a significant part of the $20 billion spent annually on videotape rentals. PPV is being marketed as the "video store at home," with suggestions to consumers that they can thus avoid the inconvenience of going out to rent tapes one day and having to return them the next.

PPV programming has been slow to develop. Fifteen years ago, the Qube PPV experiment in Columbus, Ohio (described in Chapter 3), failed because subscribers found Qube's technology awkward to deal with and because its programs were similar to those already available on HBO and other pay-TV channels. It was obvious that PPV would be economically viable only when more efficient, user-friendly systems for viewing special programs were developed. This is beginning to happen. By 1992, PPV access was available in over one-third of all U.S. cable households, and spending for its programs was doubling each year (Tables 6.2 and 6.3).

To access PPV easily, a subscriber needs a special device, which has, in the industry's phrase, full addressability, that is, equipment that allows two-way communications between the viewer and the program supplier. A "black box" (known as an addressable converter) is attached to the TV receiver. The converter provides an interactive connection between the set and the local cable office. Without it, a subscriber must make a phone call to order a program. Eventually, addressable converters will be built into television sets as standard equipment. Advanced versions of

TABLE 6.2 Pay-per-View Households

Year	Number of Pay-per-View Households (millions)	Number of Cable Households (millions)	Pay-per-View Households as a % of Cable Households
1987	5.2	41.2	12.6
1988	8.7	44.2	19.7
1989	12.5	47.5	26.3
1990	15.2	50.5	30.1
1991	17.4	52.8	33.0

SOURCE: Veronis, Suhler & Associates, Paul Kagan Associates, Wilkofsky Gruen Associates. Reprinted by permission of Veronis, Suhler & Associates.

TABLE 6.3 Growth of Annual Subscriber Spending
on Pay-per-View ($ Millions)

Year	Events	Movies	Total
1988	200.0%	51.3%	118.3%
1989	26.0	30.5	27.7
1990	13.2	27.3	18.7
1991	75.2	35.7	58.7
Compound Annual Growth	65.5	35.9	51.4

SOURCE: Veronis, Suhler & Associates, Paul Kagan Associates, Wilkofsky Gruen
Associates. Reprinted by permission of Veronis, Suhler & Associates.

converter boxes allow a subscriber to scan a menu of current PPV offerings by using a
keypad, and then select a program by punching in the program's number. The
program appears on the video screen almost instantaneously. At the same time, the
subscriber's account is debited. Quick access to programs is essential, as surveys have
shown that most PPV viewers are impulse buyers.

An early entrant into the interactive PPV market was The Box, a music video
channel. Since 1989, The Box has provided subscribers with access to 200 music
videos through a "jukebox" programming machine located in cable TV operations
centers. Viewers call a 900 number and request a specific selection. The order is
processed and the music video is sent over the cable on a first-come, first-served
basis. By 1992, the service was available in 11 million homes and was generating
600,000 calls a month.[24]

"Play-along" games are another variation of PPV services. In 1990, the Interactive
Network began testing a menu of interactive games for home viewers. The network
offers a selection of football, baseball, and other sports games, in which the players at
home call the next play or guess which players will gain the most points. In addition
to sports games, the firm has designed an interactive version of the popular television
series "Murder, She Wrote," in which viewers guess the identity of the villain. Another game involves a version of the TV game shows "Wheel of Fortune" and "Jeopardy," in which players bet on the studio contestants.

The larger cable systems are moving quickly to equip their subscribers with fully
addressable PPV boxes. By 1993, the most advanced installation was Time Warner's
150-channel cable network, located in an affluent section of Queens, New York. The
system, known as Quantum, delivers up to 15 different movies on 57 PPV channels.
Subscriber costs for each showing range from $1.95 to $4.95, low enough to discour-
age visits to the local video-rental store. Quantum also offers a full menu of cable TV
fare, from the Prayer Channel ("reverent contact with God throughout the day") to
channels programmed in Greek, Hindi, Korean, Cantonese, and Mandarin. Specialized channels featuring interactive banking and travel reservation services are also
part of Time Warner's Quantum strategy.[25]

In 1993, Time Warner announced plans for a more extensive "full-service network" on its cable systems in the Orlando, Florida, area. The upgraded systems will
eliminate conventional cable channel technology in ways that allow subscribers to

choose from an unlimited menu of programs and to view their selections instantaneously. "We're creating a TV architecture that gives people what they want when
they want it. It is channelless," Greg Holmes, Time Warner's technology director,
pointed out. The new technology involved is a "video server," essentially a high-
capacity computer that stores vast amounts of images, which can be retrieved and
transmitted via digital switches and fiber-optic circuits to home viewers. The Orlando
network will concentrate initially on entertainment programming. Time Warner plans
eventually to market a full range of two-way video, voice, and text services, making
possible video phone calls, televised teaching, interactive shopping, and electronic
game-playing, among other features.[26] The company took a major step in this direction in May 1993 when it sold a 25 percent stake in Time Warner Entertainment, its
cable TV and film subsidiary, to U.S. West, a regional telephone company, for $2.5
billion. The alliance with U.S. West strengthens Time Warner's fiscal and technical
resources for introducing advanced information and entertainment programs.

Smaller cable companies are more cautious about installing advanced interactive
systems. In 1992, only 25 percent of all local cable systems were fully addressable.
Paul Kagan, a cable industry analyst, has estimated that the number of households
with full PPV access will more than double by 1997, reaching 40 million viewers and
generating a billion dollars in annual gross revenues for the cable industry.[27] Another
survey, sponsored by the National Cable Television Association, is less optimistic,
predicting 10 percent interactive cable penetration of U.S. households by the
mid-1990s.

Many industry observers see PPV as a tough sell. There is a perception by most
cable subscribers that they are already getting more entertainment programs than
they can handle, according to a survey conducted by Viewer's Choice, one of the
largest PPV program firms. Less than 30 percent of subscribers with access to PPV
had ordered the service. The survey concluded that PPV will require aggressive
marketing, with a focus on "compelling reasons" for the service.[28] Nevertheless, PPV
habits are forming among many cable subscribers, particularly sports fans. Interest
was spurred in 1991 by three world championship boxing matches. Local cable
networks charged home viewers premium rates of up to $40 per match, which
resulted in total gross revenues of a quarter billion dollars for the three events.[29] In
1992, the Summer Olympics were made available to PPV viewers, under joint arrangements between NBC Television and cable companies. The venture was a programming success and a financial failure; NBC reportedly lost $100 million on the proj-
ect.[30]

Championship boxing bouts and the Olympic Games do not happen every week.
The bread-and-butter programming of the PPV networks is new Hollywood films. The
film industry has been actively aware of this potential for new revenues. A 1992
survey by Goldman Sachs, the New York investment house, pointed out that, for the
studios, PPV showings are worth about 50 cents of every subscriber dollar collected,
whereas they collect only 20 cents of every videocassette dollar and 15 cents of every
pay-cable movie dollar.[31] In the early 1990s, several studios took minority shares in
two of the largest PPV channels—Viewer's Choice and Request. In 1991, Barry Diller,
then chairman of Fox Inc., sent shock waves through the industry when he announced that he was considering releasing new productions from his studio on PPV

cable before they are shown in theaters.[32] The film industry is also examining the prospect of directly controlling its own PPV channels, eliminating the program middlemen altogether.

Most cable industry observers believe that PPV will expand rapidly when National Football League and major-league baseball games are fully available on the service. (There has been limited programming of major-league sports on pay television for a number of years.) The television industry is lobbying against a PPV takeover of popular sports events, although it is also planning to get into its own versions of PPV viewing in the coming years. The U.S. Congress, mindful of voters' reactions to the idea of paying for sports programs they now get free, has warned the cable industry to move slowly on PPV sports shows. When big-league games become standard PPV fare, as they inevitably will, gross annual revenues could mount quickly to the multi-billion-dollar level. PPV is already a highly competitive business. By 1993, there were a half dozen independent program suppliers, offering an increasingly wide range of programming, from rock concerts to the Metropolitan Opera. Several of the big cable TV firms are also planning PPV operations. Viacom, owner of MTV and other cable channels, is actively involved in developing interactive PPV programs.[33]

In summary, PPV offers an important opportunity for the cable industry to expand its revenue base in the next few years. PPV also is part of a larger strategy, that of positioning the industry to deal with competition from over-the-air television, DBS networks, the Hollywood studios, and telephone companies.

The cable industry's most formidable potential competitor is the telephone industry, which has long-term plans for wiring all U.S. homes with a high-capacity fiber-optic cable. Fiber links have far greater capabilities than cable TV's present coaxial wires for supplying, among other services, PPV programming. Nevertheless, coaxial cables have some immediate advantages in preempting future telephone company technology, particularly once they have been upgraded through the digital compression techniques described in Chapter 3. Compression squeezes more capacity into existing wires, allowing present coaxial lines to transmit a hundred or more cable TV channels. The cable industry is betting that that increased capacity will satisfy the average subscriber's programming needs for some time to come.

Cable operators are also acting to block phone company competition by upgrading many of their systems with fiber cable. According to industry estimates, cable companies installed 75 percent as much fiber cable in 1992 as the seven regional Bell telephone companies. Tele-Communications Inc. (TCI), the country's biggest cable conglomerate, was the world's largest buyer of fiber cable that year, according to TCI president John Malone.[34]

PPV audiences are growing, but it will be years before fully addressable services are available in most U.S. homes. More immediate problems for cable TV include the need to maintain a high level of profitability. As noted earlier, the rate of growth is leveling off. The industry continues to have problems with what it calls churn—the persistent turnover in subscribers. In one six-month period in 1990, cable systems across the country had more disconnects than new subscribers, reversing a 40-year trend.[35] Many cable companies also have a heavy debt load, inherited from the high-riding 1980s, when they were expanding their systems. At that time, cable systems were being traded like baseball cards in a schoolyard, often at dizzying prices. The trading slowed down in the recessionary years of the early 1990s, leaving many systems strapped for cash.[36]

Although the cable industry overall is in good financial shape, it needs to pursue new revenue opportunities. The most immediate increase in revenue will probably come from advertising. Ad sales moved up steadily during the 1980s, from $230 million in 1982 to $3 billion in 1992.[37] Cable advertising has already expanded to the point where subscribers are objecting to "clutter"—too many commercials interfering with programs they have already paid for. A 1991 study indicated that cable has significantly more clutter than the television networks in prime time.[38]

The cable industry has introduced a new twist in electronic advertising with infomercials, 30-minute advertisements, often masquerading as talk shows that provide viewers with an 800 phone number for ordering the featured products. (Infomercials are also broadcast on regular television channels.) They are the fastest-growing segment of the $2.6-billion TV direct-response industry, which also includes the shop-at-home channels. In 1991, the Home Shopping Network introduced a 24-hour channel devoted exclusively to infomercials and related programming.[39] The infomercial format can be very profitable. One successful practitioner, beauty consultant Victoria Jackson, had sold over $150 million worth of makeup products by 1993 exclusively through her "Beauty Breakthrough" infomercials, the girl-talk sessions she hosts.[40] A unique twist was given to the infomercial format when it was used in the 1992 presidential campaign by the Democratic party for a biographic film of Bill Clinton, complete with ads offering a free copy of his economic proposals.[41]

The trend in cable advertising favors local cable systems, not the big national channels. Local business firms can reach on local channels the specialized audiences they want, a benefit not usually available on the national channels. In addition, cable ad rates are considerably lower than those charged by local television stations. A 30-second prime-time advertisement on a cable channel typically costs $500, about one-fourth the television rate.[42] Despite these relatively low charges, cable system operators were earning over $800 million annually in local ad revenues by 1992.

Advertising will continue to be a strong revenue source for cable operators as they add more channels to their systems through digital compression technology. They are looking for new programming opportunities to fill the expanded channels. One relatively unexplored area is programming for school classrooms. Public television's school programs have served as an educational resource for many decades, but they are usually limited to a single channel in a community. As a result, it has been difficult to tailor educational TV programs to meet diverse school curriculum needs. In a 150-channel cable environment, that difficulty is largely overcome. Fifteen or 20 channels could be made available during the day for specific curricular or enrichment programming. The prospects for greater cable TV involvement in educational programming have been strengthened by Cable in the Classroom, a clearinghouse for school projects, funded by the cable industry.[43]

A unique cable TV educational service is the Mind Extension University, the creation of Denver cable executive Glenn Jones. By 1993, the Mind Extension University had become one of the fastest-growing basic cable services in the country, available to over 17 million subscribers on more than 600 cable systems. Local cable operators pay three cents a month for each of their subscribers to carry the channel. Originally developed for high schools in remote areas, the channel is used increasingly in city schools. The Mind Extension University provides 10 hours of high school programming during the day, with courses ranging from physics to art history and Japanese. The courses are beamed by satellite to schools with TV monitors, VCRs, computers, and talk-back units, which enable students to ask questions during class.

In the evening, the Mind Extension University's adult education classes take over the channel. Advanced degree programs have been developed by a consortium of universities, including Colorado State University, the University of Maryland, and George Washington University. Additional credit and noncredit classes are offered on Mind Extension channels by more than 20 universities. Viewers enroll for these courses at much lower cost than they would pay if they attended regular classes.[44]

Cable television is essentially a local business, extending no further than the end of its community network. However, some large cable conglomerates have begun to find profitable business opportunities around the world. The ESPN sports network delivers programs by satellite to Latin America and Europe. Time Warner has been aggressive in seeking overseas business. In 1991, the company entered the European cable market as a partner in a joint venture to manage a system in Hungary. Its HBO subsidiary has operated a successful program distribution network in Central and South America since 1988.

In 1991, Ted Turner's Cable News Network inaugurated full-time video service to Latin America, operating in what the network describes as a "hybrid English-Spanish" format. Moving beyond the network's English language programming, seen in over 70 countries, the service was CNN's first attempt at foreign language broadcasting.[45] Turner Broadcasting and other cable producers are making coproduction arrangements with foreign producers for programming that can be marketed worldwide. In 1992, the company announced a joint venture in Russia to build and provide programming for what it claimed would be the first private-sector independent station in Moscow.[46] A year later, Turner began transmitting two of its most profitable and popular services—the Comedy Channel and the TNT movie channel—to European viewers via the Luxembourg-based Astra satellite. Such projects, according to one Turner executive, are transforming the firm into a "vertically integrated global company that will produce and distribute programming around the world."[47]

Meanwhile, at home, the cable industry is looking to high technology as a means of improving its product offerings and profits. These prospects include two aforementioned developments—greater channel capacity through digital compression techniques and full addressability for PPV services. The industry is also considering two other revenue resources—high-quality digital music transmissions and telephone service. Columbia University communications expert Elie Noam predicts that cable systems will compete directly with telephone companies as cable's technical facilities are upgraded in the coming years.

Digitally compressed cable channels and PPV addressability are the most immediate concerns of the industry. The two projects are, in fact, connected. PPV will not be a viable business for most cable systems until their channel capacity is expanded. In 1992, only about 25 percent of all cable systems had a capacity of 54 channels or more. Two-thirds of the systems had been 30 and 53 channels. Further channel expansion will involve time, money, and a gamble on consumer tastes. "Channel rebuild," to use the industry's phrase, will cost about $500 per subscriber and will take at least several years to accomplish. Wall Street analysts estimate that channel rebuild will cost the industry about $3.5 billion.[48]

Cable system owners worry about consumer acceptance of the new channels, especially consumers' reactions to the inevitable rise in subscriber rates. Over the years, surveys have shown that most cable subscribers limit their viewing to about a half dozen channels. What will their response be to 150 channels? And what kind of programming will be available for the expanded capacity? Despite its concern over these questions, the industry is publicly optimistic about the new services. Hal Krisberg, president of Jerrold Communications and an industry leader in new technologies, predicts the average cable system will transmit as many as 130 channels later in the decade. He also predicts that, in addition to present channel services, there will be 50 new PPV channels, 35 additional advertiser-supported basic channels, and an additional 10 new channels dedicated to high-definition special events programs.[49] This upgrading will, in turn, put pressure on local cable operators to make their systems fully addressable for PPV programs.

Channel expansion will also spur the adoption of other new services. One of them is digital cable radio, which will do for home stereo what cable has done for TV. In a cable radio system, the cable TV wire is split in half. One half is linked, as before, to home TV sets, and the other half is connected to stereo systems. In this way, hundreds of compact-disc-quality sound programs can be accessed for a relatively modest monthly fee. When a number of companies began offering digital cable radio services in selected communities in 1991, consumer acceptance was strong.[50]

In summary, the cable TV industry is restructuring itself with new facilities and products. Besides supplying more revenue sources, these moves are strengthening the industry to meet marketing challenges from phone companies and other media competitors in the next decade. Cable TV has prospered on assurances of municipally granted monopoly franchises for its local networks. By 1993, fewer than a hundred of the industry's 9,400 franchise areas had competitive cable systems. There is, however, a growing trend among city councils and other local franchise authorities to license competing systems. Even more formidable competition is expected to come from outside the cable field, for instance, from services supplied by multichannel microwave distribution systems (MMDS), fiber-optic circuits operated by telephone companies, and broadcasting satellites that beam programs from space directly to homes.

In recent years, the FCC has issued operating licenses to several hundred wireless cable systems, which use over-the-air microwave channels to deliver programming to homes. (The FCC is involved because it has legal authority over the allocation of the radio frequency spectrum, including microwave.) Most MMDS networks originally served outlying rural districts, beyond the urban and suburban areas where cable TV networks are located. More recently, MMDS entrepreneurs have moved into metropolitan areas, where they compete directly with cable TV. Wireless cable has certain advantages in the competition. Installation costs are much cheaper—about $600 per subscriber versus $3,000 for an average cable wire installation. And subscription fees are also generally lower for wireless services.

The wireless cable industry faces barriers to its plans for competing more directly with cable TV networks. Technologically, most MMDS circuits can provide only a fraction of the 50 or more channels available on conventional coaxial cable systems. The current expansion of cable TV channel capacity will widen this gap in favor of cable. MMDS operators have also been effectively denied access to many of cable TV's popular entertainment services. Cable TV channels are usually owned by large national conglomerates, which also control local cable systems and which do not relish the idea of wireless cable competition. This problem was addressed in 1993 congressional legislation that required cable firms to make their productions available to competitors (including MMDS systems) on an equitable basis. Despite that requirement, wireless systems will probably be a relatively minor competitive factor for cable television in the coming years.[51] In 1992, most of the wireless systems were in rural areas, beyond the reach of cable TV facilities. The MMDS operators' campaign to win over a significant share of big-city subscribers had also lagged, with only 350,000 subscribers signed up.[52]

A more significant threat to cable TV systems in the latter half of the 1990s may be information and entertainment programs transmitted by direct broadcast satellites (DBS). Unlike the satellites that provide most cable systems with their national programming, the broadcast satellites bypass the cable system by transmitting programming directly to homes. In the 1980s, the cable TV industry considered cooperating with the proposed DBS networks, in effect trying to preempt them.[53] The negotiations eventually failed, but were revived again in the early 1990s. National cable program suppliers are well aware that over one-third of U.S. households do not subscribe to cable TV. Broadcasting satellites, transmitting into backyard earth stations, are the most efficient way of reaching that untapped market. The problem for local cable operators is that direct satellite services could also attract present cable TV subscribers. A deterrent to DBS competition is that many of the most popular cable channel programs, such as HBO and ESPN, are owned by media conglomerates that have important financial stakes in local cable systems. Although congressional legislation and a 1993 federal antitrust decision mandate that they do so, cable networks will be reluctant to share their best programming with satellite system operators.[54]

National DBS networking will become a reality by the middle of the decade. The major network will probably be operated by DirecTV, a venture sponsored by Hughes Communications, a division of General Motors. DirecTV plans three satellites that will offer more than 150 home information and entertainment channels, beamed into small customer-owned earth stations. Several other DBS networks may also be launched in the next few years. As noted earlier, their success is heavily dependent on reaching agreements that will give them access to the popular entertainment programs controlled by the big cable TV conglomerates and the Hollywood studios. The availability of these programs will determine the marketability of each broadcasting satellite network. Getting access to them can be difficult, as the managers of Primestar, an ambitious satellite venture, learned in 1990 when their DBS project failed because it lacked attractive programming.[55] In 1993, the new DirecTV network took a long step toward avoiding the same pitfall when it signed agreements with

Paramount Pictures, the Disney organization, and several basic and PPV channels for program services on its satellite channels.

Adequate program resources are less a problem for another potential competitor to cable TV, namely, the old-line television networks. The broadcast networks are seeking additional revenue streams by creating new services that will supplement their core business. The most commonly cited example is over-the-air HDTV, which may be marketed primarily as a PPV service. Network broadcasters could eventually supply HDTV service to almost every home in the country, whereas cable TV currently reaches only about 60 percent of households. However, cable may beat the TV networks to the punch. The networks will not have the technical facilities to broadcast any significant HDTV programming before the end of the decade. By then most large cable systems will have upgraded their present channel capacity through digital compression technology, which gives them the capability to provide high-definition services. Cable industry executives tend, however, to see slow growth for HDTV programming for the rest of the 1990s. In a 1992 industry panel on the subject, most panelists agreed that HDTV penetration on cable systems would involve less than 5 percent of total programming channels.[56]

Competition between the broadcast networks and cable TV is somewhat lessened because the two media have many interests in common. Retransmission of network and local TV broadcasts is still an important cable service. The networks, meanwhile, have begun producing programs for cable TV. In 1991, ABC and CBS made deals with the Nickelodeon and USA channels, respectively, to share programming.[57] At another level, the networks will probably make major investments in local cable TV systems, following the 1992 relaxation of FCC restrictions on such ownership. These developments suggest that the future relationship between broadcast networks and cable TV will be marked more by accommodation than by competition.

Despite differences in other areas, the cable TV and television industries are united on one issue: their opposition to telephone company plans to expand independently into home information and entertainment services. By 1993, most of the regulatory restrictions on such phone company activities were lifted or modified, as described in Chapter 4. The phone companies have made clear their intention to become both producers and transmitters of advanced information and entertainment services, competing with both cable TV networks and over-the-air broadcasters.

Both cable operators and TV broadcasters understand that the telephone industry may be their primary competition in supplying information and entertainment services to homes. This has spawned acrimonious debates, with cable and broadcasting leaders accusing the phone companies of trying to take over the home market. The dispute reached a crescendo in late 1991, when the FCC issued its video-dial-tone proposal, which would allow phone subscribers to call up a menu of video services in much the same way they now call up friends and neighbors. Cable and broadcasting executives saw this as the proverbial camel's nose under the tent, the beginnings of a telephone industry takeover of their turf.[58] Their fears were further confirmed in 1993 when Southwestern Bell, a regional phone company, announced that it was buying three cable systems in the Washington, D.C., area for $650 million. It was the first time that a Baby Bell company had moved directly into the cable TV business under a federal ruling that permits them to do so outside their normal phone service area.

Despite the blustery debates, there is an emerging consensus on how these opposing interests can be reconciled. The FCC video-dial-tone proposal allows limited joint ventures between cable and telephone companies. As noted above, the FCC has ended most of its regulatory restrictions against television network ownership of cable systems. At the same time, pragmatic partnerships are being formed between phone companies and cable systems. TCI, the country's largest cable conglomerate, is cooperating with two phone companies—AT&T and U.S. West—in a Denver experiment to test advanced video-program delivery to homes.[59] In 1993, Time Warner began an experiment on its Queens, New York, cable system, in cooperation with MCI, whereby subscribers are able to bypass the local phone company in making long-distance calls. Cable TV networkers have also overtaken the phone companies in upgrading their home delivery systems to fiber-optic standards. This move puts the cable operators in a strong position to offer advanced services such as high-definition video later in the decade.[60]

The eventual resolution of what the industry calls "the cable/telco debate" will take place in the political arena. The issues are too important to the future of the national information system to be left to marketplace economics. Dozens of bills on the subject have been introduced in Congress. The FCC is also part of the decision process in its role as the national regulator of television, cable TV, and phone company activities. Since all legislative and regulatory decisions involving these competitors will be challenged by them in the courts, cable-telco issues will not be fully resolved until the late 1990s, if then.[61]

A compromise will finally emerge, in the time-honored U.S. political tradition. The telephone companies will have to accept regulatory restrictions on their advanced services to homes as a hedge against their domination of the business. Those limitations will determine how, or even whether, they can produce information and entertainment services, in addition to providing transmission circuits. Cable television's role in the compromise is less clear. The big cable conglomerates already control access to a major share of local cable subscribers, as well as to most of the popular cable TV information and entertainment services. This gives them a strong advantage over their potential phone company competitors, restricted as the latter most certainly will be by regulatory rules in supplying program services.

The odds would seem to favor cable systems as providers of both the channels and the programming for advanced services to homes. But such an outcome may be changed by other factors. The cable business has been lightly regulated—over and above its municipal franchises—for decades. Its managers have argued, with considerable success, that their activities are protected by the First Amendment prohibitions against government interference with the media.[62] They have defended the monopoly status of local cable franchises with claims that cable TV is subject to competition from other media sources, particularly television and radio. That view was generally supported in the deregulatory atmosphere ("getting government off the backs of industry") encouraged by the Reagan and Bush administrations, both of which sought to ensure media diversity through marketplace competition rather than by regulation.[63] The Clinton administration has generally favored modifying the cable industry's oligopolistic control over both local networks and the most popular programs shown on cable channels—a policy signalled by the 1993 settlement of a Department of Justice antitrust case in which the major cable companies agreed to make their programs available to competitors.

High political and economic stakes are involved in the running debate over who will supply advanced information and entertainment services to homes. White House and congressional policies will seek to accommodate the interests of all the major players: telephone companies, cable systems, television broadcasters, and the other mass media sectors. The rhetorical emphasis will be on marketplace competition, but the critical factor will consist of the regulatory restrictions that will govern the activities of the telephone companies.

The cable industry will probably be the near-term winner, roughly up to the end of the decade. By upgrading many of its present coaxial cable circuits to a hundred or more channels in the next few years, cable TV can provide a broader range of information and entertainment services in ways that will satisfy a majority of its customers.[64] The telephone companies will gain less in the short run, primarily because they will not be able to compete fully with cable TV's expanded channel capacity in this decade. The phone companies' plans to wire up all U.S. households with fiber-optic cable will take at least 10 years to complete.[65] When completed, however, such a network may be capable of delivering a much higher level of advanced services to homes than cable TV channels can. The question is whether cable TV, with its lesser capabilities, will not have effectively preempted the consumer market, particularly for entertainment programming, by the time this happens. In the years it will take to complete the telephone fiber network, the cable industry may have reinforced its position as the primary producer and transmitter of information and entertainment services for homes.

Most likely there will be something for everyone as compromises are worked out to fit the interests of all the industries involved. The phone companies will be allowed to expand their advanced home services. The cable companies will continue to be in a strong competitive position. Hollywood, television broadcasters, publishers and other traditional media will produce entertainment and information products for the new home market. Consumers will benefit from new information and entertainment services. Nevertheless, the United States will still not have a full-scale national information utility down to the household level. It is true that the cable industry has brought more diversity to the U.S. media scene. So far, however, it has done this basically on its own terms. There is merit in the industry's argument that there is now more competition among the U.S. media than ever before—more television, radio, independent filmmaking, print publications, and so on.

However, electronic news and entertainment access to U.S. homes is dominated by the cable industry at present. That control is unlikely to diminish soon despite congressional efforts in 1992 to strengthen regulatory control over the industry, as described earlier. Given their vertically structured operations, a half dozen major cable TV networks make the important decisions on what kind of program services do, and do not, appear on their channels. They control both the physical channels and a large share of the programming delivered on those channels. Moreover, they have a history of blocking program offerings that go against their economic interests. As media watcher Pat Aufderheide notes, cable operators are basically

> holding (independent) programmers hostage until they get a piece of their (profits). . . . They then keep rival programmers off their systems and refuse to sell their programming to rival delivery systems. This is the situation antitrust legislation was designed to prevent: letting the common carrier—say, the owner of a railroad or pipeline or telephone system—have a grip on what's carried and for how much.[66]

This pattern is similar to that which characterized the introduction of other modern media technologies. In the early 1920s, AT&T sought monopoly control over the new radio broadcasting industry. The television networks tried to maintain direct control over local stations in the 1960s. The major Hollywood studios bought up local movie theaters to ensure outlets for their films. In each case, government actions effectively modified these attempts at vertically integrated media monopolies.

In summary, the cable TV conglomerates have consolidated control of major transmission and program resources, and they are tightening their grip, despite recent attempts by federal and state regulatory authorities to force them to make their programs available to DBS operators and other competitors. The cable TV firms may compete among themselves, but it is a limited form of competition, which tends often to protect them collectively against outsiders. That trend is not only a business marketplace issue. It also concerns the U.S. marketplace of ideas. It puts at risk the principle of open access for all citizens to a broad range of competitive information resources. As such, it concerns the evolution of a diverse national information utility. And that utility should be opened up to all communications—voice, video, and data—from any source as a fundamental First Amendment principle. It should, in effect, have the basic characteristics of the present telephone system. In regulatory terms, the phone companies are common carriers, required to provide access so that any customer may send or receive a message. The phone companies are, moreover, regulated as to the rates they charge in order to ensure nondiscriminatory economic access.

The new national information utility should be organized under roughly comparable rules. How will the cable companies, with their present power to determine access to their channels, fit into this framework? A study by Bowling Green State University researchers suggested that the cable conglomerates be separated from their programming operations in order to ensure full common-carrier diversity in the emerging information utility.[67] Meanwhile, there is increasing pressure to put limitations on the cable conglomerates' ability to dominate channel programming. In April 1993, the FCC, acting under a congressional mandate, began drawing up rules designed to force the cable TV industry to make its programming available to its principal competitors, including the wireless cable, direct broadcast satellite and telephone industries.

The debate on these issues has just begun. Its resolution will determine the future of the cable industry and all other media services in the new information environment.[68]

NOTES

1. "Cable Television Information Bulletin," Federal Communications Commission, January 1990, p. 2.
2. William C. Wood and Sharon L. O'Hare, "Paying for the Video Revolution: Consumer Spending on the Mass Media," *Journal of Communication* 4, no. 1 (Winter 1991): 24–30.
3. *Industrial Outlook,* U.S. Department of Commerce, Washington, D.C., January 1992. See also "Cable Growth to Level Off, Commerce Study Says," *Broadcasting,* 30 December 1991, p. 6.
4. "Television," *Consumer Reports* 56, No. 9 (September 1991): 576–585.
5. "Pay Cablers Float on Profits Despite Leaky Subs," *Variety,* 6 April 1992, p. 31.
6. "More Bad News on Cable: Wireless Systems Loom as New Competitive Threat," *Barron's,* 14 May 1990, p. 14.
7. "Ted Turner, on Top of the World," *Washington Post,* 13 April 1989, p. C-1.
8. "Time Marching on with Video," *New York Times,* 2 January 1980, p. C-1.
9. "Rock On," *Economist* (London), 3 August 1991, p. 62.
10. "Is Redstone Studio-Prone?" *Variety,* 13 January 1992, p. 85.
11. "Fledgling Cable Networks Are Poised for Flight," *New York Times,* 3 June 1990, p. H-1.
12. Edward Diamond, "How CNN Does It," *New York,* pp. 30–39.
13. Barbara Zelizer, "CNN, the Gulf War, and Journalistic Practise," *Journal of Communication* 42, no. 1 (Winter 1992): 60–81.
14. "Top of the News," *Economist* (London), 9 May 1992, p. 89.
15. "C-SPAN Picks Up Network News Slack," *Variety,* 17 February 1992, p. 32.
16. For a useful summary of the combined programming and local cable system holdings of the large cable conglomerates, see "The New World of TV," *Consumer Reports* 56, no. 9 (September 1991): 583–585.
17. "Time Marching on with Video."
18. "Television's Real-Life Cable Baron," *Business World,* special supplement to the *New York Times,* 2 December 1990, p. 38.
19. "Fear, Loathing and Respect for Cable's Leader," *Washington Post,* 23 January 1992, p. 1.
20. "TCI Pushes P-P-V Subs," *Variety,* 21 October 1991, p. 55.
21. "A Man to Watch," *Barron's,* 16 March 1992, p. 10.
22. "The King of Cable Scrambles to Shore Up His Fortress," *Business Week,* 27 July 1992, pp. 74–75.
23. The quoted figure is from "Cable Stocks—Still an Attractive Investment," a research report issued by Salomon Brothers, the New York investment bank, in December 1991.
24. "Interactive TV Excites a Growing U.S. Market," *Television Business International* (February 1992): 9. See also "Video Jukebox Proves Its Worth," *InfoText* 3, no. 3 (June 1992): 12.
25. "Quantity Time on Cable," *Washington Post,* 2 February 1992, p. C-1.
26. "Time Warner Plans 2-Way Cable System," *Washington Post,* 27 January 1993, p. F-1.
27. "P-P-V on Verge of Big-$ Breakthrough," *Variety,* 22 July 1991, p. 47.
28. "Pay-per-View: Never Say Never," *Variety,* 7 October 1991, p. 38.
29. "PPV Bolstering Weak Pay TV Performances," *Broadcasting,* 22 July 1991, p. 11.
30. "Advantage: Pay-per-View? Don't Count on It," *Business Week,* 28 September 1992, p. 44.

31. "Cable Battles Stir PPV $ Lust," *Variety,* 23 March 1992, p. 1.
32. "Diller's Next Moves: Cable Network Putting Theatricals on PPV First," *Broadcasting,* 29 April 1991, p. 6.
33. "Viacom Interacts with Future," *Variety,* 29 June 1992, p. 29.
34. "U.S. Cable TV into New Age," *Advanced Television Markets* (London) (June 1992): 12.
35. "Gone with the Cash," *Economist* (London), 3 November 1990, p. 73.
36. "Cable Networks See Dimmer Future," *New York Times,* 22 July 1991, p. D-1.
37. "A Change in Administration at a Cable TV Trade Group," *New York Times,* 14 October 1991, p. D-7.
38. "Cable Faces C Word: Clutter," *Broadcasting,* 21 October 1991, p. 45.
39. Beatrice Kanner, "30 Minutes," *New York,* 21 October 1991, p. 24.
40. "The Stepford Channel," *New York Times,* 4 October 1992, p. F-1.
41. "Clinton Video Now an Infomercial," *New York Times,* 24 August 1992, p. D-7.
42. "Cable TV Captures Advertisers," *Washington Post,* 14 July 1991, p. H-1.
43. "Cable Carves a Niche as a Classroom Tool," *Business Week,* 26 August 1991, p. 33.
44. "Cable Service Goes for 'Distance Learning,'" *Variety,* 6 January 1992, p. 24.
45. "CNN Goes Latin via PanAmSat," *Broadcasting,* 9 January 1989, p. 73.
46. "U.S. Group Plans Moscow TV," *Financial Times* (London), 23 July 1992, p. 5.
47. "Cable Networks' Future: Original, International," *Broadcasting,* 2 December 1991, p. 42.
48. "Cable Dough to Spur Tech's Rise," *Variety,* 7 October 1991, p. 37.
49. Ibid. See also "The Quickening Pace of Digital Compression," *Broadcasting,* 9 December 1991, p. 28.
50. "Cable's New Frontier: Wiring the Wireless," *Business Week,* 2 July 1990, p. 36.
51. "More Bad News on Cable: Wireless Systems Loom as New Competitive Threat," *Barron's,* 14 May 1990, p. 14.
52. "No Jackpot in This Lottery," *Washington Post,* 19 April 1992, p. H-3.
53. "Cable-Satellite Agreement Boosts Prospects for Direct-to-Home Service," *Aviation Week and Space Technology,* 9 February 1987, pp. 145–149.
54. Leland L. Johnson and D. R. Castleman, *Direct Broadcasting Satellites: A Competitive Alternative to Cable Television?* Report R-4047-MF/RL (Santa Monica, Calif.: Rand Corporation, 1991).
55. "Primestar—T Minus 7 and Counting," *Broadcasting,* 29 October 1990, pp. 29–30.
56. "Penetration to Hit 78% by 2000," *Broadcasting,* 8 June 1992, p. 10.
57. "Will Affair with Nets Tarnish Cable's Image?" *Variety,* 26 September 1991, p. 31.
58. "Why Cable Companies Are Playing So Rough," *Business Week,* 12 August 1991, p. 66.
59. "Telco CEO Urges Joint Ventures with Cable," *Broadcasting,* 7 October 1991, p. 30.
60. "Western Cable Show: Fiber Is Cable's Edge in Competitive World," *Broadcasting,* 3 December 1990, p. 39.
61. "Re-Regulating Cable: A Political Response to a Wired Nation," *Washington Post,* 22 January 1992, p. 1.
62. *Electronic Media Regulation and the First Amendment,* Forum Report No. 14, Aspen Institute Program on Communications and Society, Washington, D.C., 1991, p. 8.
63. "Cable Competition, Not Regulation," *Broadcasting,* 25 March 1991, p. 80.
64. "Cable's Secret Weapon," *Forbes,* 13 April 1992, pp. 80–81.
65. The timetable for construction of the telephone fiber network and the policy implications are discussed in Henry Geller, *Fiber Optics: An Opportunity for a New Policy.* Annenberg Washington Program, Washington, D.C., November 1991, pp. 23–25.
66. Pat Aufderheide, "We Don't Have to Care, We're the Cable Company," *The Progressive* 55, no. 1 (January 1991): 29.
67. Dana Roof, Denise Trauth, and John Huffman, "In Pursuit of Diversity: An Argument for

Structural Regulation of the Cable Television Industry," School of Mass Communications, Bowling Green State University, August 1991.

68. For a useful survey of the evolution of cable TV policy, see "Defining Cable Television: Structuration and Public Policy," *Journal of Communication* 39, no. 2 (Spring 1989): 10–26.

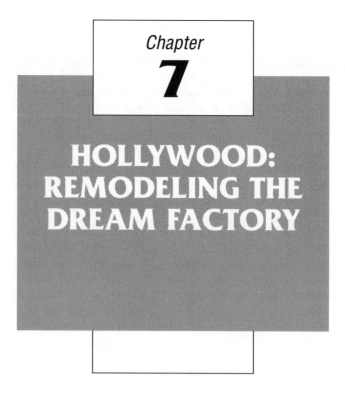

HOLLYWOOD: REMODELING THE DREAM FACTORY

Like most of its films, "Hollywood" is a fiction. No major motion pictures are made these days in Hollywood, a generally run-down district on the northern edge of Los Angeles. The film industry long ago moved its operations to other parts of the Los Angeles area, to other U.S. cities, and overseas. About 25 percent of the industry's annual production takes place outside the United States.

The word "Hollywood" is, however, a convenient shorthand for describing an industry that has been the lodestar of the U.S. entertainment world for almost a century. Besides motion pictures, Hollywood produces most of the major entertainment products used by the television, cable TV, videocassette, and music recording industries. Its unique quality over the years has been its ability to attract a broad range of creative talents. When Orson Welles, a young theater and radio director, first saw the RKO Radio studio in 1939, he described it as the greatest electric train set a boy ever had.[1] He proceeded to use his toy to write, direct, and act in *Citizen Kane*, probably the best film ever to come out of Hollywood.

Citizen Kane was an artistic success, but it was also initially a commercial failure—a reminder that Hollywood is also a business, dominated in its day-to-day decisions by bottom-line economics. The industry earned $14 billion from all of its activities in 1991, a small segment of the $250-billion global entertainment business, but an inadequate measure of its overall impact as an economic and cultural force.

The tensions between hard-line economics and artistic creativity are more pronounced in the film business than in any other media sector. After a century, there is still no agreement, inside or outside the industry, on how it works. William Goldman, the screenwriter, observed that the defining rule in explaining Hollywood is that nobody knows anything.[2] The industry's chief Washington lobbyist, Jack Valenti, has described it as a business that flies on gossamer wings. Hollywood is the land of the hunch and the wild guess. An idea that is creative (and many that are not) must survive a tortuous process of assembling money, scripts, production facilities, actors, and distribution arrangements before it is realized on film. Even once the process is finished, 6 out of 10 Hollywood feature movies end up in the red.

In any normal business, such a record would be a formula for instant failure. Not so in Hollywood. In part this is because of the industry's arcane accounting procedures in which even a film that makes a lot of money over and above its production and distribution costs can still end up on the books as a financial loser. The most controversial example in recent years was the 1990 Eddie Murphy film, *Coming to America,* which cost $48 million to make. In a court suit about the distribution of the film's $300-million gross profits, Paramount Pictures claimed that the film lost $18 million.[3] Hollywood economics are based on the somewhat touching faith that a few blockbuster movies will cover whatever losses a film studio suffers on the rest of its products. In fact, this often happens. In 1990, Twentieth Century–Fox had the usual quota of money-losing productions, but its earnings shot up 182 percent, largely due to receipts from one successful film, *Home Alone.*[4]

Despite its convoluted ways of doing business, the film industry has shown remarkable staying power over the decades. Predictions of Hollywood's decline and fall have been a recurrent theme for most of its history. The industry is, nevertheless, more prosperous now than at any time in the past, in large part because it has expanded beyond feature films and to new revenue sources—from videocassettes to Disneyland-type theme parks.

As recently as 1980, 80 percent of Hollywood's cash came from U.S. ticket sales. In the 1990s, only 30 percent does.[5] The industry is threatened with a steady erosion of its core audience, that is, the people sitting in theaters watching shadows on a screen. By 1991, only 20 percent of filmed-entertainment revenues (most of it earned by the Hollywood studios) came from traditional box office receipts. The rest was earned through home video and television sales (Table 7.1). By 1993, there were fewer American moviegoers than at any time in recent decades, with total domestic ticket sales falling below the billion mark.[6] (By contrast, over 4 billion tickets were sold to a much smaller population in 1946.) There has also been a falling off in Hollywood's traditionally strong hold on overseas audiences. In 1991, international box office sales were $1.22 billion, down from $1.45 billion the previous year. Moreover, that audience loss, both at home and abroad, has involved mainly younger filmgoers, the industry's primary target.

Meanwhile, the industry is undergoing major structural changes. For most of its history, Hollywood has been largely a business unto itself, with few outside connections. This is no longer true. Six of the eight largest studios have recently become parts of large corporations, each of them involved with other entertainment products that they hope to merge with their new Hollywood interests.

TABLE 7.1   Growth of U.S. Spending on Filmed Entertainment

	Box Office	Home Video	Television*	Total
1991 Expenditures ($ millions)	4,803	10,995	8,975	24,773
1986–91 Compound Annual Growth (%)	4.9	17.0	6.1	9.9
1991–96 Projected Compound Annual Growth (%)	6.9	8.1	7.1	7.5
1996 Projected Expenditures ($ millions)	6,720	16,230	12,630	35,580

*Includes program licensing and barter syndication.
SOURCE: Veronis, Suhler & Associates, Motion Picture Association of America, McCann-Erickson, Wilkofsky Gruen Associates. Reprinted by permission of Veronis, Suhler & Associates.

The film industry's major long-term problem, however, consists of the strong competition from new media technologies. Hollywood has dealt with similar challenges in the past, most notably in the 1950s when it began to lose audiences to television viewing. At first, the studios tried to check the loss by limiting TV showings of their vast stock of old feature films. Within a few years, however, the studios realized that they had more to gain from joining forces with the television industry than from fighting a losing battle. The old films were released, and Hollywood became the largest single producer of new television products for both the domestic and foreign markets.[7] The film industry was thus able to co-opt television technology to its own advantage. It may, however, have a harder time coming to terms with its current challengers such as HDTV, DBS's, PPV cable programming, and the new mix of multimedia computer products.

The most striking example of the impact that the new technologies have had on the film industry is videocassettes. By 1996, home video is projected to be a $16-billion business, more than double the film box office revenues (Table 7.1). Moreover, videocassette viewing involves people watching Hollywood entertainment at home rather than in a theater. The change is dramatic. U.S. households rent an average of 22 videotapes a year, according to a 1992 Louis Harris poll.[8] During the first half of January 1992, the U.S. public rented 197 million videocassettes. Assuming, conservatively, that there were two viewers for each rental, this adds up to a cumulative audience of almost 400 million home viewers in two weeks, or 40 percent of the total U.S. movie theater audience for the whole year.[9] With movie theater audiences falling off, Hollywood is increasingly dependent on the videocassette business, which in turn is almost totally dependent on film industry products.

There are signs that the home videocassette market is leveling off, after years of double-digit expansion. The market has become saturated, with relatively fewer feature films that attract large home audiences. The videocassette industry is also being challenged by still newer technologies that can supply the same services more conveniently. A major challenger will be cable TV's PPV offerings. Promoted widely as "the video store in the home," PPV exploits the fact that its programs are available simply by making a telephone call or by pressing numbers on a TV set keypad. PPV services also provide a wide range of "live" programming such as sports events, concerts, and other entertainment features, all competing for consumer dollars that, in past years, went largely to Hollywood.

The Hollywood studios are being affected by other shifts in consumer entertainment patterns. The decline in broadcast television viewing is affecting the film industry—the largest single supplier of entertainment programs to the New York networks. Given their fragile economic situation, the networks are balking at the increasingly higher costs of the programs they buy from Hollywood.

Finally, the film industry has to come to terms with a new wave of technologies that will affect both its products and the ways in which they are distributed. HDTV will involve major changes in the products that Hollywood supplies to television and cable networks. Multimedia computers and CD-ROM disks open up new opportunities for interactive entertainment and information programming. Time Warner, the largest U.S. media conglomerate, produces compact disk programs that draw on the talents of its Warner Brothers film division. Other studios are examining the prospects for supplying program materials that can be adapted to advanced Nintendo-type games and to the virtual reality market.

Meanwhile, the industry is taking another look at its traditional audience—the people who pay to watch a film in a theater. There has been relatively little change in the way movies are shown since the time of the introduction of wide-screen technology 40 years ago. Films are still delivered in large reel cans to theaters to be projected from a booth in the rear of the hall. That may change in the next few years as the film studios look into the economic advantages of transmitting films from a central point by satellite to earth stations on theater roofs, thereby eliminating reel cans and projection booths. Another possibility is to deliver movies to theaters on laserdiscs sent through the mail. (Unlike film, laserdiscs do not deteriorate.) Satellite and laserdisc delivery of films is several years down the road, but the industry is already involved in another innovation: theaters designed to show special films on giant screens that are often four or five stories high. By 1993, there were almost a hundred theaters with these big-screen facilities in the United States and abroad.[10]

A more elaborate innovation is the "leisure simulator," a moving platform that uses the same technology as an aviation flight simulator. Reconfigured as a small film theater rather than an airplane cockpit, the movements of the six-axis platform are coordinated with a wide-screen film, giving the audience the impression that they are moving with the film's action. By 1993, over 30 leisure simulators had been installed around the world by a British firm—Hughes Rediffusion Simulation.[11]

In summary, the film industry is at the edge of a major transformation in the products it produces and the ways in which it distributes them. Previously it has had to cope with one innovation at a time. Now the industry is dealing with a range of new technologies, each of which represents both a threat and an opportunity for its future operations. As noted earlier, one relatively simple device—the videocassette—has eroded theater ticket revenues significantly while at the same time providing a new source of profits. In 1991, the studios earned $3.4 billion, or 23 percent, of their domestic revenues from video sales and rentals.[12] Meanwhile, the industry's chances of recouping its lost theater audiences in the United States are slim, given the current competition from videocassettes and the prospect of even more sophisticated home-delivered entertainment resources in the future.

Can Hollywood make a profitable adjustment to these new realities? It is not an industry that has been noted for taking the long-range view. Its operating mode is frenetic, hypersensitive to current film trends and shifting enthusiasms that can change overnight, from cowboy epics to horror films to intergalactic space adventures. Fortunes are made or lost on whether the newest money-making trend can be exploited further, or whether a new trend can be launched. Hollywood has always been about winners and losers in this gamble.[13]

The film industry will not easily shake off its addiction to betting on film trends. Nevertheless, it is slowly changing some of its high-stakes gambling habits, in part because the large corporations that now control the studios are taking a closer look at production and distribution costs. Of the 10 leading global media conglomerates in 1992, 7 now have direct or indirect interests in Hollywood, along with their publishing, television, and cable TV holdings.[14]

In the film industry's so-called golden age (roughly from 1930 to 1950), the big studios were generally independent, with very little outside interference beyond any from the New York bankers to whom they were usually beholden for financing of their films. The studios controlled their own production facilities, and they kept their own stables of writers, actors, and directors. The bigger film companies also controlled many of the theatrical outlets where their films were shown, until federal antitrust laws forced them to end the practice. The studios were run by strong personalities, who decided, for better or worse, what pictures would be made. Studio heads such as Walt Disney, Louis B. Mayer of MGM, Darryl Zanuck of Twentieth Century–Fox, and Adolph Zukor of Paramount all added their own distinctive imprints to their studios and to the industry at large.

By the 1970s, Hollywood's golden years were a romanticized memory. Outside financial interests were now buying heavily into film companies; the Coca Cola Company was, for instance, a major investor in Columbia Pictures. Many of the old-line companies had lost both control of their production facilities and much of their individual styles. As director Billy Wilder noted ruefully at the time, "Studios are nothing but the Ramada Inn: you rent space, you shoot and out you go."[15] Despite these changes, Hollywood continued to be generally successful in producing feature films for itself and then video products both for broadcast television and, more recently, for the cable TV networks.

Inevitably, Hollywood's money-making formulas attracted the attention of the corporate conglomerates that began to dominate the U.S. media sector after 1975. The idea of integrating its products with other media operations was not entirely new to the film industry. In 1911, publisher William Randolph Hearst expanded his newspaper and magazine empire by setting up Cosmopolitan Films, an important feature-film studio in early Hollywood history.[16] Hearst did not shrink from using his print publications to publicize Cosmopolitan films. His attempts to use his various media holdings to support one another, however successful, were amateurish compared to the strategies enlisted by present-day media conglomerates. Today's code phrase is "information packaging." The emphasis is on establishing synergies between the conglomerates' various media holdings, with each one supporting the others in the production and marketing of their products.[17]

One Hollywood production company learned how to create synergies between its products long before any of the new media conglomerates had ever moved into the industry. It was the Disney studio, which has been exploiting the multimedia possibilities of Mickey Mouse, Donald Duck, Bambi, Roger Rabbit, and the other denizens of its cartoon bestiary for over half a century. Disney operations have changed dramatically in recent years, but the company has not lost its founder's touch for using diverse media outlets—from comic books to theme parks—to publicize its film products and boost its revenues. The studio's ability to spin off products from its films is one of the perennial wonders of the industry. Since the release of its 1989 feature-length cartoon, *The Little Mermaid,* Disney has licensed a quarterly Little Mermaid magazine, 19 dolls, 20 books, and a Saturday morning television series.[18] Disney is the only major Hollywood studio that has so far been able to resist the recent wave of corporate takeovers in the industry. It is, in effect, its own media conglomerate.[19]

The other big studios have all become parts of larger corporate enterprises. The process began a dozen years ago when Gulf & Western Inc. bought Paramount Pictures, one of the most consistently successful studios in the film business. Gulf & Western (now Paramount Communications) also owns the largest U.S. book publisher—Simon & Schuster—as well as a number of independent television stations. The firm demonstrated its media savvy when it expanded its "Star Trek" television series into six films, as well as into books, cartoons, and sponsorship of a Master Charge credit card. Gulf & Western's best-known foray into the media acquisitions business was its failed 1989 proposal to buy Time Inc. Paramount was the target of an $8.2 billion bid for its assets in 1993 by Viacom Inc.

Several years earlier, Australian-born Rupert Murdoch gave added momentum to the acquisition trend in 1986 when he bought a half interest in Twentieth Century–Fox, and, subsequently, when he gained full control of the studio. As a result of the Twentieth Century–Fox acquisition, Murdoch's firm, News Corp., became the largest and most extensive of the media conglomerates, with major holdings that include newspapers, magazines, television, and other media enterprises.[20]

The Murdoch enterprises lost this distinction, however, when Time Inc. and Warner Communications negotiated a stock merger to form Time Warner Inc. in 1989. At the time of the merger, the two firms had a combined annual revenue of $13 billion, putting them easily into the lead as the largest global media conglomerate. Time Inc. brought to the merger its extensive magazine and book publishing expertise as well as cable TV properties that included the Home Box Office network and a large number of local cable systems. Warner added its experience in film production and distribution, as well as its ownership of one of the world's largest record companies. The merged companies also provided another superlative to the merger—a $12-billion debt load that has hampered their ability to expand synergistic entertainment-packaging plans as fast as they had hoped.[21] Largely as a result of this heavy debt, Time Warner did not make a profit in its early years.

There are no typical entertainment conglomerates. The film industry is too diverse and too spread out for any cookie-cutter patterns. This was proven conclusively in recent years with the unexpected arrival of Japanese companies on the Hollywood scene. In quick succession, two major electronic manufacturers—Sony and Matsushita—took control, respectively, of Columbia Pictures and MCA, the owner of Universal studios. Foreign investment in the film industry was not unknown before these takeovers. The studios regularly courted European and Japanese inves- tors to finance individual films. There was relatively little comment when Rupert Murdoch's News Corp., a group with strong British ties, bought Twentieth Century– Fox, or when TVS Entertainment, a British television firm, paid $320 million for MTM Enterprises in order to acquire its large library of old television programs such as "The Mary Tyler Moore Show" and "Hill Street Blues."[22]

Attitudes toward the Japanese takeovers were different. When Sony assumed control of Columbia Pictures, there was an outcry about "buying the soul of Amer- ica," together with dark hints by some industry observers that Sony and Matsushita would turn their studios into Japanese propaganda outlets. A *Newsweek* magazine poll reported that 48 percent of Americans saw the Sony acquisition as "a bad thing." The Japanese takeover of the two studios was the motivation for a congressional bill that proposed a 50 percent cap on foreign ownership of U.S. "cultural business enterprises," pointedly including film studios. The proposal was roundly criticized by the film industry.[23] Hollywood's attitude was summarized by film producer Freddie Fields: "Sony isn't going to orientalize the movies at Columbia. . . . This is business and the infusion of foreign money is exciting."

Why did the Japanese come to Hollywood? A Japanese plan to mount an assault on American culture, if it ever existed, is the most far-fetched explanation. A more pragmatic view is simply that several film studio properties were ripe for takeover— part of the overall shakeout that has characterized all parts of the U.S. entertainment industry in recent years. The two Japanese firms saw advantages in investing in an industry with good economic prospects. Sony and Matsushita made it clear from the start that they were investing for the long run. "We Japanese plan and develop our business strategies ten years ahead," Sony chairman Akio Morita declared in 1989, "while Americans seem to be concerned only with profits ten minutes from now."[24]

Moreover, the Japanese brought cash to the table. The Sony takeover of Colum- bia involved $3.4 billion, plus $1.3 billion in assumed debt. It was the largest single Japanese investment in any U.S. company at the time. A year later, Matsushita raised the stakes, with its $6.1-billion purchase of MCA.[25] As far as Hollywood is concerned, money has little color or nationality. Both the Sony and Matsushita deals were friendly takeovers, unlike many other entertainment industry acquisitions.[26] An unusual as- pect of the takeovers was that Sony and Matsushita left the day-to-day operations of their studios in the hands of U.S. managers, the first time that had happened in any Japanese acquisition of a major foreign company.

The strategy aims of the so-called Japanese invasion of the film industry went beyond the goal of developing an integrated global production and media distribution network. This had been the strategy adopted by Gulf & Western, Rupert Murdoch's News Corp., and Time Inc. in their studio acquisitions. The Japanese firms had a broader objective. Both companies are major producers of CD players, video re- corders, and other consumer entertainment equipment. (Matsushita is best known in the United States for its Panasonic products.) Their declared intention in buying up major film studios was to promote and protect sales of the electronic equipment they now make or plan to make. They wanted to have an ensured supply of the entertainment software that would be used with their machines. As one Sony executive noted at the time of the Columbia studios takeover, "hardware and software are parts of the entertainment industry that can no longer be talked about separately."[27]

Sony had made its first major move in this direction in 1988, with its $2-billion purchase of CBS Records, the world's largest recording company. The next logical step was to move into Hollywood, the production source for the most popular (and profitable) film, television, cable TV, and videocassette programs. In addition to having direct access to new productions, the two companies also acquired the studios' vast libraries of old movies. Sony's purchase of Columbia included the studio's inventory of 2,700 feature films, from *Rambo* to *Lawrence of Arabia,* as well as 23,000 television episodes.

The Sony and Matsushita takeovers were the first in the entertainment industry that attempted to vertically integrate the business at all levels, from equipment production to distribution of the final product. Only one other equipment company—Philips, the European electronics giant—has made a similar, though less ambitious, effort to acquire entertainment software. Philips owns Polygram Records, one of the five major record labels, and has invested in a U.S. firm, Whittle Communications, which specializes in educational programming that can make use of Philips' new CD products.[28] Philips has also invested in Hollywood films through its Polydor affiliate.

As a result of recent mergers and takeovers, Hollywood studios are now largely controlled by outside interests. The new owners have brought a new managerial philosophy to the industry. They see their studios as resources whose products will support, and be supported by, other media-related products at both the production and distribution levels through cross-marketing and coordinated product introductions.

The results of this managerial change, so far, are mixed. The Japanese, in particular, have experienced difficulty in integrating their management skills as electronics manufacturers with Hollywood's often bizarre operating styles.[29] Sony has had to invest an additional billion dollars in Columbia Pictures, now renamed Sony Pictures, to meet rising costs. Its film venture has, nevertheless, been financially successful in its early years. Sony Pictures captured 20 percent of U.S. box office receipts in 1991; its operating profits at that time had increased by one-third since it acquired Columbia in 1989. Meanwhile, Sony has generally maintained its commitment not to interfere with the U.S. management style of its Hollywood operations.[30] Whether Sony and Matsushita are able to sustain their commitment to U.S. managers will be an important factor in the long-term success of their plunge into the film business.[31]

The new Japanese presence in Hollywood also shows up in substantial investments in other U.S. media companies. The Disney studio has been a heavy borrower of Japanese money.[32] In 1991, two major Japanese companies—Toshiba and C. Itoh—each invested $500 million in Time Warner, making them 12.5 percent shareholders in the firm. The arrangement somewhat dilutes the claim made by Time Warner executive Steve Ross in a congressional hearing that the Time Warner merger would create an "all-American company" to compete in global media markets.

The corporate realignment of Hollywood studios has changed the studios' relative standings as production units. By 1993, Time Warner's film division had become the leading individual studio in terms of domestic box office shares. However, Sony's Columbia acquisition in 1989 gave it two distribution channels (Columbia and Tri-Star), which together made it the overall box office leader. The most consistent performer among the major studios in recent years has been the Disney organization, with three production labels—Touchstone, Disney, and Hollywood. However, Disney has had a more difficult time keeping pace with its strong growth in the 1980s.[33]

In these corporate comings-and-goings, a sad loss has been the decline of Metro-Goldwyn-Mayer (MGM). Once the greatest studio of them all, MGM has been reduced to a bit-player role. Since the early 1980s, it has been the victim of junk-bond deals and corporate fraud by a series of owners.[34] In recent years, MGM has received less than 3 percent of the industry's domestic box office shares. In addition to the major studios, the film industry consists of a large number of independent operators. In some years, the "indies," such as Cannon and Goldwyn, produce twice as many films as the big studios. Independent studios were responsible for some of the biggest hits of the early 1990s, including *Dances with Wolves, Robin Hood: Prince of Thieves,* and *Terminator 2: Judgment Day.*

Both the big studios and the smaller independents share a perennial problem: how to predict the public's tastes and, more specifically, what films it will pay to see. Dore Schary, a film executive in the 1950s, once declared that America is a happy-ending country. Acting on that assumption, he produced happy films that made a lot of money for MGM, his employer. Formulas for success are more complicated now. The U.S. demographic pattern is changing radically, along with the ways in which Americans allocate their time and money for leisure-time activities. Hollywood must also take into account the increasingly intense competition these days from other media technologies for the public's attention.

There are also troublesome, if unofficial, censorship problems. Filmmaking was inhibited for decades by the Motion Picture Production Code, which rated films on a morality scale. The code was eliminated in the 1960s, replaced by a more lenient rating system. Recently, however, new calls for censorship have come from a wide assortment of interest groups, including Native Americans, African Americans, animal rights proponents, and the gay community. Each is intent on registering disapproval of alleged slights to their interests, in the hope of shaping (or reshaping) their public images as displayed in films.[35]

Although the urge to follow the newest trend is strong, the studios usually fall back on tried-and-true formulas. The most enduring and successful of these is the big, visually exciting blockbuster film with a strong story line. Original scripts are still important, but the best of these films tend to be based on an old reliable—the novel. At a time when people have less time to read fiction, they rely on the film industry to bring it to them in a quicker and more easily digested form. An independent producer Frank Price noted, "Movies have become the short stories of the video age."[36] The search for good stories can be a gold mine for writers. Novelist Michael Crichton was paid $1.5 million by Universal Studios for the rights to the 1993 film *Jurassic Park,* a story about genetically engineered dinosaurs.

Mr. Crichton's bonanza is a sign of the industry's struggle with the rising costs of everything associated with filmmaking. The result, as one Hollywood wag put it, is a tightening of the Gucci belts throughout the movie business. The industry's primitive financial structure is no help. With some exceptions, new films are financed one at a time. The average production budget for a film by the early 1990s was $20 million. Collectively, this adds up to big business: the total gross revenues from all film-related sources is over $25 billion a year.

Hollywood's basic product is still the standard feature film, a consumer item that depends for its success on the fickle whims of an ever-shrinking theatergoing audience. This fickleness is magnified by the influence of a relatively small group of film critics, whose opinions can often make or break a film in the first few days after its release. As critic Nigel Andrews noted:

> It is a demented cultural-economic climate. Critics are sometimes asked why they express negative or carping opinions about a work of cinema. The answer is: because they are the only people allowed to do so. No one else connected with the industry, when assessing a film, is permitted to point out that the Emperor is naked; or even to offer hints that the weather is a little chilly, your majesty, and you may want to throw on a scarf.[37]

Given the risks involved, financing a film is usually an exercise in cuckoo-cloudland economics. The takeover of the big studios by cash-rich corporations in recent years has added some stability to the process, but the risks remain. As noted earlier, over half of the industry's film productions do not earn enough to pay their production and distribution costs. The rate of return demanded by outside investors is often in excess of 20 percent—a requirement that would be regarded as highway robbery in any other industry.[38]

Nevertheless, investors keep taking risks on film projects, intrigued by Hollywood's perennial ability to come up with the occasional financial blockbuster. The 1992 hit *Batman Returns* cost about $75 million to produce and earned $46 million in box office receipts during the first weekend of its showings.[39] Popular films can also be solid long-term investments. The low-budget cult film *The Rocky Horror Picture Show* has earned Twentieth Century–Fox $37 million at domestic box offices since its release in 1976. The long-run investment champion is the 1937 Disney cartoon classic *Snow White and the Seven Dwarfs,* which had taken in $62 million in theater receipts by 1992.[40] This is over 30 times its original production costs.

The international market has always been a critical component in Hollywood's financial success. By the 1930s, overseas receipts accounted for more than half of the industry's revenues.[41] There are film industries in over 60 countries, but typically they restrict themselves to local subjects in their productions. It was Hollywood that invented the international film. The names of such stars as Charlie Chaplin, John Wayne, Marilyn Monroe, and Arnold Schwarzenegger are as familiar in New Delhi and Paris as they are in Boston and Des Moines. Unlike their foreign competitors, the Hollywood studios hired foreign directors, actors, and writers and then proceeded to make films in all parts of the world.

But it is Hollywood's portrayal of life in America that has made the biggest impression. More than any other factor, Hollywood films have set the world's popular impression of U.S. culture. The impact has not always been flattering. In 1967, when an American cowboy film was being shown to Viet Cong prisoners of war, the audience cheered for the Indians.[42] But among most moviegoers abroad, the reaction is more sympathetic. For journalist A. M. A. Aziz, who grew up in India, cowboy films depicted a heroic America:

> It is sweet to recall those movie impressions of America—the America of the cowboys and their adventures. . . . Of course, there were villains and crooks in the movie stories. But the villain did not typify the average American in the boyhood image. On the other hand, the hero did. Then came the more serious type of American. He was the village sheriff, wore a top hat, and gathered some half a dozen other top-hatted persons around a table to discuss a grave problem. The gathering of the top-hats inspired confidence that the problem, however grave, would be solved; and so it was.[43]

The world's continuing fascination with U.S. films is such that Hollywood is the biggest single contributor to the U.S. net trade surplus in media exports.[44] U.S. films account for only about 15 percent of annual global production, but that is a poor measure of Hollywood's artistic and marketing influence. In a typical week in 1993, U.S. films were the top hits in 10 of the 13 large cities abroad monitored by *Variety*, the show business newspaper. Despite their often superior quality, few foreign films do as well. Many U.S. films are more financially successful abroad than they are at home. The Disney production *Who Framed Roger Rabbit?* earned $189 million overseas in its initial showings, compared to $157 million domestically.[45]

Hollywood's foreign earnings have been somewhat erratic in recent years, due at least in part to a persistent economic recession in Europe. The industry is also threatened by political restrictions on its product sales abroad, usually in the form of quotas designed to protect local film producers. In 1989, 12 European Community countries established a 50 percent quota on foreign (i.e., Hollywood) entertainment programs on their television stations. The French government followed up in 1991 with a similar quota, set at 60 percent, which was officially explained as an action to preserve the integrity of the French language. Despite these and other restrictions on its products abroad, Hollywood earned $3.27 billion in worldwide feature film rentals in 1991.[46]

The restrictions have had less effect in curbing U.S. film sales than might be expected. Hollywood is still the leading international producer of the most popular attractions. Moreover, the demand for its products continues to expand. New markets have been created by the increase in private television stations in Western Europe, where the number of channels will have expanded from 40 in 1983 to an estimated 120 by 1995. Most of these new stations buy U.S. productions.

Large parts of the world previously off-limits to Hollywood, such as China, Eastern Europe, and the former Soviet Union, are potentially huge markets. In 1992, a Disney subsidiary, Buena Vista International, concluded a 10-year barter deal with Russian Television and Radio, giving the Russians the option of showing six hours of Disney programming a week in exchange for exclusive rights to sell advertising to accompany the programs.[47] The Disney studio began marketing its cartoons to Chinese television in 1986, attracting 300 million viewers a week.[48] The company halted the arrangement in 1990, in part to protest the fact that Disney-trademarked products were being counterfeited by Chinese industries. Disney resumed its operations in China in 1992, with a schedule of television programs, together with plans for a Chinese language Disney magazine and 20 stores that will sell Disney T-shirts and other products.[49]

Another factor favoring Hollywood export marketing is the rapid expansion of movie theaters abroad. The new emphasis, particularly in Europe, is on multiscreen cinemas, a phenomenon largely unknown overseas until recently.[50] Foreign sales now figure equally with the U.S. market in Hollywood's plans. The chief difference between the two, according to film executive Stan Golden, is that "domestically, we're facing consolidation, contraction and network erosion; in most of the rest of the world, we're dealing with expansion, with more customers and more outlets."[51]

The Hollywood studios are also turning their attention toward what the industry calls its peripherals—products that are spun off from the basic filmmaking activities, from Disneyland-type theme parks to music recordings. Currently, the most important of these spinoffs is the videocassette. Consumer surveys in the early 1990s underscored how videocassettes are changing consumer entertainment habits. A 1991 survey, sponsored by the Electronic Industries Association, indicated that consumers preferred home video screenings to theater outings by a margin of more than three to one. Only 22 percent of the respondents, given a choice, preferred to leave home for a movie. The survey also indicated that a substantial majority of the tape-renting public take home more than two movies a month while the majority of moviegoers get to a theater less than twice a month.[52]

As noted above, Hollywood is a major beneficiary of the $12 billion in annual cassette sales and rentals, because it supplies most of the programming. Sales and rentals of popular films can be a very profitable business for the major studios. In 1992, the Disney company sold 20 million copies of its full-length *Beauty and the Beast* cartoon feature, earning $270 million for the firm's Buena Vista Home Video division. No theatrical release in Hollywood history has ever been so profitable. Overall, Buena Vista's total videocassette revenues were $1.1 billion for the year, making it the film industry's most profitable single operation.[53]

Videocassette revenues are important for the film industry, but they can be expected to decline steadily in the coming years. More and more, home viewers are turning to PPV showings of Hollywood movies and other attractions on their cable TV channels. PPV has been slow to develop, primarily because its early technology could not deliver programs quickly on demand. With that problem largely resolved, PPV usage is expanding, with a half dozen channels serving tens of millions of homes. The number of PPV services will increase as cable companies upgrade their systems from the present 50 or 60 channels to 150 or more—a development already well under way.

Hollywood has been ambivalent about the coming change from videocassettes to PPV services. Clearly, the industry stands to make a lot of money by offering films and other programs to PPV channels. The studios face decisions over whether they should develop their own channels or at least invest in the currently operating channels. This latter strategy is being tested by Paramount Pictures and MCA, which in 1991 made a joint investment in TVN, a 10-channel PPV distributor.[54] A year later,

Paramount negotiated agreements that allow it to license PPV rights directly with cable systems, bypassing the normal PPV middleman vendors.[55] Meanwhile, TCI, the largest U.S. cable operator, announced in 1993 that it would invest $100 million in Carolco Pictures in exchange for four feature PPV premieres.

The reluctance of other studios to become more involved in PPV distribution may stem from the fact that the number of households actively using PPV services is still relatively small, totaling less than a third of the country's 60 million cable TV homes. The studios' attitude about controlling distribution of their own products could change as PPV's audience increases. The economic advantages to the studios of bypassing the current PPV channels and initiating their own services would then be hard to resist.

A more immediate opportunity for increasing studio revenues lies with another entertainment business—music records. Hollywood has always had close ties to the record industry, from the days when record companies promoted 78 RPM recordings of such film-song staples as Bing Crosby's *White Christmas*. Records are big business, with $24 billion in annual global sales, including $6 billion spent in the United States.[56] Moreover, it is a growth industry, which is changing dramatically. One reason is the popularity of MTV, the cable TV, music video channel, which has given popular music new exposure in recent years.

As a result, Hollywood is now more deeply involved in the record industry than ever before. The three most recent takeovers of major film studios have involved companies with significant record operations—Time Warner, Sony, and Matsushita. Time Warner owns Warner Records and Sony has its Sony Record label. As part of its acquisition of MCA/Universal Pictures, Matsushita bought control of Geffen Records, with its strong stable of recording artists, including Guns 'N Roses, Aerosmith, and Cher. In each case, the companies saw their record business as an important part of a strategy to develop multimedia packages for their films, publications, and other operations.

These deals whetted other Hollywood studios' interest in records. The Disney studios, which had a small children's record division, created an adult-oriented record label—Hollywood Records—in 1989. Morgan Creek, an independent studio, launched its own Morgan Creek label. The Fujisanki Communications Group, Japan's largest media conglomerate, entered the market when it bought a 25 percent stake in a major British label—Virgin Records. These moves sharpened the already aggressive competition that characterizes the record industry, dependent as it is on the whims of young people who buy fully half of its products.[57]

The risks were dramatized in Sony's 1991 deal with its resident superstar Michael Jackson. Mr. Jackson's albums *Big* and *Thriller* were the firm's most recent hits, with the former selling 38 million copies. In his contract renegotiations, Jackson demanded and got a new record label of his own, along with arrangements to create his own feature films, theatrical shorts, and other media products. Sony officials confidently predicted that the new contract could generate a billion dollars in sales. (Record companies deal in very round numbers.) However, the deal also involved the very real risk that Michael Jackson's particular talents might cease to attract his youthful audiences. The contract ran against the industry's accepted truism that every new musical trend takes the record business by surprise, including the rise and inevitable fall of its big stars.[58] This did not deter Time Warner in 1992 from renegotiating its contract with its superstar, Madonna. The arrangement, reportedly worth $60 million, gave the pop singer control over her own multimedia entertainment company.[59]

Hollywood's rekindled love affair with the record business is helping to push the major film studios into new technologies. The recording industry has already gone through one major technological change recently, with compact discs' replacing long-playing records and cutting deeply into the audiotape market. Now the industry has to come to terms with other, more advanced high-technology products, notably CD-ROM disks, which will combine music, video, and data capabilities.

The transition is already under way. Eventually, it will involve the Hollywood studios and their record subsidiaries in an entirely new line of products. One of these is digital tape recordings, which produce the same crisp music as CD records. Unlike CDs, digital tape machines can record and copy music in the home—a capability that Sony and other manufacturers hope will bring about another revolution in home entertainment.

Competing with digital tape recorders for market share is another technical innovation—the CD minidisc, which is about half the size of the familiar CD music record. For the minidisc, as with digital tape, audio engineers have compressed music into far fewer ones and zeros, those symbols of digital information. The technique involves leaving out sounds that are not heard anyway because they are masked by other sounds in whatever is being recorded. Philips, the European electronics firm, introduced its DCC minidisc in 1992, followed by Sony's Minidisc entry.[60]

Minidiscs will make their mark on the record business, but they in turn may be challenged by a technology that relies on PCs not only to play music but to compose it. According to a 1991 Gallup survey of U.S. musical trends, the fastest-growing music product is software for PCs. At the time, 11 percent of U.S. households had at least one person who used a computer to make music. Given the right software, an Apple PC can compose, arrange, produce, and record a song. Similar techniques have been standard procedure in film and record studios for a number of years.[61]

The trend toward computerized music has been accelerated recently by a new generation of electronic musical instruments, crammed with semiconductor chips, which have accounted in recent years for over half of U.S. instrument sales. When these machines are plugged into a small computer, they perform and store a musical score as it is written on a PC monitor. A bizarre twist on these electronic devices is karaoke. A Japanese innovation, karaoke plays recordings of songs with the vocals removed, thus allowing would-be Madonnas, Michael Jacksons, and Frank Sinatras to sing along with a musical accompaniment. In what may turn out to be a culturally misguided attempt to prevent amateur errors, engineers at MIT's Media Lab are experimenting with models that will prevent any wrong note from being heard.

Karaoke and the other new music devices are steps toward the evolution of computerized multimedia products. The film studios, the record companies, and every other media industry will eventually be involved in technologies that will integrate video, audio, and print in mass consumer information and entertainment products. The transition to these products has begun. The early versions of CD-ROM disks with multimedia capabilities are already being marketed. The next step is the development of home telecomputers—living room machines that will function as a combined television set and computer, with programming delivered by television stations, CD-ROM disks, fiber-optic cable, or direct-broadcasting communications satellites.

Will Hollywood become a major production center for multimedia programs? The answer is not yet clear. The film industry's primary expertise is in making movies. The new multimedia technologies are only partly about making movies; they also involve new techniques for integrating sound, video, graphics, and print. More than any other media industry, Hollywood believes it has the creative and technical know-how to put this combination together. George Lucas, creator of the *Star Wars* sagas, is confident he can transfer his filmmaking talents to the task of creating the proto-type of a CD-ROM multimedia curriculum that will offer one week of education for an eighth-grade class:

> It's kind of what I brought to the movie business. I said when I began, "Why can't I make the most exciting two-hour movie?" And I did it. And then I realized that I can take the same technique and move it into the classroom just by respecting the material.[62]

Hollywood's role in the multimedia environment will be set by the industry's new owners—Time Warner, Rupert Murdoch, Sony, and Matsushita, among others. Each of them is organizing resources to become producers and distributors of multimedia information products. Among the large conglomerates, Time Warner has been the most aggressive in promoting a multimedia strategy, through its Time Warner Interactive Group subsidiary. The group has developed a "library" of interactive CD-ROM disks, which has concentrated on musical compositions (e.g., Benjamin Britten's *The Young Person's Guide to the Orchestra*), with text, pictures, and additional audio segments providing background notes on the composition.

The new multimedia firms are finding that information packaging is hard to organize; old habits die hard among the various media units they control. Nevertheless, the momentum for multimedia products is building, and competition among the companies involved will be intense.[63] Not all of the competition will come from firms with Hollywood facilities. One new entrant in the field is a television-based firm, Cap Cities/ABC, which is producing a range of multimedia CD-ROM disks. Another group of players will be the big computer companies. IBM and Apple, among others, have been negotiating with Hollywood studios since 1991 on plans to produce interactive software for the new generation of multimedia computers.[64]

One of the challenges facing the film industry is finding the most efficient way of distributing its new multimedia products to consumers and particularly to homes. Laserdiscs, capable of a full range of interactive video, text, and sound, are a possibility. Laserdiscs are, however, expensive, and they require costly recording machines. The most immediate avenue available to Hollywood is cable television. Another source is the telephone companies, many of whom are preparing to compete with cable TV in the potentially lucrative market of supplying multimedia products to U.S. households via high-capacity wires. For the present, the cable companies are in the most favorable position for supplying these services. By upgrading their present cable facilities through digital compression techniques, they can make a hundred or more new channels available. Time Warner already has a 150-channel system in New York, which carries PPV entertainment as well as interactive multimedia products.

Hollywood has successfully adapted to a number of technological revolutions in its history. The most notable was the introduction of sound movies in the 1920s, an event that turned the industry around in a few months. The transition to new multimedia products will take longer, given the costly production, marketing, and distribution problems involved. However, the technology is ready, poised to change the way Americans and the rest of the world deal with information and entertainment resources.[65]

The film industry has the know-how and the resources to exploit the new technologies. It will still make movies, but it will be producing, packaging, and distributing them in new ways. The industry's reputation as the world's premier dream factory will remain. Hollywood is a survivor. As one of its legendary film directors, Billy Wilder, once said, "I can assure you that, on the day the world ends, somebody will be out there shooting second unit."[66]

NOTES

1. Barbara Leaming, *Orson Welles: A Biography* (New York: Viking Penguin, 1985), 212.
2. William Goldman, *Adventures in the Screen Trade* (New York: Warner Books, 1983).
3. "Buchwald vs. Paramount: Coming to a Conclusion," *Washington Post,* 2 March 1992, p. B-1.
4. "Recession Comes to Tinsel Town," *Financial Times* (London), 1 December 1991, p. 7.
5. "Gone with the Cash," *Economist* (London), 3 November 1990, p. 74.
6. "Hollywood's Third Best Year," *Washington Post,* 5 January 1993, p. C-2.
7. Wilson Dizard, *Television—a World View* (Syracuse, N.Y.: Syracuse University Press, 1966), 118.
8. "No Place Like Home, Poll Says," *Variety,* 30 March 1992, p. 23.
9. "Sales, Rentals Hit Highs," *Variety,* 27 January 1992, p. 19.
10. "Today the Stones. Tomorrow, Stallone?" *Business Week,* 16 December 1991, p. 52.
11. "In Tomorrow's Motion Picture Theater, the Theater Is Also in Motion," *Intermedia* (London) 21, no. 2 (March-April 1993): 46.
12. "Videotapes Growing Rival: Pay-per-View TV," *New York Times,* 30 March 1992, p. D-8.
13. "Fun and Profit," *Economist* (London), 29 October 1988, pp. 21–24.
14. "Yesterday the World," *Financial Times* (London), 31 January 1992, p. 11.
15. Chris Columbus, "Wilder Times," *American Film* 6, no. 2 (March 1980): 28.
16. Leo Bogart, *The American Media System and Its Commercial Culture,* Occasional Paper No. 8, Gannett Foundation Media Center, March 1991, p. 4.
17. "Big vs. Little: Surviving in a World of Media Giants," *Television Business International* (London) (October 1990): pp. 54–66.
18. "Disney in the Swim with 'Mermaid' Merchandise," *Variety,* 13 April 1992, p. 12.
19. For a survey of recent Disney studio changes, see Ron Grover, *The Disney Touch: How a Daring Management Team Revived an Entertainment Empire* (New York: Business One Irwin, 1991).
20. "How Murdoch Makes It Work," *New York Times,* 14 August 1988, p. F-3.
21. The Byzantine negotiations involved in the Time Warner merger and its aftermath are described in Connie Bruck, "Deal of the Year," *New Yorker,* 8 January 1990, pp. 66–89;

also Connie Bruck, "Strategic Alliances," *New Yorker,* 6 July 1992, pp. 34–56. For an account of the merger, which emphasizes the alleged loss of editorial independence by Time Inc. publications, see Richard Clurman, *To the End of Time* (New York: Simon & Schuster, 1992).

22. "Invasion of Studio Snatchers," *Business Week,* 16 October 1989, p. 53.
23. "Valenti Hits Foreign-Ownership Bill," *Variety,* 11 November 1991, p. 20.
24. Quoted in "Chief of Sony Tells Why It Bought a Part of America's Soul," *Financial Times* (London), 4 October 1989, p. 6.
25. For an interesting description of the political as well as economic factors involved in the Matsushita acquisition, see Connie Bruck, "Leap of Faith," *New Yorker,* 9 September 1991, pp. 38–74.
26. "Media Colossus," *Business Week,* 25 March 1991, pp. 64–70.
27. "The Entertainment Industry," special survey in *Economist* (London), 23 December 1989, p. 10.
28. "Philips to Buy 25 Pct. of 'Channel One' Firm," *Washington Post,* 6 February 1992., p. D-11.
29. "Can Sony Make Hollywood Pay?" *New York Times,* 23 February 1992, p. F-8. See also "Sony Struggles with the Rewind Button," *Financial Times* (London), 20 February 1992, p. 18, and "The Rising Sun Setting on Sunset Strip," *Variety,* 15 June 1992, p. 1.
30. "Sony's Twins Hit Terrible Twos," *Variety,* 9 September 1991, p. 1. See also "Will Intramural Squabbling Derail Debt-ridden Sony?" *New York Times,* 11 August 1991, p. F-5.
31. "Is Sony Finally Getting the Hang of Hollywood?" *Business Week,* 7 September 1992, p. 76. See also "Hollywood Hot Topic: Japanese Cold Feet," *New York Times,* 9 July 1992, p. C-15, and "Shadow Shogun Casts Light on Matsushita," *Variety,* 5 October 1992, p. 41.
32. "Mickey Mouse Goes to Japan," *Corporate Finance* 4, no. 12 (December 1990): 25.
33. "Disney Is Looking a Little Fragilistic," *Business Week,* 25 June 1990, pp. 52–54; also "No Mickey Mouse Company," *Barron's,* 24 June 1991, p. 8.
34. Peter Bart, *The Calamitous Final Days of MGM* (New York: William Morrow, 1990).
35. "Hollywood's Sensitivity Training," *Washington Post,* 28 December 1991, p. C-1.
36. "Loved It, Darling, Let's Shoot," *Economist* (London), 12 October 1991, pp. 94–95.
37. Nigel Andrews, "Stop Mugging the Paying Public," *Financial Times* (London), 1 January 1992, p. 21.
38. "Venturing into Capital," *Television Business International* (April 1991): 40.
39. "Batman Is Back, and the Money Is Pouring In," *New York Times,* 22 June 1992, p. D-1.
40. "Top 100 All-Time Film Rental Champs," *Variety,* 6 January 1992, p. 86.
41. For a useful description of Hollywood abroad, see William Read, *America's Mass-Media Merchants* (Baltimore: Johns Hopkins University Press, 1976).
42. "Viet Cong Weeps for Redskins," *Variety,* 25 January 1967, p. 2.
43. A. M. A. Aziz, *A Pakistani Journalist Looks at America* (Dacca: Al-Helat, 1960), p. 3.
44. "The World Is Hollywood's Oyster," *Business Week,* 14 January 1991, p. 97.
45. "Studios Look to Foreign Markets," *New York Times,* 7 March 1990, p. D-1.
46. "Majors Global Rentals Totaled $3.27 Bil in '91," *Variety,* 15 June 1992, p. 3.
47. "Russian TV & Radio Inks Deal with BVI," *Variety,* 18 May 1992, p. 33.
48. "Disney Co. Cartoons Are Going to China in Commerical Foray," *Wall Street Journal,* 23 October 1986, p. 1.
49. "Mickey Makes the Long March Back to China," *Financial Times* (London), 21 March 1992, p. 5.
50. "Tinseltown Invasion: Box Office Boffo in Europe," *Washington Post,* 11 November 1991, p. G-1.
51. "Yank Distribs Read Signs of Growth Abroad," *Variety,* 3 February 1991, p. 39.
52. "No Place Like Home," *Washington Post,* 23 January 1992, p. D-7.

53. "Disney Leads Shift from Rentals to Sales in Videocassettes," *Wall Street Journal,* 24 December 1992, p. 1.
54. "Hollywood Tries to Fit PPV into Its Game Plan," *Broadcasting,* 29 April 1991, p. 37.
55. "Paramount to Make Its Own PPV Deals," *Broadcasting,* 2 November 1992, p. 51.
56. These 1990 record industry estimates are from the International Federation of the Phonographic Industry. See "Cassette Tape World Sales Decline," *Financial Times* (London), 3 October 1991, p. 4.
57. "Can These Upstart Record Labels Survive?" *New York Times,* 5 January 1992, p. F-5.
58. "Michael Jackson Gets Thriller of Deal to Stay with Sony," *New York Times,* 21 March 1991, p. C-17.
59. "Madonna Makes a $60 Million Deal," *New York Times,* 21 April 1992, p. C-11.
60. "Almost Grown—a Survey of the Record Business," *Economist* (London), 21 December 1991, p. 14.
61. Ibid., 15–16.
62. "George Lucas on Issues, Ideas and Indiana Jones," *New York Times,* 27 January 1992, p. C-17.
63. "Cross-Media Megadeals Stoke the Synergists," *Variety,* 10 February 1992, p. 1.
64. "Multimedia Beats a Path to Hollywood," *Financial Times* (London), 14 May 1992, p. 9.
65. "Hollywood Romancing Silicon Valley," *Variety,* 28 September 1992, p. 77.
66. "The AFI Life Achievement Award," *American Film* 13, no. 6 (July 1987): 22.

Chapter 8

GUTENBERG'S LAST STAND?

Networked computers will be the printing presses of the twenty-first century."[1] That prediction, made in the early 1980s by communications scholar Ithiel de Sola Pool, was dismissed at the time by most publishing industry experts as a futuristic fancy. Professor Pool's prediction is, however, being realized faster than even he might have anticipated. The traditional publishing sectors—newspapers, magazines, and books—are adjusting their operational styles to computer realities, as well as coping with competition from a growing number of new electronic information providers.

The changes do not, however, signal the end of print. Johannes Gutenberg lives on in familiar morning newspapers, in weekly magazines, and in the 50,000 books published annually in the United States. The U.S. printing and publication industries remain comfortably profitable, with revenues of over $175 billion in 1991.[2] The idea that computers and other electronic devices might transform America into a "paper-less society" has been turned on its head. Computers and Xerox-type machines have, in fact, created a massive paper glut, simply because so many people want to store computer-generated information as hard-copy print in old-fashioned file cabinets. As a result, the United States currently accounts for one-third of the 165 million tons of paper produced annually around the world.[3]

Paul Saffo, research fellow at the Institute for the Future, noted a new synergy between traditional printed information and the advanced electronics:

> Paper won't disappear, but paperless media will soak up more of our time. We will eventually become paperless the same way we once became horseless. Horses are still around, but they are ridden by hobbyists, not commuters. . . . Now it is cheaper to store information electronically. Paper has become an interface—an increasingly transient, disposable medium for viewing electronically compiled information. We are entering the future where information is reduced to paper only when we're ready to read it, and then the paper is promptly recycled.[4]

Meanwhile, the electronification of print is beginning to take hold. Media scholar Anthony Smith compared this process of change with two earlier communications upheavals: the one brought about by the invention of writing and the second, caused by Gutenberg's printing press:

> The computerization of print is truly a third revolution in communications of similar scale and importance, in that it raises comparably fundamental issues concerning the social control of information, the notion of the individual creative function, the ways in which information interacts with human memory.[5]

The computer, Smith added, calls for a complete reorganization of the concept behind the print medium. Although computers were used initially by the industry to turn out products in their traditional form, print computerization opens up innovative possibilities for collecting, storing, and marketing information for mass audiences.

As has happened in every other media sector, print publishers have been generally slow to understand these implications. They regarded computerized technologies primarily as cost-cutting operational aids while they continued to produce the same products. The Xerox-type copier was considered a substitute for carbon paper, rather than as a cheap and easy way for people to produce and distribute copies of printed materials cheaply. As a result, xerographing of books and newspaper articles has been a factor in the erosion of publishing revenues. Publishers saw the value of computers in improving old-line production methods, but they lagged in recognizing the implications of Professor Pool's vision of the computer's role in creating a new media culture.

As an example, the prospects opened to publishers by computer-driven multimedia disks are only beginning to be understood. The pioneering work in this field has been done by Sony, a Japanese electronics manufacturer. The company's Electronic Book Player is a portable machine that fits in the palm of the hand. Each of the player's disks stores and displays 100,000 pages of text, 32,000 graphic images, or a combination of both. "It weighs eight million pounds less than your average library," Sony's advertisements proclaim. The ultimate electronic "book" may resemble the prototype Dynabook, the brainchild of Apple Computer scientist Alan Kay. A hand-held device, the Dynabook stores and displays prodigious amounts of information gathered by individuals for their personal needs and gives access to a full range of outside databases.[6]

The publishing industry's reluctance to branch out into computerized products stems in part from the disappointing experience of early entrants into electronic publishing during the 1980s. Those early projects generally failed—the victims of limited technology, poor marketing, and a largely uninterested consumer audience. The few projects that succeeded were those that identified a specialized audience with the interest, and the money, to make good use of electronic information targeted toward their needs. An early example of this was the LEXIS data network, introduced in 1973, which provides lawyers with quick access to court decisions in ways that have since made printed law digests in book form largely obsolete.

Eventually, electronic publishing will require massive restructuring of the print industries. It will also involve a psychological shift on the part of publishers. As Times-Mirror Co. executive Jerome Rubin pointed out:

> Growth in publishing—and, in some cases, survival—will lie in our ability to work in multiple dimensions. . . . Gutenberg provided a means of creating identical multiple copies. Electronic technologies, on the other hand, provide a means of creating infinite *variations* of the same material. Different versions are thus created continually, and each one can be stored in the computer. There is no one "author," nor is there any "definitive version" of the material. We are returning in spirit to Plato's Academy and the pre-copyright world of oral dialogue.[7]

The computerization of print is also influenced by other developments affecting the future shape and direction of the publishing industries. The most important one is the changing profile of U.S. society. The prosperity of the media industries after World War II was stimulated by unprecedented population growth. The postwar baby boom generation provided a large, affluent, and receptive audience for traditional print products—newspapers, magazines, and books—as well as for television and other electronic media. Demographic patterns were, moreover, relatively stable during this period. Families with several children were still the norm, represented by the personification of the cottage-with-white-picket-fence "American dream." Changes in that pattern began emerging a generation ago and are now pervasive. Population growth in the 1990s will average 7 percent, the slowest rate in the country's history. That change is accompanied by a major transformation in the U.S. population profile. Married couples with children now account for only 27 percent of all households; almost 30 percent of married couples have no children. Another 25 percent of the population are unmarried.

This fragmentation of traditional population patterns is having a major impact on newspapers, magazines, and other publishing sectors. A special factor is the new importance of ethnic minorities. About 80 percent of the U.S. population increase projected between now and the year 2010 will be represented by the African-American, Hispanic, and Asian communities.[8] One result has been the growing importance of ethnic publications, similar in pattern but greater in volume than the surge experienced earlier in this century when many immigrant groups had their own language newspapers and other publications. The Washington, D.C., area now has five weekly Spanish language newspapers. It also has a lively Korean media sector, which includes five daily and three weekly papers, three radio stations, and two television production units.[9] Overall, the Washington area has more than two dozen foreign language newspapers.

Along with these demographic changes are shifts in work-and-leisure patterns, which affect reading habits. A 1992 study by the Washington-based Economic Policy Institute found that the average U.S. worker puts in about 140 more hours on the job every year than the worker of two decades ago. Commuting time has also increased, so that Americans annually have almost 160 fewer hours—or one month less—for leisure activities.[10]

In summary, a new demographic environment is affecting the form, content, and distribution of media products. Print publishing in particular is feeling the impact of these population and life-style changes. For example, big-city afternoon newspapers in the United States are closing down, the result of large-scale migrations to the suburbs together with the availability of evening television news, which offers a quick version of the day's events.[11]

These developments have also transformed the publishing industry's financial prospects. In the past, publishing revenues were based largely on products aimed at broad general audiences centered around family households. As older life-styles erode, newspapers and magazines have fewer readers whose interests can be met with general information. Mass publications are losing readers to other print products that appeal to the ever-narrowing specialized interests of select audiences—scuba divers, Barbie doll collectors, or Corvette drivers, to name a few of the many groups that now have their own publications.

Special interest publications are not new, of course. The difference in recent years is that, collectively, they have overtaken general interest newspapers, magazines, and books as the dominant growth sector in U.S. publishing. Newspapers have responded with special editions, edited for particular audiences. General magazines are dividing up their readerships by zip codes and by income groups in order to satisfy advertisers who are no longer willing to pay for an undifferentiated mass readership. These are expensive efforts, which have escalated production and distribution costs. Since the mid-1980s, single-copy magazine prices have increased by over 70 percent.[12] Book and newspaper prices are not far behind.

Advertising revenues are still the financial mainstay for newspapers and most magazines, but they have shrunk alarmingly in recent years. These publications, along with television, benefited from an extraordinary expansion in the amount of money spent on advertising, beginning in the mid-1970s. Overall U.S. advertising expenditures grew by an average of 13.5 percent annually from 1975 to 1984, most of it involving television, newspaper, and magazine ads.[13] Since then, general advertising spending by these media has been reduced to the point where it barely keeps pace with inflation. The persistent economic recession of the early 1990s added to the slowdown.

The shifting advertising pattern has had a marked impact on the current and future fortunes of the publishing industry. Aside from the immediate loss of revenues, the industry has been affected by a sharp change in advertising strategies in recent years. The shift is away from traditional media to marketing techniques aimed more directly at specific consumer targets. That strategy includes greater reliance on direct mail campaigns, telephone marketing, sweepstake contests, and shop-at-home catalogs. Supermarket bonus coupons have become a major merchandising tool; in 1991, U.S. advertisers distributed over 284 billion coupons, of which 7.5 billion were cashed in.[14] These alternative advertising techniques have been expanded more recently to include specially prepared videocassette presentations as well. When the Chrysler Corporation wanted to reach potential customers for its new minivan models in 1991, it sent to a targeted list of potential customers 400,000 videocassettes describing the product.

The fastest-growing type of alternative advertising is telemarketing—the selling of products or services by telephone. Telemarketing techniques include unsolicited sales calls to customers as well as 800- and 900-number calls initiated by customers. There are over a million 800-number services operating throughout the United States. The newer, 900-number industry is a billion-dollar enterprise whose primary service is not pornography-pandering, as popularly believed, but the dispensing of all kinds of information.[15]

The telemarketing industry did not exist 20 years ago. Today it employs 3.5 million people, who collectively rang up $435 billion in sales in 1991.[16] The industry's success is based on a combination of advanced telecommunications technology and computers. Increasingly, its telephone operations are carried out by robotic machines, using computerized speech to process orders. One such device, developed by a British company, can handle up to 120,000 calls a day, compared with the 2,000 previously taken by a staff of 16 telephone attendants.[17] Telemarketing techniques are being expanded to include direct marketing to and from personal computers. Computer-driven marketing is an important element in services such as Prodigy—the IBM/Sears Roebuck consumer data network. Prodigy carries telemarketing advertising on almost all of its data displays. Another threat to print-media revenues is the telephone industry's expansion into electronic yellow pages services, a consumer information network that will compete directly with newspaper classified advertising.

Taken together, telemarketing and the other alternative advertising techniques constitute a significant economic threat to newspapers, magazines, and other print publications. A 1991 *Business Week* analysis of major consumer industries found that traditional media advertising accounted for only 30 percent of marketing budgets, down 13 percent from 10 years previously.[18] General print publications will continue to be attractive outlets for many advertisers, particularly those offering products (soft drinks, cigarettes, etc.) aimed at large consumer groups. But the overall trend in the budgeting of advertising expenditures is away from mass audience newspapers and magazines.

This scaling back of advertising revenues has forced a shakeout throughout the publishing sector. A considerable number of magazines and newspapers, including some of the best and most venerable, have disappeared entirely, usually the victims of changing advertising patterns. Meanwhile, many of the surviving publications have turned to mergers and buyouts to ease their financial troubles. These takeovers are often carried out by large media corporations, which integrate publishing into larger multimedia operations that include television, film, and cable TV resources as well as newer, computer-driven technologies.

In summary, the publishing industry is undergoing major changes, spurred by new consumer patterns, financial upheavals, and the pressure of new technologies. These factors are common to all parts of the industry—newspapers, magazines, and books—but the situation in each sector is distinct enough to warrant examining each one separately.

First, newspaper publishing, still the centerpiece of U.S. print media activities: It is the industry that has historically defined the standards and obligations of media in U.S. society, long before radio, television, and the other mass communications services came along. Newspapers are woven into the warp and woof of the U.S. experience, from Ben Franklin's *Pennsylvania Gazette* to the present pattern, which extends from the *New York Times* to the *Unterrified Democrat,* a weekly that has been flaunting its defiant title in rural Missouri for over a century.

No other medium has the capability to collect, record, and distribute information at so many different levels, from the daily activities of small towns to national and international events. In aggregate, newspaper files contain the most complete written memory of U.S. society. When the *Boston Globe* decided some years ago to catalog and upgrade its century-old newspaper morgue, it discovered that it had 9 million clippings in 700,000 folders, along with 800,000 photographic prints.[19] The *Globe*'s files are, in raw form, a chronicle of modern Boston and its surrounding area.

For all its past glories and lapses, U.S. newspaper journalism is now in a period of massive transition, challenged by present-day electronic media and faced with competition from newer, computer-driven information resources. The debate is already under way about how (and even whether) newspapers can cope with the new challenges. There are no simple answers. Newspapers will continue to be a major presence in U.S. media for a long time to come. Through the mid-1990s, they can expect to have a compound annual growth rate of about 7 percent (Table 8.1). To survive over the long run, however, they will have to adjust their production and editorial styles to the new computer-based competition and to the changing demographics and life patterns of their readers.

A half century ago, newspapers were the primary sources of news, opinion, and light entertainment for most Americans. More important, they were the preeminent institution for setting the nation's political and social agendas. The only competitive mass medium was radio, whose news influence was spotty. Many homes received a morning and an afternoon paper. Newspaper market penetration in 1945 was 135 percent, meaning that more papers were sold every day than there were households. Circulation continued to climb until the early 1960s and then began to level off. Market penetration did not keep pace with the rapid population growth at the time— the famous postwar baby boom. By 1970, newspaper circulation had fallen below the total number of households.

The accepted wisdom in the industry at the time was that circulation would rise again as postwar baby boomers grew up and became, like their parents, regular newspaper readers. This did not happen. The baby boomers turned to television for their news. Young women (who composed a disproportionately high share of home newspaper readership) went to work outside the home. By 1989, newspaper penetration of households had fallen to 67 percent, less than half the percentage at the end of World War II.[20]

Many Americans had begun to lose the habit of newspaper reading. That decline

TABLE 8.1   Growth of Total U.S. Spending* on Newspapers

	Daily Newspapers	Weekly Newspapers	Total
1991 Expenditures ($ millions)	39,612	3,540	43,152
1986–91 Compound Annual Growth (%)	2.9	5.6	3.1
1991–96 Projected Compound Annual Growth (%)	6.7	7.0	6.7
1996 Projected Expenditures ($ millions)	54,820	4,965	59,785

*By advertisers and readers.
SOURCE: Veronis, Suhler & Associates, Newspaper Advertising Bureau, Paul Kagan Associates, Wilkofsky Gruen Associates. Reprinted by permission of Veronis, Suhler & Associates.

was analyzed in a 1991 study of reading habits commissioned by the American Society of Newspaper Editors (ASNE). The survey went beyond the well-known facts about overall readership losses. It also probed the habits of individual groups, including regular and occasional readers as well as nonreaders. The study found that there is a solid core of loyal readers, about 55 percent of U.S. adults, who regard newspapers as an important part of their life. The next group, characterized as "at-risk readers," pick up a paper several times a week but find little value in what they find there. As the ASNE study noted wryly, "They are not our fans. They are primarily interested in news that helps them cope with everyday living."[21] The remainder of those surveyed are nonreaders or very occasional readers, who are unlikely to take up the newspaper habit.

The key finding in the survey, however, is the steady loss in readership among younger people, those younger than 35. The majority of at-risk and potential readers are in this group, the most critical age category for the future of U.S. journalism (Figure 8.1). They are, moreover, the group that will be the most difficult to attract, primarily because their life-style tends to be fast moving and volatile, unsuited to regular newspaper reading habits. Young adults are caught up in constantly shifting patterns influenced by such factors as job changes, two-income households, child care, divorce, and frequent household moves. The survey suggested a number of ways in which more young readers could be attracted to newspaper reading, such as flashier page formats and features that focused on personal-living issues. The survey was not optimistic, however, that the current loss of readership could be turned around or even stemmed.

The problem was summarized by Lou Heldman, an official in the Knight-Ridder newspaper organization:

> We know how to win Pulitzers. We know how to topple politicians. We know how to do gut-wrenching stories. What we don't always know is how you get people to read serious journalism.[22]

Some newspaper executives dispute the importance of the overall decline in readership. They argue that newspapers are retaining their hold on their most important

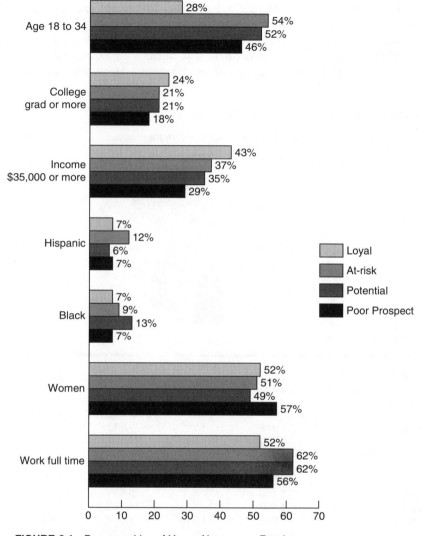

FIGURE 8.1 Demographics of Young Newspaper Readers

SOURCE: American Society of Newspaper Editors

reader groups—the middle class and the affluent, who have the bulk of buying power and are therefore most sought after by advertisers. True as this may be, it has not prevented a steady decline in newspaper advertising revenues in recent years. Newspaper ad revenues did benefit from the 1980s' economic boom, but by 1990, they had turned sharply downward. That year, for the first time in decades, the American Newspaper Publishers Association (ANPA) reported no increase in ad revenues[23] (Figure 8.2).

In recent years, newspaper profits have been depressed more deeply than the general economy. Even the *New York Times,* with its strong upscale readership, had a

27 percent drop in net profits in 1991, largely because of lower ad revenues. Despite such economic woes, daily newspapers continued to lead all other media in overall advertising revenues, with a 25 percent share in the early 1990s. Television ranked second, with 22 percent, and direct mail was third, with 18 percent.[24]

The most important change in the industry has been the closing down, or

FIGURE 8.2 Newspapers' Share of Advertising Expenditures

1989 and 1990 Sales and Percentages

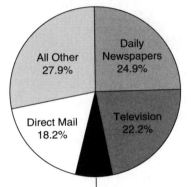

Radio 6.8%

	1989 (millions)	% of Total	1990[1] (millions)	% of Total	% of Change
Daily Newspapers					
Total	$ 32,368	26.1	$ 32,280	24.9	(0.3)
National	3,948[2]	3.2[2]	4,122	3.2	4.4
Local	28,420[2]	22.9[2]	28,158	21.7	(0.9)
Magazines	6,716	5.4	6,885	5.3	2.5
Television					
Total	26,891	21.7	28,755	22.2	6.9
Network	9,110	7.4	9,565	7.4	5.0
Spot	14,966	12.1	15,780	12.2	5.4
Syndication	1,288	1.0	1,610	1.2	25.0
Cable	1,527	1.2	1,790	1.4	17.2
Radio	8,323	6.8	8,765	6.8	5.3
Farm Publications	212	0.2	215	0.2	1.4
Direct Mail	21,945	17.7	23,590	18.2	7.5
Business Publications	2,763	2.2	2,875	2.2	4.1
Outdoor	1,111	0.9	1,155	0.9	4.0
Yellow Pages	8,330	6.7	8,850	6.8	6.2
Miscellaneous	15,271	12.3	16,120	12.4	5.6
Grand Total National	69,218[2]	55.9[2]	73,792	57.0	6.1
Grand Total Local	54,712[2]	44.1[2]	55,688	43.0	1.8
TOTAL—ALL MEDIA	$123,930	100.0	$129,480	100.0	4.5

[1]Preliminary estimates.
[2]Revised figures.
SOURCE: McCann-Erickson Inc., Newspaper Advertising Bureau and Veronis, Suhler & Associates. Reprinted by permission of Veronis, Suhler & Associates.

consolidation, of many afternoon papers in larger cities. Numerically there are almost twice as many afternoon papers (1,080) as morning ones (560) across the nation. Most of the afternoon papers are located in smaller towns, where there is no compelling reason to put out a morning publication. The total circulation of afternoon dailies nationally is half that of the morning papers.[25] The demise of big-city afternoon papers is only one part of the structural change taking place in the newspaper industry. Historically, the industry's pattern has been a mix of many independent papers in smaller cities, together with national chains, which dominated the big-city markets. The latter were often owned by "press lords," in the image of William Randolph Hearst and E. W. Scripps, who took a direct interest in the editorial side of their enterprises.

The mix of independent and chain newspapers still characterizes the industry, but its composition is changing. Unlike most of their predecessors, many of the larger newspaper chains are now part of conglomerates with multimedia holdings. The most striking example is the Gannett Co., which owns (in addition to *USA Today* and 87 other daily newspapers) 10 television stations, 16 radio stations, the Louis Harris polling organization, its own news service, and the largest billboard advertising group in the country. The New York Times Co. is more than the *Times.* It is the owner of the *Boston Globe* and 32 smaller papers, a half interest in the *International Herald Tribune,* 17 magazines, 5 television stations, a radio station, and a thriving data information service. Newspaper firms with extensive holdings in other media operations include the *Washington Post, Chicago Tribune, Los Angeles Times-Mirror,* and the Knight-Ridder chain. There are very few newspaper-only chains left: one of the largest is the little-known MediaNews Group, based in Houston, with 15 dailies in nine states, including the *Denver Post* and the *Houston Post.*[26]

Some media observers believe editorial independence is threatened by chain ownership.[27] There are enough documented examples of such threats to justify these concerns. More characteristically, however, the new multimedia groups are led by corporate executives who are not inclined to interfere in editorial policy. Their focus is on bottom-line profitability. They are more cost conscious than owners of independent papers, and they tend to invest heavily in improving product quality.[28]

Nevertheless, the potential loss of editorial independence by chain-owned newspapers should not be underestimated: As media critic Ben Bagdikian pointed out:

> The problem is not evil media empires. Nor is it the nature of any one corporation. The real problem is that more and more of the country's mass media is being controlled by fewer and fewer corporations. . . . Economists know perfectly well what happens. When a handful of companies have most of the business and the remainder is divided among hundreds or thousands of small companies, it is market domination. The dominant companies control prices and the nature of the product. But in this case, the product happens to be the country's reservoir of news, information, ideas and entertainment.[29]

The new corporate owners of newspapers are reshaping the form and direction of the industry. ANPA estimated in 1991 that about 75 percent of U.S. daily newspapers were owned by chains, compared with 60 percent a decade earlier. As a result of mergers, bankruptcies, and buyouts, only 39 cities had competitive daily papers in the early 1990s. Newspaper chains also controlled about half of the country's 7,000 weekly newspapers, almost all of which had been independently owned in the early 1980s, according to the ANPA survey.[30] Unlike other media conglomerates, such as Time Warner and Rupert Murdoch's News Corp., most U.S. newspaper chains are less inspired by the gospel of synergistic information packaging. These chains usually operate their publications on separate tracks and put relatively little effort into coordinating the production and marketing of their individual papers.

Faced with declines in readership and revenues, the newspaper industry is looking for ways to maintain its competitiveness in a changing information environment. Increasingly they are turning to new technologies, both to upgrade their present products and to improve production and marketing efficiency.[31] For two decades, newspapers have moved steadily toward computerization of their internal operations, to the point where newspaper production is now almost totally automated, from newsroom word processing to computerized delivery programs. The changes have had a strong influence on the ways in which reporters cover stories and particularly on their new ability to tap into computerized information resources.[32]

The next step for publishers was to redesign their newspapers, with a particular focus on increasing their appeal to younger audiences. A 1991 survey by a research group at the University of Missouri's journalism school indicated that 69 percent of the papers surveyed had added or expanded their color capabilities or changed their basic design during the previous five years. Three-quarters of those papers use Macintoshes or other PCs to create improved graphics.[33] Even the *New York Times,* a longtime holdout against glitzy journalism, has redesigned itself in recent years, with more graphics and magazine-style layouts. The *Times* is also devoting more space to local news, an acknowledgment that, despite its journalistic preeminence, it reaches only 1 in 10 households in the New York area. The *Times*'s transformation has been accelerated by the 1991 opening of an automated $450-million printing plant in Edison, New Jersey, where computers and robots perform most of the tasks previously done by humans.

The most controversial attempt at creating a new kind of newspaper was the launching of *USA Today* by the Gannett chain in 1982. The paper was the brainchild of Allen Neuharth, Gannett chairman and one of the most flamboyant figures in recent U.S. journalism. (His autobiography is entitled *Memoirs of an SOB.*) Neuharth deliberately set out to offer a print version of television news and features—short, eye-catching, and light on details. With its editorial material delivered by satellite to printing plants throughout the United States and abroad, the paper is bought every day by about 2 million people, the largest circulation of any U.S. daily. *USA Today* has been, however, an expensive test of how a newspaper can attract audiences in a media-saturated environment. By 1992, it had reportedly suffered estimated after-tax losses of $800 million and had never turned an annual profit.

In recent years, *USA Today* has offered more substantive news reporting, a distinct change from its earlier emphasis on lighter-and-brighter journalism. The paper now provides better coverage of national and international affairs and of economic developments affecting its readers.[34] That change is part of a larger trend in the newspaper industry, reflecting the realization that its primary strength is in providing substantive, detailed information on a wide range of current events.

Newspapers are also adopting technologies that enable them to deliver timely information in innovative and profitable ways. Their early attempts at electronic delivery were trial-and-error experiments.[35] The *New York Times* began the first major experiment in computerized access in the mid-1970s, with its New York Times Information Bank, providing summaries and full texts of current and past articles for subscribers with small computers. In 1980, an Ohio paper, the *Columbus Dispatch,* made available its entire daily editorial content to home computers around the country on the CompuServe data network. Viewers could call up a news menu from which they could select the stories they wanted to see.[36] Other major papers, including the *Washington Post* and the *Wall Street Journal,* also make news and feature offerings available on computer networks. A 1991 survey by ANPA found that 140 papers were providing on-line access to full-text databases of their editorial contents.[37]

Several newspaper organizations have expanded their computerized products to provide information beyond their in-house editorial material.[38] The most aggressive of these projects has been managed by the Knight-Ridder chain, which bought a major on-line database, DIALOG, in 1988. Knight-Ridder's aim is to become a major player in the business information field, competing with computerized services offered by the Reuters news agency and by Dow Jones, owner of the *Wall Street Journal* and other business publications.[39] Other newspapers are marketing selected summaries of their editorial products by means of facsimile machines. As noted in Chapter 3, these experiments have had only limited success. The most successful sellers of fax-delivered news have been newsletter publishers, whose stock-in-trade is providing specialized groups of customers with news of fast-breaking events in their professional fields.

A growing number of newspapers are using 800- and 900-number telephone networks to offer information products to consumers. The range of services they supply is wide and growing. By 1993, the *Washington Post* had 13 free, 800-number services, ranging from sports scores to current mortgage rates. The *Post*'s services have averaged over 6 million calls annually in recent years. The *Los Angeles Times* began by offering free, 800-number access to its editorial contents and then shifted in 1991 to pay-per-call 900-number access at $1.50 per minute.[40] The *Atlanta Journal and Constitution* offers advance snippets of weekend sermons—a service paid for by the city's churches and synagogues. The *New York Times* and the *Washington Post* provide a 900-number guide to good dining, at 75 cents a minute. The *Daily Camera* in Boulder, Colorado, supplies classified personal ads via a 900 number for a fee. In 1992, the *Ladies' Home Journal* asked readers to call a 900- number to give their opinions on the subject of abortion rights. The request triggered 30,000 responses.[41]

Profitable as these services are, they have relatively little impact on the problems that newspapers face in adjusting to a changing information environment. A major issue for the industry concerns the current competition between the telephone and cable TV industries for the lead role in supplying video, data, and voice services via electronic circuits to U.S. homes.[42] Newspaper executives consider the development a long-term threat. Their concerns were summarized by George W. Wilson, chairman of the ANPA task force on telephone competition:

> The flood of new electronic products and services that the regional Bell telephone companies are creating will be nothing less than tomorrow's system for distributing information to every American home. . . . Depending on how they are used, these distribution systems will strengthen or shatter the traditional links between newspapers, their advertisers and their readers. In short, the phone companies could reshape the media triangle.[43]

Mr. Wilson and his fellow publishers fear that the phone companies could attract a large proportion of classified advertising—an important source of newspaper revenues—by offering customers access to cheap, easy-to-use electronic bulletin boards. In response to this perceived threat, the newspaper industry has mounted a full-scale lobbying campaign designed to put limits on phone company involvement in information services.[44] Newspapers may also find themselves competing with a range of portable information machines, which can receive, store, and distribute multimedia materials of all kinds. One of these devices, developed by Apple Computer, is the Personal Digital Assistant (PDA). It is a hand-held computer that allows the user to plug into the PDA's own stored information or to communicate by phone or wireless cable with other information sources.[45]

These developments have led to renewed interest in the prospects for newspapers, based on electronic production and delivery techniques. The idea of electronic home delivery was tested in the late 1970s by the Knight-Ridder newspaper chain. Known as Viewtron, the service offered news and features delivered to home computer terminals over telephone lines. Viewtron was essentially a videotext system, with the added attraction of offering materials tailored to individual subscriber interests. The project was eventually closed down, bedeviled by poor technical performance, high costs, and consumer indifference. As noted previously, other newspapers have had only modest success in selling videotext information to subscribers with PCs.

The new interest in electronic newspapers is based on the growing popularity of laptop and other notebook-sized computers. The key is portability. Unlike conventional PCs, notebook computers can store and display newspaper materials that can be read anywhere. As media consultant Jonathan Seybold points out:

> I can't think of any reason why anyone would want to read a newspaper on a video screen, but there are a lot of reasons to read a different product on a screen that you can carry around.[46]

A critical requirement is that the flat-panel displays on portable computers must be clear and bright. By the early 1990s, computer manufacturers had begun to meet this goal through advanced chip technology. Early prototypes of electronic newspapers display a sharp, 8½-by-11-inch newspaper "front page" as a menu from which subscribers select the news and features they want to see. The subscriber can then read, print, or store the information. Electronic versions of traditional newspapers would be delivered to subscribers by cable TV systems, DBS, or advanced telephone circuits.

Electronic newspaper enthusiasts see a bright future for the new technology. Others are more skeptical about any sudden transition from traditional print to electronic modes. The higher cost of electronic services will be a factor. As Walter Baer, a media expert at the Rand Corporation, noted,

> When you're dealing with high-value information for business and professional people, electronic information is workable. But most consumers don't find information so valuable that they want to pay more than 50 cents for the newspaper. Newsprint will be around until well after the turn of the century.[47]

This view is echoed by newspaper analyst William Blankenburg of the University of Wisconsin. In the current evolution that the industry faces, he said,

> the comprehensive daily newspaper is not viable. Only pieces of it will survive, probably in targeted combinations, perhaps for a very long time. Some of its functions will be carried out by other means in the converged megamedium. The vertical integration of the newspaper industry will end, and with it, presumably, the local monopoly that owed to economies of scale in production. In the hazy future, the optimist will see the public freed from the shackles of old monopolistic media that constricted the flow of information vital to democracy. But the pessimist worries that a huge information utility controlled by mammoth venal corporations will widen the gaps between rich and poor, invade privacy, and destroy the communities of interest that shared the comprehensive daily newspaper.[48]

Newspaper executives are increasingly aware that they will be more involved in new electronic information systems. By 1993, the *New York Times,* the *Washington Post,* and the Hearst newspaper chain were actively involved in electronic newspaper research. Despite its earlier failed experiment with Viewtron, the Knight-Ridder chain was testing the new technology at its *San Jose Mercury* facility. The *Chicago Tribune* had developed a partnership with an electronic information service to make its news services available to subscribers.

Whether through traditional print or by way of the new electronic techniques, the newspaper industry will play a major role in the new-media environment. No other media sector has the overall experience or resources that newspapers bring to the production and distribution of information for both business and home consumers. The industry stands to benefit greatly if it exploits this advantage and becomes a central player in new forms of electronic journalism during the coming decade. As Roger Fidler, director of new media development for the Knight-Ridder chain, noted:

> I don't see print disappearing. But I see it taking a different form. The question is not whether there will be newspapers in the next century, but who will publish them. I'm not convinced the majority of the newspaper companies today will be in business in the next century.[49]

The magazine industry is also in a state of transition, sharing with newspapers the problems created by demographic shifts, the competition for advertising dollars, and challenges from the electronic technologies. Newspapers have a certain advantage in the new environment in that they usually operate within a limited geographic area, with the opportunity to adjust their content on a daily basis. Magazines deal with larger, more varied national audiences, whose attitudes and preferences are harder to define.

General magazines such as *Time, Newsweek,* and *Reader's Digest* still have, collectively, the largest share of readers. The major trend in the magazine business, however, is the division of its audiences by interest groupings. Almost every conceivable group, from bird watchers to sky divers, has one or more magazines targeted toward its interests. The industry is fragmented into thousands of national, regional, and local special interest publications. Even the larger general magazines are edited and distributed in different editions, with targeted editorial content and advertising in segmented editions. *Farm Journal,* for instance, publishes different editions for dairy, hog, beef, and high-income farmers. Some industry strategists foresee the day when magazines will be routinely personalized for subscribers, with no two copies alike.

In common with other media, the magazine industry flourished in the boom years of the 1980s, when over 2,500 new publications were launched. Most of them had disappeared by the early 1990s. The more enduring legacy of the 1980s was the scramble by multimedia corporations to buy up successful magazine properties. The most spectacular single sale was the $3 billion paid by Rupert Murdoch's News Corp. for *TV Guide* in 1988.[50] The deal of the decade, however, was the 1989 merger of Warner Communications and Time Inc., resulting in the world's largest media conglomerate. Their corporate marriage began with high hopes. As Nicholas Nickels, one of the Time Inc. executives involved in the deal, declared at the time, "In 1995 and the year 2000, when we have access to every home in the world on a direct-to-consumer basis, that's when the big numbers kick in."[51] On paper, Time and Warner were the perfect multimedia fit. Warner was a major film, television program, and music record producer. Time Inc. had a stable of highly successful magazines, including *Time, Fortune, People,* and *Sports Illustrated.* It was also a major book publisher and one of the largest owners of cable TV systems and owner of HBO, the leading networker of satellite-delivered cable programming. The Time Warner deal was a bizarre financial arrangement, tied to an exchange of stock, which left the merged company with over $10 billion of debt. There were, moreover, serious questions about a mismatch between a pop entertainment conglomerate and a major U.S. publisher, with attention focused on the continued editorial integrity of the latter. The tumultuous early years of the Time Warner merger served only to reinforce these doubts.[52]

In the 1990s, the magazine industry has continued its shift away from general interest publications to more specialized ones. In particular, computer magazines have proliferated, along with those emphasizing personal health, sports, and financial planning. There has also been a new emphasis on retirees and other older readers: circulation skyrocketed for *Modern Maturity,* the publication of the American Association of Retired Persons. Bridal magazines also flourished as the marriage rate increased in recent years. One 1990 issue of *Bride's and Your New Home* made the *Guinness Book of World Records* as "the weightiest publication ever," at 1,024 pages.

The 1990s have been shakeout years for the magazine industry. Most of the new publications that started up in the 1980s have disappeared, along with many of the older ones. With over 3,000 surviving publications, the industry remains basically healthy, but many of its publications are having a difficult time fitting into the new information environment. The search is on for new editorial formulas to match the changing demographics and life-styles of their customers. Meanwhile, the economics of magazine publishing are also changing. Magazines, like newspapers, are affected as advertisers turn to direct mail and other so-called alternative advertising techniques. One result is that subscription charges loom much larger as revenue producers. In the 1970s, it was advertising that produced two-thirds of overall magazine revenues; by the late 1980s, subscription revenues were higher.[53]

Another trend of the 1990s has been the steady internationalization of the magazine business. *Time, Newsweek,* and *Reader's Digest* have each published international editions for over 40 years. More recently, they have been joined by *Business Week* and *Scientific American,* each with three overseas editions. *Cosmopolitan* proclaims the gospel of the Cosmo Girl in its 25 international editions.[54] International Data Group, a Boston firm specializing in information technology journals, publishes over 140 magazines in 55 countries.[55] Meanwhile, foreign publishers have been moving into the U.S. market. They include Hachette, a major French publisher; Rupert Murdoch's News Corp., and Britain's Reed Elsevier group. Reed's American affiliate, Cahners Publishing, specializes in trade journals, with a stable of 69 publications ranging from *Variety,* the show-business journal, to *Modern Materials Handling.*

Increasingly, magazines are turning to new technologies to improve their editorial content and their revenues. Most magazine production is now computer driven, from desktop layouts of editorial copy to the final printed product. Computerization has made it easier to produce segmented editions, with subscription lists categorized by income level, geographical location, or other specialized divisions. *American Baby,* a monthly with a circulation of 1.1 million, is often segmented into 100 different versions of a single issue.

New printing techniques make it possible to tailor issues to fit the interests of individual customers. The first major test of individualized printing took place in 1990, involving *Time, Sports Illustrated,* and *People,* all published by Time Warner. Each subscriber found his or her name in an advertisement for Isuzu automobiles, together with a special insert listing the Isuzu dealer nearest the subscriber's home.[56] *Forbes* magazine added an electronic touch to its advertising strategy when it included a bound-in floppy disk in a June 1992 issue sent to 700,000 subscribers. The disk offered interactive ads, with animated color graphics, from 10 advertisers.

In another experiment in customized publishing, *Newsweek* offers its subscribers the option of eight extra ad-free pages in each issue, tailored to their personal interests. The required technology involves computerized binding of the magazine, keyed to the subscriber's mailing label. This Newsweek Focus service initially offered supplements on new books, science and technology, personal finance, and international news, at an annual cost of $5 for each supplement.[57]

The magazine industry is showing increased interest in other electronic technologies that can open up new markets, building on the industry's editorial expertise. McGraw-Hill and other large chain publishers offer videotext versions of their publications to computer owners. The next step for such publishers is to use their editorial resources to produce CD-ROM versions or to create special disks. The leader has been Time Warner, drawing on its diverse editorial resources. In 1991, the company marketed "Desert Storm: The First Draft of History," a week-by-week retelling of the Persian Gulf war on a CD. Earlier, *National Geographic* magazine collaborated with IBM to produce a CD-ROM called "Mammals," which contained hundreds of still images, plus video segments and animal sounds.[58]

In 1993, *Newsweek* became the first general-interest magazine to offer editorial material on a CD-ROM. The "*Newsweek* Interactive" disks are sold by subscription four times a year. Each disk is devoted to an in-depth review of a single subject. *Newsweek*'s disks, and similar innovative projects, indicate that the magazine industry has a potentially important role to play in the new world of electronic multimedia information and entertainment, albeit with formats that will be quite different from the ones it uses now.

Desktop publishing will eventually be the norm in the magazine business, expanding beyond its current use in producing newsletters and other specialized publications. By 1993, a number of general circulation magazines were being produced on desktop computers, including Conde Nast Publications' *Allure,* Hearst Magazine's *Victoria,* and Time Inc.'s *Entertainment Weekly.* Time Inc. editors sponsored a one-week experiment in April 1993 in which they used advanced editorial, imaging and transmission technologies to produce a high-quality, four-color, 92-page general interest prototype publication, working entirely with electronic equipment. They were able to integrate all of the major editorial and production operations—from writing to page layout—on one desktop computer system.

The most venerable of the media industries is book publishing. For all the many advantages of new electronic media, none has improved on the book and its practical attributes as an information storage device: portability, inexpensiveness, range of subject matter and never having to be sent out for repairs.

The U.S. book industry is big and diverse, with $20 billion in domestic annual sales in 1991. The industry experienced strong growth in the 1980s, a pace it has not been able to sustain more recently (Table 8.2). About 50,000 books are published annually in the United States.[59] Educational and professional books account for over half of this volume. Trade books—those sold for general consumption—are a relatively small part of the industry's output; fewer than 5,000 fiction books are issued every year. Over 20,000 firms publish one or more books annually. New, less expensive production techniques, such as desktop publishing, make it easier for new entrants to break into the field.[60] Most of them remain minor players in the industry.

The book trade is dominated by a half dozen major publishers. Significantly, five of these six big firms are parts of larger companies, which are active in other media. The takeovers of old-line publishing houses over the past 15 years have irrevocably changed the industry's staid, literary-oriented image. The distinctive styles of such firms as Charles Scribner, Viking, Grove Press, and Doubleday have been either lost or watered down. No longer is Random House defined as the publisher of William Faulkner, W. H. Auden, or Sinclair Lewis. Alfred A. Knopf (now part of the Random House complex) once had an outstanding reputation as a publisher of high-quality literature, particularly works by foreign authors. Knopf's output in more recent years has included *Miss Piggy's Guide to Life* and the voyeuristic sex surveys of Shere Hite

TABLE 8.2 Growth of U.S. Spending on Books

	Consumer Books	Professional and Educational Books	Total
1991 Expenditures ($ millions)	12,735	7,530	20,265
1986–91 Compound Annual Growth (%)	10.0	6.8	8.7
1991–96 Projected Compound Annual Growth (%)	8.1	6.7	7.6
1996 Projected Expenditures ($ millions)	18,785	10,390	29,175

SOURCE: Veronis, Suhler & Associates, Book Industry Study Group, Wilkofsky Gruen Associates. Reprinted by permission of Veronis, Suhler & Associates.

The largest and most successful of the publishing houses in recent years has been Simon & Schuster, now owned by Paramount Communications, the multimedia conglomerate with extensive Hollywood and television holdings. Since Paramount acquired it in 1975, Simon & Schuster has shed its longtime image as primarily a trade book house in order to become an eclectic publisher of educational and professional books and data services. With $1.5 billion in annual sales by the early 1990s, the firm accounts for about a third of Paramount's revenues.[61] Despite its overall profitability, Simon & Schuster is not immune from poor earnings as a result of faulty editorial judgments. In 1991, it issued Ronald Reagan's memoirs, *An American Life*, after reportedly paying the former president $5 million for the manuscript. The book was a commercial failure, easily outsold by another White House memoir, *Millie's Book*, about Barbara Bush's English springer spaniel, published by a different firm.

Such failures have not discouraged other publishers from paying big advances for what they hope will be surefire hits. In 1992, HarperCollins negotiated a $24-million contract with romance writer Barbara Taylor Bradford for three novels. Earlier, pop biographer Kitty Kelley signed a $4-million contract with Warner Books for an unauthorized look at the British royal family.[62]

Other media conglomerates with publishing interests include Time Warner (Little, Brown, and other imprints), Newhouse Publications (Random House), and the Reader's Digest Association, with its perennial Condensed Books editions. These conglomerates have not been overly successful in transferring their synergistic media-packaging plans to include their book products, possibly because book publishing is not as amenable to multimedia exploitation as television, records, magazines, and other holdings are. One exception has been Paramount Communications' exploitation of its "Star Trek" television series, which has been spun off into Simon & Schuster books, as well as into films, cartoon magazines, and a credit card.

In recent years, foreign publishers have expanded into the U.S. market. Doubleday and Bantam Books are owned by Bertelsmann A.G., a German conglomerate, which started as a publisher of bibles two centuries ago. Bertelsmann is now a major international media power, second in size only to Time Warner in its global multimedia holdings. Britain's Maxwell Communications controlled Macmillan Publishing until the collapse of its media empire put all its holdings in doubt following the death of Robert Maxwell, its flamboyant founder, in 1991. Pearson, the London publishing, banking, and industrial group, owns a number of important U.S. book imprints, including Penguin, Viking, New American Library, E. P. Dutton, Longman, and Addison-Wesley.

The U.S. book industry today is, in many ways, stronger and more successful than at any time in its history. It faces major changes in the next decade, however, as new information technologies erode its traditional print formats. The industry has been largely successful in automating its internal operations in ways that have low-ered production and distribution costs. Book production is now mostly computer-ized, from authors' word processors to final printing and distribution. The process, known in the trade as electronic manuscript management, tracks a book's production on a day-by-day basis, including keeping current tallies on costs, man-hours, and production schedules.[63] One result is that publishers now find it easier to customize textbooks for individual courses. McGraw-Hill, a major textbook publisher, has been offering this service to college professors for several years. The Council on Foreign Relations, a small but prestigious publisher of textbooks, can produce an individu-alized anthology of articles selected by a professor, including his or her personal introduction to the book.

The next step is the creation of books that are not produced or distributed in traditional print formats. This is made possible through the convergence of a new generation of computer-based technologies, including flat-panel video displays, which are much thinner than a hardcover book; more powerful computer chips; and software that can display electronic "pages" on almost any computer. Primitive ver-sions of electronic books are already on the market. Sony has introduced the Data Discman, which operates with small CDs that contain movie guides and other refer-ence works. There is a growing "library" of books that have been transferred to videotext on CD-ROM disks, primarily in the reference book category. The largest publisher of electronically generated books is the relatively unknown Franklin Elec-tronic Publishers, which, by 1993, had sold more than 5 million books, primarily reference works.

In 1992, the first multimedia "books" appeared on the market. One of the pioneers is a Santa Monica publisher, Voyager, whose initial list included a science fiction trilogy, Douglas Adams's *The Hitchhikers Guide to the Galaxy;* a technological thriller, *Jurassic Park,* by Michael Crichton; and an annotated version of *Alice in Wonderland.* Each was produced with Apple Computer's Macintosh software, which can integrate print copy with animated drawings, sound effects, and so-called hyper-text links that let readers quickly locate materials that directly interest them. Accord-ing to Voyager executive Bob Stein, "Apple, completely unintentionally, created the first electronic book."[64]

Traditional publishers have been slow to move into the new electronic book field, although all of the larger firms are looking at the possibilities. A few have made more substantial commitments. In 1992, Random House announced that it would make its Modern Library book classics available in electronic form, to be read on Apple Computer's portable machines.[65] Earlier, Paramount Communications, owner of Simon & Schuster, paid $75 million for Computer Curriculum Corporation, a firm specializing in computer-based curricula for schools. The acquisition is part of the firm's long-term plan to move into the integrated learning systems field.

Industry observers still have doubts, however, as to whether and when book readers will be ready to substitute electronic pages for printed ones. The accepted wisdom in the industry is that electronic books will be limited, at least in the near term, to reference works and other professional publications. "We see this marketplace really growing as a business-to-business marketplace," according to Stephen DiFranco, manager of new applications development for Sony Corp. "Trying to change how we culturally read and entertain ourselves is not as easy and will take a little longer."[66]

Despite these hesitations, most observers see the electronic book as a permanent, growing part of the publications industry. The ability to add sound, graphics, and animation to the printed word can result in a new kind of literature that goes beyond the linear storytelling of traditional books. Some experts suggest that "books" will evolve that only remotely resemble their traditional text-based ancestors.

One observer of this trend, computer expert George Landow, noted that "movement from the tactile to the digital is the primary fact about the contemporary world." He envisions a transformation in the ways we deal with the kinds of information presently encapsulated in printed books:

> Electronic text processing marks the next major shift in information technology after the development of the printed book. It promises (or threatens) to produce effects on our culture, particularly on our literature, education, criticism and scholarship, just as radical as those produced by Gutenberg's movable type.[67]

As they make their plans for the new electronic products, old-line book publishers face competition from some formidable outsiders. These include the major computer and software companies such as IBM, Apple, and Microsoft, all of whom have set up electronic publishing subsidiaries. Other competition may come from electronics manufacturers, such as Sony and Matsushita, which are interested in publications software to support their CD players and other consumer equipment. Philips, the European electronics giant, paid $175 million in 1992 for a 25 percent share in Whittle Communications, a U.S. publisher, with the clear purpose of using Whittle's editorial expertise to develop information materials for Philips's new line of interactive compact disks.[68]

The decisions that book publishers must make in the face of the new electronic technologies are similar to those that managers in newspaper, magazine, and other print enterprises must make. Each sector of the publishing industry brings special strengths and vulnerabilities to a new information environment in which Gutenberg's great invention will be transformed in the coming years.

NOTES

1. Ithiel de Sola Pool, *Technologies of Freedom* (Cambridge, Mass.: Harvard University Press, 1983), 224.
2. *1992 Industrial Outlook*, International Trade Administration, U.S. Department of Commerce, Washington, D.C., January 1992, p. 152.
3. The 1989 figure is from the *Pulp & Paper International Fact & Price Book*, cited in

"Another Journey on the Roller-Coaster," *Financial Times* (London), special supplement on world paper production, 24 May 1991, p. 2.

4. "The Electronic Future Is upon Us," *New York Times,* 7 June 1992, p. F-13.

5. Anthony Smith, *Goodbye Gutenberg* (New York: Oxford University Press, 1980), p. xii.

6. Frank Rose, "Pied Piper of the Computer," *New York Times Magazine,* 8 November 1987, p. 56.

7. Jerome S. Rubin, "Publishing as a Creature of Advanced Technology," in *Toward the Year 2000: New Forces in Publishing* (Gütersloh, Germany: Bertelsmann Foundation, 1989), p. 41.

8. "Threat to Mass Circulation on Demographic Landscape," *New York Times,* 7 January 1990, p. C-22.

9. "Korean Media Clamor to Deliver News from Home," *Washington Post,* 2 December 1991, p. C-1.

10. Juliet Shor and Laura Leete-Guy, "The Great American Time Squeeze: Trends in Work and Leisure, 1969–1980," research report for the Economic Policy Institute, Washington, D.C., February 1992.

11. John Morton, "40 Years of Death in the Afternoon," *Washington Journalism Review* 13, no. 11 (November 1991): 50.

12. Jib Fowles, "The Upheavals in the Media," *New York Times,* 6 January 1991, p. D-13.

13. For a survey of recent changes in the advertising industry, see Martin Mayor, *Whatever Happened to Madison Avenue?* (Boston: Little, Brown, 1991).

14. "America Is Coupon Crazy," *New York,* 7 September 1992, p. 18.

15. "For 900 Numbers, the Racy Gives Way to the Respectable," *New York Times,* 1 March 1992, p. F-8.

16. Teresa Riordan, "Dread Ringers," *Washington Post Magazine,* 23 February 1992, p. 14.

17. "Robots Pick Up the Call," *Financial Times* (London), 23 February 1992, p. 29.

18. "What Happened to Advertising?" *Business Week,* 23 September 1991, p. 68.

19. Smith, *Goodbye, Gutenberg,* 112.

20. "Rethinking Newspapers," *New York Times,* 6 January 1991, p. C-1.

21. *Keys to Our Survival* (Reston, Va.: American Society of Newspaper Editors, July 1991), 3.

22. "Slicing, Dicing News to Attract the Young," *Washington Post,* 6 January 1991, p. A-1.

23. "Rethinking Newspapers," *New York Times,* p. C-6.

24. *Facts About Newspapers—1991* (Reston, Va.: American Newspaper Publishers Association, April 1991).

25. "At Many Papers, Competition Is at Best an Illusion," *New York Times,* 22 September 1991, p. E-18.

26. "We're the Only One Left," *Forbes,* 17 February 1992, p. 42.

27. See Ben H. Bagdikian, *Media Monopoly,* 2d ed. (Boston: Beacon, 1987); also Ellis Cose, *The Press* (New York: William Morrow, 1989).

28. David Pearce Demers, "Corporate Structure and Emphasis on Profit and Product Quality at U.S. Daily Newspapers," *Journalism Quarterly* 68, no. 1/2 (Spring/Summer 1991): pp. 15–26.

29. Ben H. Bagdikian, "In the Time Deal, the Public Is the Loser," *New York Times,* 19 June 1989, p. D-6.

30. "The Weekly Newspaper Becomes a Hot Property," *New York Times,* 15 May 1989, p. C-11.

31. Tom Koch, *Journalism in the 21st Century* (New York: Praeger, 1991).

32. Katherine Corcoran, "Power Journalists," *Washington Journalism Review* 13, no. 11 (November 1991): 28–32. See also Jean Ward and Kathleen A. Hansen, "Journalist and Librarian Roles, Information Technologies and Newsmaking," *Journalism Quarterly* 68,

no. 3 (Fall 1991): 491–498, and "Quantum Leaps: Computer Journalism Takes Off," *Columbia Journalism Review* 31, no. 1 (May/June 1992): 61–63.

33. Jean Gaddy Wilson and Iris Igawa, "Strategy No. 9: Redesign," *Presstime,* American Newspaper Publishers Association (September 1991): 34.

34. "We Want News, McPaper Discovers," *Washington Post,* 26 December 1991, p. A-1.

35. For a description of early efforts at electronic publishing, see Walter S. Baer and Martin Greenberger, "Consumer Electronic Publishing in the Competitive Environment," *Journal of Communication* 37, no. 1 (Winter 1987): 49–63.

36. "First U.S. Experiments in Electronic Newspapers Begin in Two Communities," *New York Times,* 7 July 1980, p. B-13.

37. The survey is cited in "Don't Baby the Baby Bells," report issued by the American Newspaper Publishers Association, 7 October 1991.

38. "Database Dollars: Whose Are They?" *Columbia Journalism Review* 31, no. 3 (September/October 1992): 21.

39. "Knight-Ridder's Knight in Electronic Armor?" *Business Week,* 18 November 1991, p. 100.

40. "Los Angeles Times Migrates to 900," *Infotext* (October 1991): 20.

41. "Women Now Talk Back to *Ladies' Home Journal,*" *New York Times,* 22 June 1992, p. D-8.

42. Penny Pagano, "Electronic Warfare," *Washington Journalism Review* 14, no. 4 (April 1992): 18–23.

43. "Looking to the Future," *Communications News,* 1 May 1989, p. 4.

44. "Power of the Press vs. the Baby 'Behemoths,'" *Broadcasting,* 24 February 1992, pp. 28–29.

45. "America's Empire Strikes Back," *Economist* (London), 22 February 1992, p. 64.

46. "A Media Pioneer's Quest: Portable Electronic Newspapers," *New York Times,* 28 June 1992, p. F-11.

47. Ibid.

48. William B. Blankenburg, "The Viability of the Comprehensive Newspaper," research paper presented at the Association for Education in Journalism and Mass Communications annual conference, Montreal, Canada, August 1992, p. 7.

49. Doug Underwood, "The Newspapers' Identity Crisis," *Columbia Journalism Review* 30, no. 6 (March/April 1992): 27.

50. "Magazine Madness: The Story Behind the Buyout Binge," *Business Week,* 18 March 1985, p. 149.

51. Quoted in Richard Clurman, *To the End of Time* (New York: Simon & Schuster, 1992), 33.

52. The history of the Time Warner merger is documented in Clurman, *To the End of Time,* ibid.

53. "Magazines Raise Reliance on Circulation," *New York Times,* 8 May 1989, p. D-11.

54. "Defining the Cosmo Girl: Check Out the Passport," *New York Times,* 12 October 1992, p. D-8.

55. "U.S. Trade Journals Go Abroad for New Growth," *New York Times,* 3 February 1992, p. D-8.

56. "Magazine Advertising: Up Close and Personal," *Washington Post,* 29 December 1989, p. F-1.

57. "A Customized *Newsweek* for Subscribers," *Newsweek,* 27 April 1992, p. 1.

58. "Big Media Firms Try 'Publishing' in CD Offshoot," *Wall Street Journal,* 18 March 1991, p. 17.

59. *U.S. Industrial Outlook,* International Trade Administration, U.S. Department of Commerce, Washington, D.C., January 1992.

60. "Computers Let a Thousand Publishers Bloom," *New York Times,* 7 October 1987, p. D-1.

61. "Profits—Dick Snyder's Ugly Word," *New York Times,* 30 June 1991, p. C-4.

62. "Publishers Just Can't Say No to Some Huge Book Deals," *New York Times,* 18 May 1992, p. D-1.
63. "The Designing Computer," *New York Times,* 30 June 1991, p. C-4.
64. "Is the Electronic Book Closer Than You Think?" *New York Times,* 29 December 1991, p. E-5.
65. "Business Digest," *Washington Post,* 6 May 1992, p. F-2.
66. "Plugged-in Publishing," *Washington Post,* 5 July 1992, p. H-1.
67. Quoted in Robert Coover, "The End of Books," *New York Times Book Review,* 21 June 1992, p. 1.
68. "1991 Bright for Philips," *Variety,* 2 March 1992, p. 44.

Chapter
9

THE OPEN-ENDED FUTURE

Mass communications in the United States is clearly in the middle of a massive transition. The older media face wrenching changes as they adapt to the advancing technologies, their changing audiences, and the new challenges by computer-based information providers.

This shift has been under way, in fits and starts, for a long time. The difference now is that the pace is accelerating. The pressures placed on the media by computers and other advanced technologies are no longer fringe phenomena. They are the dominant force shaping the future of the media industries. In turn, they are altering the form and direction of U.S. society: how we see ourselves, what we think is important, and where we get the information that directs our daily decisions and activities.

We are at the edge of this change. Mass media patterns have been changing steadily in recent years (Table 9.1). Predicting future media patterns is a risky business. Anyone trying to do so 25 years ago would have had little or no forewarning of such developments as satellite broadcasting, cable TV networks, compact discs, videocassettes or personal computers, among other innovations that are setting the pace for current media developments.[1] We also need to avoid illusions about these new media, what French sociologist Jacques Ellul calls "the technological bluff." The introduction of any technological change exacts a price, he pointed out. Each innova-

TABLE 9.1   Changes in Communications Industry Spending

Industry Segment	1987	1988	1989	1990	1991	CAGR*
Television Broadcasting	4.0%	6.5%	2.5%	4.8%	−5.4%	2.4%
Radio Broadcasting	3.7	8.2	6.7	4.8	−3.2	4.0
Cable Television	11.8	20.2	14.6	11.1	10.4	13.6
Filmed Entertainment	15.6	13.4	12.2	6.2	2.4	9.9
Recorded Music	19.7	12.3	5.2	14.6	3.9	11.0
Newspaper Publishing	7.5	6.4	4.5	1.1	−3.6	3.1
Book Publishing	10.0	9.8	12.0	5.6	6.4	8.7
Magazine Publishing	6.1	5.7	9.3	3.4	−1.1	4.6
Business Information Services	13.9	10.5	8.1	6.7	6.4	9.1
Total Spending	9.2	9.2	7.7	5.1	0.9	6.4

*Compound Annual Growth Rate.
SOURCE: Veronis, Suhler & Associates, Wilkofsky Gruen Associates. Reprinted by permission of Veronis, Suhler & Associates.

tion adds something on one hand and subtracts something else on the other. In any event, all such innovations have unforeseeable effects.[2]

The current transition to a new media environment differs from past experiences, when technologies were phased in slowly. The introduction of media forms such as radio, TV, and cable was more orderly. Sufficient time elapsed between one and the next to sort out the economic and social consequences of each. The media industries now face a convergence of many technologies, which are arriving at a speed and with an urgency that narrow the time needed to assess how they will fit into an already complex pattern. This much is clear: technology is opening a wide range of options for both media producers and consumers—a welcome challenge for a democratic society that values choice and variety, particularly in information matters.

These technological options will eventually be sorted out, primarily through trial-and-error testing in the marketplace. As that occurs, there will be a vastly different pattern to the ways that the media industries organize, package, and distribute their information and entertainment products. That pattern will be shaped by political and economic elements as well as technological factors. It is this restructuring of the basic communications network that is, for the present, the most important event forcing change in media patterns. The next two decades will see the completion of a universal information utility, a resource that can be compared roughly to the networks that supply us with electricity, gas, and water. The new facility will be a high-tech extension of the telephone network, with capabilities that will extend far beyond voice telephony to include a full range of high-capacity video, graphics, and data services. Originally designed to serve big business and government needs, the network is now reaching down to homes and other consumer locations. There is a steady massification of advanced information services, including the media.[3]

Until recently, the media industries have operated largely outside this network. Although they have used it extensively for their internal operations, they have continued to issue their products in traditional formats—print, nitrate film, videotape, and the like. It is now apparent that distribution of these separate media products is beginning to merge into a single electronic "pipe," the nervous system of the evolving information utility, whose digital signals will be transformed into print, video, or sound resources for consumer use. In the process, the traditional media are being integrated into a vastly expanded communications and information sector.[4]

The prospect causes considerable hand-wringing in some quarters about the decline of the mass media, the rise of megamedia conglomerates, the beginnings of electronic Big Brotherism, and similar themes. Admittedly, there are troubling aspects to the ways in which electronic technologies could lead to more centralized controls of media and other information resources.

In fact, the probable scenario is more optimistic. Electronic production and delivery of information open vast opportunities for the traditional media as well as for their new competitors. Old ideas about the appropriate role of the media will have to be adjusted accordingly. Until now, mass communications has been defined as the industrialized production, reproduction, and multiple distribution of messages through technological devices.[5] The focus has been on information products produced in a relatively few centralized locations and distributed through separate one-way channels to large groups of consumers. The new technologies change this. Old distinctions disappear. Facsimile machines combine printed text and telephones. Interactive compact disks bring together the resources of personal computers, television, and printing devices. The telephone system becomes something else, used increasingly for nonvoice transmissions between information machines rather than for person-to-person conversations.

Media resources are being reassembled in a new pattern, consisting of three main parts. The first consists of the traditional mass media; these will remain for many years the most important element in the pattern in terms of their reach and influence. The second consists of the advanced electronic mass media; this part of the pattern operates primarily within the new information utility, competing increasingly with older media services. Finally, there is the emergence of newer forms of personal electronic media, formed by clusters of like-minded people in order to fulfill their own professional or individual information needs. Each of these aspects of the evolving mass communications pattern deserves separate scrutiny.

First, the traditional media—broadcast TV, film, radio, and print. Collectively, they are a formidable presence, with annual revenues of over $100 billion in the United States. These services will continue to expand, particularly in international markets. In a 1992 survey of global media prospects, the London *Economist* sees major gains for the U.S. media industries:

> Entertainment is America's second-biggest export earner, after aerospace. Thanks to technology, the media industry is also merging with the (even bigger) global information business, which includes computers and telecoms. In 1990, that combined total was worth $1.3 trillion. By 2000 it may reach $3 trillion—or roughly $1 out of every $6 of global GNP.[6]

The traditional media are the continuing link in the transition to a new mass communications environment. As we have seen in our survey, media industries are facing up to the need for change in the ways they produce and distribute their wares. It is not just a question of marketing old products in new ways. Increasingly, the content and purpose of the products themselves are changing. What is the daily newspaper's role in an information-saturated environment? How do television and cable TV deal with the fragmented information and entertainment needs of their viewers? How does the book business come to terms with the fact that its most profitable activity—the assembling of ideas and facts into small paper packets—can often be done more efficiently by computerized data banks held in the palm of the hand?

The second part of the new media pattern involves electronic mass communications services: consumer data banks, multimedia computers, and so forth. For the present, they make up a small part of the pattern, but they are steadily challenging the old media order. Electronic production and distribution of information are still focused primarily on the needs of large organizations, public and private. Within a decade, however, the mass consumerization of computer-based information and entertainment resources will become a commonplace fact. The transition has been slow in coming, early ventures in the field having been bedeviled by inadequate technology and consumer resistance, both of which are now being overcome.

The first computer-literate generation is already moving into the media marketplace. They are men and women who are at ease with keyboards, data disks, and video monitors. Their skills, learned in schools and offices, are now being transferred home. Consumer data services such as Prodigy and CompuServe, using ordinary telephone lines, are following. Over 3 million homes now subscribe to these services, not as exotic innovations but as useful, taken-for-granted aids to daily living.

The resources that the new computer-based technologies provide for this audience are still mainly print data, with some graphics capabilities. The next step consists of multimedia capabilities, combining data, sound, and video services in one electronic package. These services will be delivered to multimedia PCs or to telecomputers, the replacements for today's TV sets, with large, high-definition screens that are better adapted to entertainment programs. Such machines will be standard fixtures in most U.S. homes early in the next century, providing services from traditional media organizations as well as from their new electronic competitors.[7]

Finally, we will see the emergence of personal electronic media as a new form of mass communications. These are networks put together by individuals and groups that bypass the whole range of commercial information and entertainment providers. A small but important example is the 50,000 electronic bulletin boards now available to computer owners throughout the United States.[8] The most spectacular example of mass networking is the Internet, a network of networks. Internet is a high-speed data communications grid linking over 10,000 other networks, private and public, around the globe. Originally developed by the U.S. government for communications between domestic research institutes, Internet has blossomed into the world's largest data facility, with an estimated 10 million users. Internet and other data highways have turned small computers into electronic meeting places. Once the playtoys of small groups of computer buffs, bulletin boards are now available to millions of people. Exchanges of information are still made mainly by videotext. In the next few years, the range of capabilities of these networks will expand to video and sound as a new generation of multimedia computers becomes available.

Computer bulletin boards and similar developments are an electronic extension of a long tradition of "small media" that have always operated around the fringes of the larger media services. The small media include amateur and citizen-band radio grids, facsimile networks, and the vast range of special interest newsletters, magazines, and bulletins serving, collectively, tens of millions of people. These traditional small-media outlets will continue, but they will be supplemented, and perhaps eventually be replaced, by the new computer-based alternatives.

The definition of mass media will have to be modified to accommodate this changing pattern of consumer information facilities. Mass communications is undergoing mutations that are changing its traditional patterns and purposes. Increasingly, the new personal networks are taking on the characteristics of traditional mass media. These networks serve, collectively, large audiences with specific information needs, from the frivolous to the profound. They also spur the trend toward the fractionalization of mass audiences, which has been characteristic of the media in recent decades. In the process, personal networks are beginning to compete more directly with the larger mass media as information resources.

Electronic bulletin boards are only part of this restructuring of media resources. The new personal networks also include networking by touch-tone and cellular phones, audio and video cassettes, personal fax machines, small-group satellite conferencing, and low-powered television transmitters designed to serve specialized audiences. Some of these technologies may fall by the wayside, as they are replaced by more efficient methods. It will be years before their total impact can be adequately measured given the innovative, unpredictable ways they are used by individual groups, from nuclear disarmament activists to stamp collectors.

Personal electronic networking is a present-day reality, and it is changing the information habits of millions of people. Only when we shuck conventional ideas about the media can we recognize that these networks are a new form of mass communications, providing decentralized, interactive information resources that expand and often take the place of traditional mass media services. Whole telecommunities are being formed around these new resources. One early project in the 1980s, Eaglecrest, in the Sierra Nevada of California, was planned around advanced communications facilities that permitted telecommuting to old-fashioned workplaces. It also provided families with personal access to other network resources beyond anything formerly available to them.

Potentially, the new networking adds a powerful democratic dimension to U.S. society. Thirty years ago, Marshall McLuhan sent out an early-warning signal when he declared that Xerox-type machines would make Everyman his own publisher. McLuhan could not have imagined the wider prospects opened by newer technologies such as personal computers, compact disks, videocassettes, and facsimile machines. Each offers variations on the theme of liberation of individuals and groups from the need to rely on centralized media. These technologies expand the possibilities for personal initiative in creating, storing, and distributing information. The balance of power in controlling information is beginning to shift in favor of individual users.

The shift is not without its dangers. For all their faults, the mass media constitute a critical social force within a democratic society. They serve not only as information providers but also as a kind of Elmer's glue, binding people into a coherent sense of shared interests. The new personal electronic networks can also serve this purpose, or they may erode it. As communications researcher Gladys Ganley noted:

> In free societies, access to information tends to be regarded as democratizing, and therefore desirable. But such instantaneous access on such a wide scale has never before been possible and could create such unsettling shifts that the overall results might not be all positive. . . . Spread to millions of individuals throughout the world, each literally following his or her own agenda, such power could remove the glue of social cohesion, provided by limited numbers of organizations and governments. . . . Power to the people could mean that nobody is in control, with unpredictable political consequences.[9]

In a society dedicated to the extension of the marketplace of ideas, we have no choice but to accept the social risks of the new personal electronic networks.

The telecommunications industry is already restructuring its facilities to serve this new market, making it easier to form individualized networks. Electronic mail and other networking arrangements are an everyday fact of life. A breakthrough occurred in 1991 when the MCI telephone network began marketing its Friends & Family service, which offered greatly reduced rates to individuals who wanted to form their own personalized network. The company signed up 5 million customers within a few months.[10] It takes no great stretch of the imagination to see this voice service extended to data and video networking over the company's fiber-optic network. In 1992, Pacific Bell, California's telephone company, linked up with IBM and Northern Telecom to test a new multimedia consumer network integrating voice, data, and video services.[11]

Another service, scheduled for activation in the mid-1990s, may be a major channel for personal electronic networks. It is called Interactive Video Data Service (IVDS), authorized by the FCC in 1992. IVDS permits viewers to use their regular television set for interactive video links with a variety of resources, from home shopping services to educational courses. Although promoted primarily as a business marketing device, IVDS may also be used to develop consumer information and entertainment services that compete with more conventional media.

Given these developments, what will the new media pattern look like? Where will the traditional media fit in an electronic framework in which large providers and small consumers share networks? Predictions swing between extremes. At one end, there is visions of a democratic Nirvana with computerized access to vast information resources shared by everyone. At the other extreme is dark warnings of a system in which individuals and groups are fragmented into information islands, unable to connect with one another, unaware of common concerns, and lacking any shared cultural reference points. Most likely, our media future lies somewhere in between.

Michael Janeway, dean of the Medill School of Journalism, points out that "any vision of achievement of a 21st Century Great Society via computerization must be iffy, if only because technologists' ability to predict human tastes and social behavior is so notoriously poor."[12]

Dean Janeway's point is important. The effects of the new media pattern are long term and largely unpredictable. Clearly, however, the process of change is under way. Every day, uncounted numbers of decisions are being made that move us closer to a radically different mass communications structure.

The transition will be a bumpy one for both traditional media organizations and their new challengers. They will be guided primarily by the imperfect signals coming from the marketplace. What sells? What doesn't? What is the competition up to? Do we try something new or do we sit tight? The marketplace is still a useful indicator of social needs. However valuable a new product or service may appear to be, it does not become a viable choice until a seller puts a price on its value and a significant number of buyers agree. The new media services are no exception to that process.[13]

Marketplace economics will thus be a major force in determining the shape and purposes of the new mass communications structure. Market-driven decisions in the past have helped to create in the United States the most varied, open communications system in the world. In the coming years, new technologies can extend that system to a truly universal multimedia information utility. Technology and economic forces cannot, however, guarantee a fully accessible system. There will be gaps, as there are in the present system. Communications researcher Herbert Dordick points out that there are still 2 million U.S. households that do not have basic phone services, much less the prospect of plugging into exotic new information services.[14]

A case can be made for directing public-policy decisions in ways that strengthen the prospects for this advanced information system. The historical record shows that public intervention at critical points in U.S. communications development has actively encouraged better facilities and access to them.[15] The best example of this was the policy decision made over half a century ago to create the world's first interactive mass communications network. It is the U.S. telephone network, which was an elite resource in this country for 50 years after the telephone was invented. The network became universally accessible as the result of a far-reaching social decision embodied in congressional legislation—the Communications Act of 1934. The act mandated a new democratic principle: the right of citizen access to electronic communications networks. The 1934 law dealt only with the technologies of the time—telephone, telegraph, and radio broadcasting—but it has been extended, by both law and practice, to include later innovations in telecommunications.

The original policy intent of the 1934 legislation has been honored by reinterpreting the law to cover new technologies as they developed. Such ad hoc legislative adaptation is no longer adequate. The reason is that our telecommunications/information network is now much greater than its parts. And that reality should be reinforced in policy and law. The 1934 law served the country well by encouraging new technologies and by ensuring consumer access to them. It is time, however, to design effective policy instruments for a more complex information environment.

A revitalized public consensus is needed to ensure full citizen access to the high-capacity information utility now being built. There have been recurrent proposals for a top-to-bottom revision of the 1934 Communications Act to reflect present-day economic and technological realities.[16] Considering the complexity of these realities, however, it is not surprising that attempts to revise the 1934 law have failed. A more interesting and imaginative proposal, advanced by Columbia University communications scholar Elie Noam, is to define a set of general principles to guide future public policy in the communications and media fields. Specifically, Professor Noam suggests a twenty-first-century revision of the First Amendment, which would affirm the right of people to gather electronically. (Appendix A gives the full text.)

Such a public affirmation of electronic rights could be useful in defining a broad national agenda for the new information environment. Admittedly, no general principles by themselves will ensure a satisfactory outcome. The process will also be driven by the ongoing push-pull of economic and political interests, involving a continuing series of compromises and accommodations. In the accepted U.S. tradition, everyone concerned will get something; no one will get everything. A perennial consequence of the process is that public policy, as always, lags behind marketplace developments.[17]

A case in point is the present maneuvering of the telephone companies and the cable TV systems to decide which industry will have the lead role in providing the high-capacity, multimedia links into U.S. homes. The outcome of that contest is critical to the prospects for a universal information utility, with particular implications for the mass media industries. Congress, the White House, and the courts have all been involved in attempts to define public policies on the issue. Their decisions, however useful or well meaning, will serve primarily to validate what is already happening in the marketplace. In this case, the cable and phone industries are making their own deals, which, in effect, will divide the market between them.

Some form of large-scale information utility will be built, with or without a coherent public consensus. Sooner or later, however, such a consensus must be considered, which addresses the question of how the resource can open us up to a new world of information richness.

Meanwhile, the restructuring of communications channels will bring kaleidoscopic changes in the media, both the traditional sectors and their new electronic competitors. The transition to this new media environment will not be easy. Most of the old guidelines are being smudged or even wiped out. Media managers face difficult decisions on the pace at which they will adapt to technological changes. The temptation to stick with old products and practices will be strong. It will be reinforced by the resistance that consumers have put up against adopting many of the new electronic services. Surveys of cable TV subscribers over the years have shown that most viewers limit themselves to five or six channels. The idea of 150 channels, now being installed in many cable systems, leaves them nonplussed.[18] Moreover, many of the new technologies involve more expense for both media providers and consumers. Television and videocassettes gained almost instant consumer acceptance in past years because they were relatively cheap, were easy to use, and delivered a recognizable, attractive service. Mass adoption of the new electronic services is proving to be much slower.

Meanwhile, the media industries must deal with more immediate problems. These include the fragmentation of their traditional audiences, in part because of changing national demographics. Population growth in the coming decade will take place overwhelmingly within the African-American, Hispanic, and Asian communities. By the end of the century, white citizens in the bellwether state of California will probably be in the minority. Previous assumptions about leisure habits, cultural tastes, and spending patterns will have to be rethought by the media industries.[19]

As we have seen, these industries also face the well-documented erosion of their audience among younger age groups, particularly in the film, newspaper, and magazine sectors. This trend began in the 1960s with the generation whose ideas and interests were formed by Vietnam, Woodstock, and other symbols of alienation. The media industries assumed that the disaffection was temporary and that younger people would "come home" to the older information outlets in due course.

With some exceptions, this has not happened. The media audience erosion continues, particularly among news outlets. The respected Times Mirror Center for the People and the Press has been tracking this trend for decades. In its 1990 survey, the center reported that, among young people, 42 percent were nonusers of *any* kind of news media. Overall, the survey found that young Americans, aged 18–30, know less and care less about news and public affairs than any other generation of Americans in the past half century. The report concluded:

> With the advent of satellite technology, CNN, and ever-longer local news broadcasts, one might expect that young people would know more than ever before. . . . The ultimate irony of the Times Mirror findings is that the Information Age has spawned such an uninformed and uninvolved population.[20]

Hand-wringing over the shortcomings of young people is hardly new. The Times Mirror survey, like most of its kind, tends to equate current affairs literacy with usage of traditional print media—newspapers, magazines, and the like. There is some evidence, though, that technohip youth are turning to computers for their information; the Times Mirror survey found an increase in computer usage among young people, which may compensate somewhat for the decrease in newspaper reading. It is clear, however, that the under-30 generation relies less and less on traditional print media for facts and opinions about present-day issues. Moreover, this generation is a dropout audience, not one that is migrating in any great numbers to newer and better sources of information on current events. These demographic developments are forcing the media industries to reassess their product lines. What new computer-based products will sell in today's market? How much should we invest? Who is the audience and how should we reach it? The answers to these questions will determine the corporate winners and losers in the new information environment.

Current wisdom among many media observers suggests that the winners will be the new breed of big multimedia conglomerates, primarily because they may be best able to handle the diversity of new demands. These "information packagers" have evolved in two ways—by cross-ownership between media firms and by the acquisition of media by nonmedia concerns. Time Warner and Rupert Murdoch's News Corp. are typical examples of the former; Sony's and Matsushita's takeovers of two major Hollywood studios represent the latter. The heyday of media mergers occurred in the mid-1980s. Seventy-seven major deals were carried out by 13 large media firms between 1983 and 1987. More than half of the transactions involved European and Canadian companies.[21] A relatively small group of megamedia firms now have an outsized influence on the pace and direction of the industry.

Are these companies the media wave of the future? Perhaps not. Despite their size, they represent a relatively small share of the total media market in the United States and abroad. The orthodox justification for media conglomeratization is that news and entertainment companies must expand or die. They are industries with large fixed costs and high product risks. The classic examples of the latter are the Hollywood studios, most of whose films are financial failures. For all their undoubted successes, the big multimedia firms have still not mastered the trick of producing best-sellers, hit records, or blockbuster films on a consistent basis. The primary reason is not bad management or other incompetence, although that occurs. A more basic reason is that the success of the big firms' products usually depends on a fragile element—the often erratic tastes of a variegated consumer public.

Only media giants, the argument goes, can absorb failures and wait for the high returns from more successful products. This was the thinking that created the spree of media mergers and acquisitions in the 1980s. It was bolstered by the idea that synergies between different media products could be exploited by vertically integrated companies. Books could beget films that could beget cable TV profits and so on.

The idea was both intriguing and simplistic. In the years since the merger mania, media synergies have had mixed results. One of the fervent believers in synergistic operations was Rupert Murdoch. By 1990, however, no more than 15 percent of the total revenues of his multimedia enterprises came from vertically integrated operations.[22] Murdoch and other megamerger entrepreneurs may be able to improve on that record, but until now, media synergies have not been a decisive benefit for them.

Consider, for instance, the 1989 merger of Time Inc. and Warner Communications, which created the world's largest multimedia corporation. On paper it was the perfect media marriage, involving a full range of film, magazine, book, cable TV, and record resources. In the ensuing years, however, successful synergies among the Time Warner products have been few and far between, generating a small percentage of the new firm's activities. One problem is that Time Warner has been a marriage of unequals. By 1992, Warner's operations were producing two-thirds of the firm's revenues. Moreover, the new company was saddled with a staggering debt as a result of the merger. Although the original merger proposal was to have been a simple debt-free exchange of stock, the negotiations ended up with Time's borrowing $14 billion to buy Warner outright. Managing the debt has seriously hobbled Time Warner's ability to put its synergistic plans into practice. The firm did not make its first annual net profit until 1992. The merger also proved to be a psychological mismatch. The somewhat buttoned-down attitudes of Time's New York managers did not mix readily with the open-shirt-and-gold-chain style of its new Hollywood partners. The two corporate cultures clashed, causing tensions at the upper management levels and confusion in the lower ranks.[23] These tensions were heightened by the ostentatious way in which the firm's top managers compensated themselves at a time when lower-level employees were being fired. The late Steven J. Ross, who, as head of Warner

Communications, was primarily responsible for the 1989 merger, received $78.2 million in salary and bonuses in 1990.

The Time Warner merger was not a typical megamerger deal, if only because of its sheer size. It provides a case history, however, of problems that also plague other corporate attempts to get synergy out of their multimedia resources. Like Time Warner, other information packagers are finding that individual media sectors—films, books, magazines, and so on—have operational styles that are not always easy to meld into winning combinations.

Future expectations for the big-scale conglomerates will differ from sector to sector. Consider the film industry: Hollywood today, as in the past, is dominated by a half dozen major studios. Two of these, Fox and Warner, are controlled by large media conglomerates—Time Warner and Rupert Murdoch's News Corp. In both cases, the studios are doing well as independent units. There is, however, little evidence to date that they have been successful in advancing the synergistic multimedia strategies of their owners. A more interesting Hollywood story is the attempt by two Japanese electronics companies, Sony and Matsushita, to integrate their recently acquired studio properties, Columbia and MCA. In each case, they wanted to strengthen their consumer equipment operations, by ensuring a supply of entertainment software for their videocassette recorders and similar products. In both cases these experiments in vertical integration of software and hardware products have been inconclusive. Sony and Matsushita have each experienced difficulties in reconciling Japanese corporate styles with the free-swinging fiscal practices of their new Hollywood affiliates. Both companies have invested large amounts of new capital in their film operations, often with less than successful results. In 1991, for example, profits from MCA's film and television division reportedly were down 50 percent, an event that sent corporate shock waves through Matsushita's headquarters in Osaka.[24] Overall, Sony Pictures has been more successful in its entertainment operations, raising its annual operating profit from $150 million in 1989-1990 to $305 million in 1992-1993.

In the publications sector, multimedia conglomerates have had only sporadic success in developing synergies between their print products and their other media holdings. Large newspaper and magazine firms have focused primarily on buying up other publications, resulting in so-called chain ownership. The traditional argument against chain ownership has been that it discourages diversity of news and editorial opinion at the local level. This has happened to some extent in newspaper buyouts. The overall trend in chain publishing, however, is to leave editorial matters up to the local editors. If anything, this indifference has encouraged editorial blandness, a journalistic failure not limited to chain publishing.

Chain ownership of newspapers has reduced or eliminated competition in many cities. In general, this occurs because of the ability of the large chains to finance and manage their properties more effectively. However, increases in one-newspaper towns cannot be blamed exclusively on the increase in chain ownership. Another reason is the well-documented decrease in total U.S. newspaper readership.

In television broadcasting, industry dominance by the big three networks is ending. Twenty-five years ago, ABC, NBC, and CBS controlled, through direct ownership or affiliation, almost all local stations. They also produced the major share of prime-time entertainment programming. Both of these advantages have been seriously eroded in recent years. The production of and the profits from prime-time entertainment programs are now centered in the Hollywood studios, following an FCC decision that effectively eliminated network ownership of these shows. Local station affiliates are operating more independently of the networks. Cable TV has cut deeply into broadcast television's audience base. There is also new competition from a fourth network, Fox Television, and from the rapid increase in the number of independent stations. The outcome has been a greater quantity, although not necessarily a better quality, of broadcast television programming at both the national and local levels.[25]

In the area of cable television, the trend toward conglomeratization is striking. Here, a half dozen companies control most local cable networks under virtually monopolistic conditions. These conglomerates also have effective control over the most popular cable programming, particularly satellite-delivered services such as HBO, Showtime, and the sports networks. They have, moreover, tried to use this control to exclude competing program providers. This oligopolistic situation poses a serious threat to media competition and diversity. The threat is heightened as the major cable companies move aggressively to supply hundreds of channels of multimedia services to U.S. homes and other consumer locations. Under circumstances of normal competition, such extended services would be a welcome development, contributing to greater diversity of information and entertainment.

The circumstances are not, however, normal. Cable conglomerates have lobbied hard to preserve their control over local networks and the program services they supply. Their efforts are comparable to those that took place in the film and television broadcasting industries a generation ago. The big film studios controlled most Hollywood production, as well as the major theater chains through which their films were distributed. In television, ABC, CBS, and NBC had similar control over network programming and their affiliated local station outlets. The industry-wide vertical integration in films and television severely restricted outside competition. This did not change until the federal government stepped in under the antitrust laws, forcing the big studios to sell off their theater holdings. In television, the big three networks were required to open program acquisition to outside producers.

Although the cable TV industry's control over both programs and distribution outlets is similar to earlier experiences with films and television, there is an important difference. Vertical integration of production and distribution in films and television involved, in each case, a single media product. However, the cable industry's hold on vertical integration takes in *all* major media—film, television, radio, and print— which can be delivered electronically to homes and other consumer locations through high-capacity lines. Congressional legislation, passed in 1992, attempted to limit some of the more outrageous monopolistic practices by the cable industry. The effects of the legislation in curbing these excesses will not be measurable for years. Meanwhile, the telephone companies are pressing for advantages in supplying multimedia services to U.S. homes. As we saw in Chapter 4, the cable and telephone industries have enlisted powerful political and economic resources in the fight over control of high-capacity consumer circuits and the media resources that flow through them.[26] The outcome of this debate is critical to the future of U.S. mass communications.

Media conglomeratization may be affected by an opposite trend in America, namely, the backlash against big corporations in general. The assumption that mega-corporations are efficient has held sway for most of this century. That notion is now challenged by a broad range of economists, both conservative and liberal. Their consensus is based on the weak performance by many parts of the economy (auto, steel, etc.) in recent years. They now argue for the disassembling of giant corporations into smaller, more efficient parts—the "unbundling of America," as the Manhattan Institute's Peter Huber described it.[27] Such restructuring has already begun throughout the economy, and the big media conglomerates are not immune. They are, in fact, prime candidates for unbundling in future years. They may find themselves at a disadvantage when smaller, more innovative firms emerge that can deal more effectively with new technological opportunities and respond to the demographic and economic fragmentation that characterizes all media audiences now.

This may not happen for some time. Until then, large media organizations will continue to be an important factor on the U.S. media scene. There are recurrent proposals for curbing the power of megamedia firms in the interest of ensuring greater diversity of information from more sourccs. British communications scholar Anthony Smith has suggested that the alternative may be that "the democratic process itself is placed in thrall to a company or individual that may be pursuing, albeit quite legitimately, ends that are at variance with other objectives of a society."[28] The problem, according to media critic Ben Bagdikian, is not that the big firms are evil media empires but that they tend to dominate the economics, operating styles, and product content of all of the media sectors.

This conflict between individual rights and communal needs is, of course, a continuing one. The U.S. experience has been to refrain from control over media and other information resources, in the interests of diversity and individual expression. Fitting these principles into the new media environment presents special difficulties. With the expansion of electronic channels, the possibilities for misusing them become more serious as those channels become more sophisticated. Computer graphics technology has reached a point where it can create digitized representations of people and events that are fictional but virtually indistinguishable from reality.[29] First Amendment rights in the new electronic environment are still unclear. Are the new computerized media networks akin to telephone networks, with their assurance of privacy and open information exchange? Or are they the equivalents of electronic newspapers, where libel laws and other limitations apply?[30] Confusingly, they can be both, and drawing the line between the two is difficult.

These First Amendment questions are not always hypothetical. In 1991, for example, the Prodigy consumer data network became involved in a controversy challenging the right of electronic free speech. Prodigy's services include an electronic-mail network in which subscribers exchange views on a wide variety of subjects, some of them dealing with controversial issues. One such exchange was an electronic discussion of whether the Holocaust of World War II was a hoax—an outlandish theory promoted by a small fringe group. The electronic exchanges included statements that were clearly anti-Semitic. After complaints by the Anti-

Defamation League of B'nai B'rith, Prodigy's managers decided to allow the electronic exchange on the subject to continue. However, they also changed Prodigy's guidelines by banning statements that are "grossly repugnant expressions of bigotry and hate"—an action that was challenged by the American Civil Liberties Union.[31] In 1993, in another case, Prodigy closed down its "Frank Discussion" electronic bulletin board, which was intended to deal with general social issues, because many subscribers objected to the sexually explicit messages carried on the service.

These events are examples of the First Amendment issues implicit in the new electronic mass media. Outright censorship is not the only problem. Censorship usually involves an overt action that can be debated and resolved. Other issues raise more difficult questions about the suppression or alteration of the flow of information through electronic networks. Some of these techniques involve direct electronic manipulation of media messages. Other practices are more subtle, hidden in a complex pattern of conventional information. Control mechanisms can invade networks softly and invisibly, without, so to speak, leaving fingerprints or other incriminating evidence. Such intrusions are hard to identify and harder to prevent, since they often involve routine electronic functions whose threat to personal liberties is not self-evident.

Such practices are not the only barriers to full utilization of the new electronic media networks. Thirty years ago, political scientist Karl Deutsch proposed that advanced information resources must be made universally available if modern democratic societies are to thrive and survive. Information is power, he pointed out, and, more important, it is a multiplier of power. The problem is complicated by a rising flood of media messages and other information that pushes us toward the limit of human capacity to cope with them. The solution, Professor Deutsch suggested, is a new approach to what he called intelligence amplification, taking advantage of new information technologies in ways that permit more effective access to the information we need to function individually and as members of an advanced democratic society.[32]

Access to media and other information resources in the United States is unequal for many reasons. Not the least of these reasons is that tens of millions of Americans are functionally illiterate. Illiteracy is, in turn, both a cause and an effect of economic disparities. Over 2 million U.S. families do not have telephone service; many more are not connected to cable systems or other electronic channels. Therefore they lack the means to plug into present-day communications channels, much less to take advantage of advanced services.

Economist Robert Reich emphasized the impact that this information gap has on U.S. society: "No longer are Americans rising or falling together, as if in one large boat. We are, increasingly, in different, smaller boats." If present trends continue into the next generation, he notes, the top 20 percent of U.S. earners will account for more than 60 percent of all earned income; the bottom fifth, for 2 percent.[33] Increasingly, the factor that separates U.S. economic classes is information access and control. Media critic Terry Curtis suggested that we are moving toward a computer-generated caste system.[34] At the top of the scale is the information elite, which prospers because it knows how to use the new resources. Farther down the scale is the information *lumpenproletariat,* which lacks the skills and the will to cope with advanced technologies.

This may be an information age version of Darwin's survival of the fittest. However, the analogy is flawed. The information poor will not become extinct. They have political and social power to strike back. Communications technologies have augmented the ability of disadvantaged groups to demonstrate their grievances—witness the impact of TV reportage of inner-city riots and similar events.

America's disenfranchised are less willing to accept second-class status until economic and social benefits, including those promised by advanced information services, trickle down to them through the market system. In an interdependent postindustrial society, the risks of excluding these groups from the new resources are high.

The mass media have an important *mediating* role to play both in documenting the new realities and in providing a forum for discussing them. Will the new media services accept that role, so necessary to our individual and collective survival in the new postindustrial environment?

There are powerful forces, inside and outside the industry, favoring greater trivialization of information. "Infotainment" is the buzzword among media producers and advertising executives these days as they grapple with the problem of retaining their audiences in highly competitive markets. Gresham's Law, defining how the bad drives out the good, operates as readily in the media business as in any other. Will we, in media critic Neil Postman's scathing phrase, find that we are amusing ourselves to death in the new communications environment?

These issues are part of the larger question concerning how advanced information technologies can change the ways we see ourselves and how we relate to the world around us. We communicate primarily to tell stories. These stories both reflect and re-form our self-images and our communal values. For most of human history, stories were told by storytellers to small groups of listeners, gathered in a village square or by a fireside. It is only in the past 500 years that the role of the storyteller has begun to be replaced by a machine-produced resource—the printed book. Now we are moving into the age of image communications—first photography, then film and television, and now multimedia computing. These resources deliver powerful messages to enormously expanded audiences. Battered by their drumbeat pervasiveness, our defenses against them begin to break down. The result, too often, is a loss of the purposes and interconnectedness by which we were sustained—personally and as a community.[35]

As we have seen throughout our survey, the media industries are being transformed by technological, economic, and social forces. Those forces can either reinforce the dominant influence of the older centralized media or disperse it in new, more democratic ways. The options are still open. Too much of what today's media produces tends more to reflect narcissistic and escapist trends in U.S. society rather than to lead in defining the problems and opportunities before us.

The good news is that these patterns are being challenged. The new communications technologies have the ability to widen and diversify the control of information, giving more power to individual users and groups. This prospect can add a dramatic new dimension both to democratic information resources and to the shape and purpose of U.S. society in the next century.

NOTES

1. The perils of technological prediction in the electronics field are documented in Carolyn Marvin, *When Old Technologies Were New* (New York: Oxford University Press, 1988).
2. Jacques Ellul, "The Technological Order," *Technology and Culture* 3, no. 4 (Fall 1962): 394.
3. For a useful survey of the information utility's prospects, see *Universal Telephone Service: Ready for the 21st Century?* Annual Review of the Institute for Information Studies (Queenstown, Md.: Aspen Institute, 1991).
4. For a useful summary of these trends, see John D. Lockton Jr., "Information Age Developments in Telecommunications," in William Dutton, Jay Blumler, and Kenneth Kraemer (eds.), *Wired Cities: Shaping the Future of Communications* (Boston: G. K. Hall, 1986), 131–138.
5. For a discussion of the relationship between mass media and mass communications, see Joseph Turow, *Media Systems in Society* (New York: Longman, 1992), 9–10.
6. "The Media Mess," *Economist* (London), 29 February 1992, p. 17.
7. Frederick Williams, "Network Information Services as a New Public Medium," *Media Studies Journal* 5, no. 4 (Fall 1991): 137–151.
8. This estimate of electronic bulletin board use was made by Jack Rickard, editor of *Boardwatch,* a magazine about on-line services, in "Rights on the Line," *Washington Post,* 1 October 1991, p. E-5.
9. Gladys D. Ganley, "Power to the People via Personal Electronic Media," *Washington Quarterly* 10, no. 3 (Spring 1991): 20.
10. "MCI's Winning Pitch," *Business Week,* 23 March 1992, p. 36.
11. "IBM Launches Laptop in Color," *Financial Times* (London), 25 March 1992, p. 23.
12. Michael C. Janeway, "Power and Weakness of the Press," in *Media Studies Journal* 5, no. 4 (Fall 1991): 11.
13. For a spirited defense of the marketplace as a reliable arbiter for media industries, see Mark Fowler and Daniel Brenner, "A Marketplace Approach to Broadcast Regulation," *Texas Law Review* 60, no. 2: 207–257.
14. Herbert S. Dordick, "Towards a Universal Definition of Universal Service," in *Universal Telephone Service,* Institute for Information Studies annual review, 1991, p. 120.
15. For a thoughtful review of the relationship between marketplace realities and wider public needs, see Robert M. Entman and Steven S. Wildman, "Reconciling Economic and Non-Economic Perspectives on Media Policy: Transcending the 'Marketplace of Ideas,'" *Journal of Communications* 42, no. 1 (Winter 1992): 5–18.
16. For a review of these attempts, see Wilson Dizard, *The Coming Information Age,* 3d ed. (New York: Longman, 1989), 166–168.
17. Jeffrey Abramson, Christopher Arterton, and Garry Orren, *The Electronic Commonwealth: The Impact of New Communications Technologies on Democratic Politics* (New York: Basic Books, 1988).
18. "Quantity Time on Cable," *Washington Post,* 12 February 1992, p. C-1.
19. For a discussion of this issue, see Dorothy Butler Gilliam, "Media Diversity: Harnessing the Assets of a Multicultural Future," *Media Studies Journal* 5, no. 4 (Fall 1991): pp. 127–135.

20. "The Age of Indifference: A Study of Young Americans and How They View the News," Times Mirror Center for the People and the Press, Washington, D.C., June 1990, pp. 1, 3.
21. Greg MacDonald, *The Emergence of Multi-Media Conglomerates,* Working Paper No. 70, Multinational Enterprises Program, International Labor Organization, Geneva, Switzerland, 1990, p. 13.
22. "Time-Warner and the Shrinking Media World," *Broadcasting,* 13 March 1989, p. 27. The classic failure in multimedia conglomerates was the collapse of Britain's Maxwell Communications in 1992, following the death of its founder, Robert Maxwell. The details surrounding this event were documented by investigative reporter Bronwen Maddox in "The Big Lie: Inside Maxwell's Empire," a six-part series in the *Financial Times* (London), 14–19 June 1992.
23. The Time Warner merger and its aftermath are expertly documented in Richard Clurman, *To the End of Time* (New York: Simon & Schuster, 1992).
24. "The Osaka Decision," *New York Times,* 3 May 1992, p. F-1; also "Will Intramural Squabbling Derail Debt-Ridden Sony?" *New York Times,* 11 August 1991, p. F-5.
25. These changes in the networks' fortunes are recorded in Ken Auletta, *Three Blind Mice* (New York: Random House, 1991).
26. For a useful summary of the contending arguments, see "Cable TV Battling Phone Companies," *New York Times,* 29 March 1992, p. 1.
27. Peter Huber, "The Unbundling of America," *Forbes,* 13 April 1992, p. 118.
28. Anthony Smith, *The Age of Behemoths: The Globalization of Mass Media Firms* (New York: Priority, 1991), 71.
29. "Do Adjust Your Set," *Financial Times* (London), 30 December 1986, p. 14.
30. The debate on media freedoms in the electronic age is lively and growing. See Fred H. Cate (ed.), *Visions of the First Amendment for a New Millennium,* Annenberg Washington Program, Washington, D.C., 1992; "The First Amendment—the Third Century," special issue of *Journalism Quarterly* 69, no. 1 (Spring 1992): 5–123; "Electronic Media Regulation and the First Amendment," Forum Report No. 14, Aspen Institute Program on Communications and Society, Queenstown, Md., 1991; "Celebrating the First Amendment," *Columbia Journalism Review* 30, no. 4 (November/December 1991): 41–55.
31. "Computer Networks to Ban 'Repugnant' Comments," *Washington Post,* 24 October 1991, p. 1.
32. Karl Deutsch, *The Nerves of Government* (New York: Free Press of Glencoe, 1963).
33. Robert Reich, *The Work of Nations* (New York: Alfred A. Knopf, 1991), 302.
34. Terry Curtis, "The Information Society: A Computer-Generated Caste System," in Vincent Mosco and Janet Wasko (eds.), *The Political Economy of Information* (Madison, Wis.: University of Wisconsin Press, 1988), 95–107.
35. The point is argued persuasively in Neil Postman, *Technology: The Surrender of Culture to Technology* (New York: Alfred A. Knopf, 1992).

Appendix

PRINCIPLES FOR THE COMMUNICATIONS ACT OF 2034

A proposal made by Dr. Eli M. Noam, director of Columbia University's Institute for Tele-Information, that would establish a new legal basis for protecting citizen rights in the new electronic information environment: Dr. Noam's restatement of First Amendment principles was presented at Massachusetts Institute of Technology in October 1991.

1. PREAMBLE

We, the people, in order to create a more perfect union of various transmission and content media, have established principles by which all electronic communications should be governed, with the goals of encouraging the production of information of many types, sources and destinations; ensuring the existence of multiple pathways of information; encouraging their spread across society, the economy, and the world; and advancing social and economic well-being, technology, and education.

2. FREEDOMS OF SPEECH AND TRANSMISSION

Freedom of content is technology neutral. Government shall not prohibit the free exercise of communications or abridge the freedom of electronic speech or of the content provided by the electronic press or of the right of the people to peaceably assemble electronically.

3. COMMON CARRIAGE

All electrons and photons are created equal. Carriers operating as a common carrier must be neutral as to content, use, and users. The transmission of lawful communications shall not be restricted by a common carrier. Common carriers are not liable for the use to which their conduit is put.

Where no competition exists in a conduit, it must be offered on a common carrier basis on at least *part* of the capacity. Competitive transmission segments need not be common carriers. *But* if a transmission segment interconnects with or accesses other networks by taking advantage of common carrier access rights, then it must offer such rights reciprocally on part of its capacity, without discriminatory terms or conditions of service.

Any party complying with a conduit's reasonable technical specification may interconnect into, access, or exit any common carrier conduit segments at interface points, which must be provided at technologically and economically reasonable intervals.

4. MARKET STRUCTURE

Government shall make no law establishing a network privileged in terms of territory, function, or national origin. Nor shall it burden any network more than its competitors', except with compensation.

A conduit may offer carriage of any type of service over its conduit and may interconnect with any type of carrier. Monopolistic conduit segments can be accessed by their own content services only where adequate capacity is available for common carrier access and subject to antitrust principles.

Competitive conduits and all content can be priced freely. Prices for noncompetitive conduit segments are presumptively regulated where their increase exceeds inflation, taking into account other important factors, too. Prices for noncompetitive conduit segments cannot be set such that they distort competition for nonmonopolistic services.

For competitive conditions in a market segment to be said to exist, three or more offerers of substantially similar or equivalent services constitute a rebuttable presumption. With two, evidence of vigorous price competition is necessary.

Spectrum use is a property right that is sold or leased out by the government and can be used flexibly. Frequency zoning for the clustering of services may be instituted.

5. PRIVACY

Electronic information cannot be searched and seized arbitrarily by the state.

Electronic information is the property of its creators or assignees. Where information is created by a transaction involving two parties, they normally hold the property jointly, and the consent of both is needed for the use of the information. Each party should disclose jeopardies of privacy to the other.

6. SUBSIDIZED SERVICES

Financial support for some users (e.g., universal service) and to content providers, contents, or technologies, where instituted by government, must be generated and allocated explicitly and the burden of such support be placed on general revenue or equally on all competitors.

Where the development of new communications services or technologies requires coordination efforts and the creation of a critical mass of users, and where the service in question is of clear societal benefit, government may support such efforts in their infancy stage.

7. JURISDICTION

Information must move freely across interstate and international borders, without unreasonable burdens by state or national jurisdictions. No content or carrier should be treated in a country more restrictively than domestic providers are. But the right to equivalent treatment in another country requires reciprocity at home.

Federal jurisdiction (in the United States) sets basic national telecommunications policy where it deems national solutions to be clearly necessary. It may delegate flexibility in application and implementation to lower-level governmental bodies, which may also set policy for functions of clearly local nature.

Where a non-common carrier serves horizontal groupings of users in the same industry, its exclusion of other users is subject to antitrust principles.

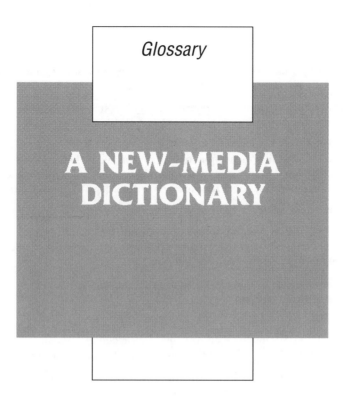

Glossary

A NEW-MEDIA DICTIONARY

Addressability. The function in a cable television system that allows a subscriber to contact, through keypad input, the system's central office in order to receive special programs (e.g., pay-per-view entertainment).

Amplitude modulation (AM). In broadcasting, a method of modulating electrical impulses in which the amplitude (power) is varied and the frequency remains constant. AM is used in the radio broadcast band (540–1,605 kilohertz), in the picture portion of television transmissions, and in shortwave broadcasting.

Analog. In telecommunications transmissions, the representation of numerical or alphanumerical values by physical variables (e.g., voltage, current). See Digital.

Artificial intelligence. A computer's capability to perform functions normally associated with human intelligence (i.e., reasoning and learning). Early attempts to replicate human thought have been overtaken by more limited but practical applications such as neural networking.

Aspect ratio. The ratio of a television screen's width to its height. Current television sets have a 4:3 aspect ratio. High-definition television sets will have aspect ratios that will provide a wider screen.

Associated Press (AP) principle. A modern restatement of First Amendment media freedoms, stemming from a 1945 court decision in which the AP was held to be in violation of antitrust laws for prohibiting service to nonmembers and allowing members to blackball competitors for membership.

Automated number information system. The process by which cable TV systems can provide interactive services (e.g., pay-per-view television).

"Baby Bells." The seven regional telephone companies created as a result of the 1984 divestiture of AT&T's local telephone holdings. The Baby Bells, known more formally as the Regional Bell Holding Companies, will be primary suppliers of phone company information and entertainment services to homes once their legal right to do so is clarified.

Bandwidth. The range within a band of wavelengths, frequencies, or energies.

Basic services. A Federal Communications Commission designation for transmission capacity offered by a common carrier (e.g., phone companies) to move information between two or more points. See: Value-added services.

Baud. A measure of signaling speed in a digital communications circuit. The speed in baud is the number of signal elements per second.

Betamax. The videocassette standard supported by Sony in the 1980s, which was superseded by Matsushita's VHS standard. Although Betamax faded as a standard for home VCRs, it continues to be used for other applications within the media industries.

Bit. A contraction of "binary digit," a bit is the smallest unit of information that a computer recognizes. A bit is represented by the presence or absence of an electronic impulse, usually symbolized by a zero or a figure one.

Broadband. A signal that requires a large bandwidth to be transmitted, alternately applied to equipment that must be capable of receiving or transmitting accurately a signal with a large bandwidth.

Byte. A group of adjacent binary digits (often shorter than a word) that a computer processes as a unit. Usually, one byte is eight bits long.

Cable antenna television (CATV). The original name for cable television systems that provided coaxial cable retransmission of over-the-air television. The name was dropped after the introduction of national satellite-delivered channels in the 1970s.

Cable-telco debate. The political and economic contest between telephone companies and the cable TV industry to gain the upper hand in supplying multimedia information and entertainment services to U.S. households.

Chapter. One independent, self-contained segment of a computer program or an interactive video program.

Chip. A silicon-based device on which microscopic electronic circuitry is printed photographically to create passive and active devices, circuit paths, and device connections within the solid structure.

Coaxial cable. Insulated cable used to transmit telephone and television signals in a high-frequency mode. "Coax" has been the standard channel carrier for cable TV.

Coder/decoder (CODEC). A series of integrated circuits that perform a specific analog-to-digital conversion, such as the conversion of an analog voice signal to a digital bit stream, or an analog television signal converted to a digital format.

Common carrier. The provision of transmission capability over a telecommunications network. A common carrier company offers public communications services. It is subject to regulation by federal and state regulatory bodies that establish operating rules and tariffs in order to make the services available at a fair price and on a nondiscriminatory basis. Telephone companies are common carriers.

Communications Act of 1934. The basic national legislation governing electronic communications. The act mandated a national telephone system—the first such legislation to recognize the importance of telecommunications for social and economic growth. In the new age of advanced electronic media, a similar consensus is needed.

Compact disk. An optical storage medium, used for music and for computer data, among other services.

Compact disc audio (CD-A). A popular compact disc format for high-fidelity digital music. Each disk offers up to 75 minutes of programmable sound with no degradation of quality during playback.

Compact disk interactive (CD-I). A disk storage medium for interactive audio, video, and data information. Pioneered by Sony and Philips, CD-I was originally developed for business training uses. It is currently being introduced into the home market, with marketing efforts focused on consumer information and entertainment applications.

Compact disk–read-only memory (CD-ROM). A prerecorded, nonerasible disk that stores up to 600 megabytes of digital data. On the market since the late 1980s, early applications have focused on reference materials, databases, and audio and video files.

Compression. The reduction of certain parameters of a signal while preserving the basic information content. The result is to improve overall transmission efficiency and to reduce cost. In media operations, the most extensive use of compression techniques is in cable TV coaxial cable, where compression can double or triple the number of available channels.

Compunications. A description, proposed by Harvard Professor Anthony Oettinger, of the convergence of computer and telecommunications technology, which results in an integrated information network.

CompuServe. A consumer data network, owned by H&R Block, which provides an extensive range of information services for PC owners.

Customer premises equipment (CPE). Any advanced telecommunications network equipment located on the premises of the customer (e.g., a PBX telephone device). The phrase is also used by telephone companies to refer to customer-provided (as opposed to company-provided) equipment in offices and homes.

Cyberspace. A computer-generated artificial environment designed to maximize the user's freedom of movement and imagination.

Data. Alphabetical or numerical representations of facts or concepts, in a manner suitable for communication, interpretation, or processing by human or automatic means.

Data communications. The transfer, reception, and validation of data between a source and a receiver via one or more data links, using appropriate code conversions or protocols.

Desktop publishing. The editing and layout of newspapers and other publications on small computers, using specialized software. Text, photos, and graphics are assembled electronically, then transmitted for final printing.

Digital. A method of signal representation by a set of discrete numerical values (ones and zeros), as opposed to a continuously fluctuating current or voltage. See: Analog.

Digital audio broadcasting (DAB). Digital transmission of sound signals by cable, terrestrial microwave, or communications satellites. DAB will eventually replace AM and FM technology in radio broadcasting.

Digital audio tape (DAT). A tape format for storing digital audio signals. Each tape can store more than 2.5 gigabytes of data. DAT is often used as a computer storage backup system.

Digital video interactive (DVI). A technology for compressing and decompressing video and audio to create multimedia applications. DVI can store up to 72 minutes of full-motion video on a compact disc. Using DVI, a viewer can interact with the image being shown. As an example, a viewer may "walk" through a computer-generated building, seeing details of the interior from any angle.

Direct broadcasting satellite (DBS). A communications satellite whose signal both radiates over a large area and is capable of being picked up by small earth stations. DBS technology has been used in recent years to deliver information and entertainment services to homes and other locations.

Direct-read-after-draw (DRAW). An optical-disc technology that allow a user to record material that cannot be erased. A high-powered laser "burns" pits into a heat-sensitive layer beneath the surface of a recordable disc. The information is then read by a lower-power laser.

Disk. A flat, circular, rotating platter that can store and replay various types of information, both analog and digital. "Disk" is often used when describing magnetic storage media. "Disc" usually refers to optical storage media.

Divestiture Agreement. The plan, finalized in 1984, in which AT&T and the federal government set the terms for AT&T's relinquishment of control over its local phone companies in exchange for permission to enter the information services market. The resultant document is also called the Modified Final Judgment.

Dynabook. A concept advanced by MIT researcher Alan Kay to describe an all-purpose handheld computer that would store vast amounts of data, as well as have the capability to access other data sources.

Dynamic random access memory (DRAM). A type of computer memory in which information can be stored and retrieved in miscellaneous order, but which must be "maintained" or refreshed by a periodic electrical charge if the memory is not read out or used immediately.

Electronic data interchange (EDI). Networks that eliminate intermediate steps in processes that rely on transmission of paper-based instructions and documents by performing them electronically, computer to computer. EDI networking is growing rapidly in the United States.

Electronic mail. The forwarding, storage, and retrieval of messages by electronic transmission systems, usually using digital techniques.

Electronic manuscript production. In book production, computerized tracking of the preparation of the book on a day-by-day basis, including keeping current tallies on costs, man-hours, and production scheduling.

Electronic news gathering (ENG). In broadcasting, coverage of events outside the studio through the use of satellite-dish-equipped trucks, providing live or taped coverage.

Electronic publishing. Replaces traditional means of delivering and storing text information by using computerized delivery. The information is held in a storage device for delivery to computer screens rather than printed on paper.

Encoding. The process of transforming an analog signal into a digital signal, or a digital signal into another digital format.

Enhanced definition television (EDTV). A variation on high-definition television, providing a better picture than current TV sets but offering less resolution than high-definition technology. See: High-definition television.

Enhanced services. A telecommunications category established by the Federal Communications Commission to describe services that result in additional, different, or restructured transmitted information or that involve user interaction with stored information, whether voice or data. See: Basic services.

Erasable rewritable optical disc (EROD). A read/write storage medium that uses a laser and reflected light to store and retrieve data on an optical disc. The discs can store more than one gigabyte of data and are generally used to replace a hard drive.

Facsimile (fax). A form of electronic mail, or remote copying. Also, the document resulting from a fax transmission.

Federal Communications Commission (FCC). The federal independent regulatory agency that licenses and sets standards for telecommunications and electronic media. FCC deregulatory policies in recent decades have had a major impact on U.S. media patterns by expanding the range of delivery services available.

Femtosecond. A millionth of a billionth of a second. The capabilities of optical-fiber systems now under development will be measured in femtoseconds (i.e., millions of times the capacity of present systems).

Fiber optics. The technology of guiding and transmitting light for use as a communications medium. Modulated light-wave signals, generated by a laser or a light-emitting diode, are propagated along a silicon-based waveguide and then demodulated back into electrical signals by a light-sensitive receiver. The bandwidth capacity of fiber-optic wire is substantially greater than that of coaxial cable or copper wire.

First Amendment. The Bill of Rights provision that is the ideological base, and protector, of information freedoms in the United States.

Flash-memory chip. A recent major advance in chip technology. Flash-memory chips retain information when a computer is turned off, unlike earlier chips. The result is to eliminate the need for disk-drive storage systems, permitting much smaller, lighter computers.

Frequency modulation (FM). In broadcasting, a method of modulation in which the frequency is varied and the amplitude (power) remains constant. In addition to its radio uses, FM is used in the sound portion of TV transmissions. See: Amplitude modulation (AM).

Generator. Any device that facilitates such a computer task as text, graphics, or program design.

Gigabit. A measure of the quantity of binary digits. A gigabit equals one billion bits per second. A gigabyte is one billion bytes.

Headend. A cable TV system's control center where program signals from satellites and other sources are transferred to the system's network.

High-definition television (HDTV). A group of technical systems, each of which can encode, transmit, and display greatly enhanced levels of information compared to conventional TV, making possible a sharper video picture, improved color fidelity, and the use of stereophonic sound. HDTV is scheduled for large-scale adoption in the United States, Europe, and Japan by the end of the decade.

Hypertext. Computer software that allows users to link information together through a variety of paths or connections. Users can randomly organize the information in a manner that conforms to their own needs. Hypercard programs ("stacks") are made up of "cards," which when activated, allow users to move to another part of the material they are working with. Hypercard programs are written in "hypertalk," a simple, object-oriented programming language.

Icon. In computer operations, a symbolic, pictorial representation of any function or task.

Image technology. A general category of computer applications that convert documents, illustrations, photographs, and other images into data that can be stored, distributed, accessed, and processed by computers and special-purpose workstations.

Information utility. The concept of a national, and eventually global, electronic network, which will supply a full range of media and other information resources to all locations (comparable to water and electricity utility networks).

Integrated services digital network (ISDN). A long-term plan for the transition of the world's telecommunications systems from analog to digital technology, permitting the integrated transmission of any combination of voice, video, graphics, and data over a common electronic "information pipe." ISDN is a software standard that will eliminate present technical incompatibilities between telecommunications systems and allow uninterrupted transfer of traffic between them.

Interactive media. Media resources that involve the user in providing the content and duration of a message, permitting individualized program material. Also used to describe media production operations that take maximum advantage of random access, computer-controlled videotape, and videodisc players.

Interactive video. A combination of video and computer technology in which programs run in tandem under the control of the user. The user's choices and decisions directly affect the ways in which the program unfolds.

Interactive Video Data Service (IVDS). A service authorized by the Federal Communications Commission in 1992, which allows home viewers to use their television sets for interactive video links to a variety of resources, from home shopping services to educational courses.

Interface. The point or boundary at which hardware or software systems interact (e.g., the connection between a computer and a terminal).

International Telecommunications Union (ITU). A United Nations agency that sets the technical and administrative standards for the global telecommunications network. The ITU has been a leader in promoting ISDN standardization. Its headquarters are in Geneva, Switzerland.

KA band. The new frontier of the radio-frequency spectrum. Located in the 20–30 gigahertz frequency bands, KA is, for the present, the upper limit of spectrum use for media and other normal communications needs. The KA frequencies are capable of handling enormous amounts of information. The other high-capacity bands currently in use are C band and KU band, both used extensively for satellite and terrestrial microwave transmissions.

Karaoke. Japanese for "empty orchestra." A videodisc-based form of entertainment that provides musical and video accompaniment for amateur singers.

Laser. Technically, *l*ight *a*mplification by *s*timulated *e*mission of *r*adiation. Lasers amplify and generate energy in the optical, or light, region of the spectrum above the radio frequencies. In a typical media application, lasers are used to read the micropits on a videodisc, which contain video or sound signals.

Light-emitting diode (LED). A semiconductor device that changes electrical energy into light energy.

Light guide. An extremely clear, thin glass fiber that is to light what copper wire is to electricity. It is synonymous with optical fiber.

Low-powered television (LPTV). Small television stations licensed by the Federal Communications Commission, using low transmitter power. LPTV stations cover relatively small geographical areas.

Media composing. A high-tech variation on desktop publishing, which incorporates sound and video resources with print and still-graphics materials.

Media Lab. A unit of the Massachusetts Institute of Technology, which has done much of the pioneering research on applying advanced technologies to media uses.

Megabit. One million binary digits or bits.

Microprocessor. An electronic circuit, usually on a single microchip, which performs arithmetic, logic, and control operations, customarily with the assistance of a small internal memory, also on the chip.

Minitel. A national information-retrieval network in France, which supplies thousands of data services to millions of homes. High-tech versions of Minitel, such as Prodigy and CompuServe, are being developed commercially in the United States.

Modem. A device that makes possible the linkage of a digital computer to the analog telephone system. As digital telecommunications networks evolve, modems will become obsolete.

Multichannel microwave distribution system (MMDS). Television delivery system that uses line-of-sight microwave circuits to transmit programs similar to those supplied on cable TV. MMDS systems have limited channel capacity, however, compared with cable systems. MMDS is often referred to as "wireless cable."

Multimedia. Information delivery systems that combine different content formats (e.g., text, video, sound) and storage facilities (e.g., video tape, audio tape, magnetic disks, optical disks).

Multiple-system operators (MSO). Large cable TV companies, each controlling many local cable TV systems across the country.

Multiplexing. A technique that allows handling of multiple messages over a single channel. It is accomplished by varying either the speed at which the messages are sent (time division multiplexing) or by splitting the frequency band (frequency division multiplex).

National Association of Broadcasters. The Washington trade association whose membership includes most of the television and radio stations in the country.

National Cable Television Association. The Washington trade association of the cable television industry.

National Information Infrastructure. A phrase coined by Michael Dertouzis, chief of the computer research lab at MIT, to describe the eventual development of an integrated multimedia telecommunications system. See: Information utility.

National Television Systems Committee (NTSC). In the 1940s, this committee formulated the U.S. television standard of 525 horizontal lines per frame at 30 frames per second. The NTSC standard will eventually be phased out with the introduction of high-definition television, which offers twice as many horizontal lines.

Optical memory. Technology that deals with information storage devices that use light (generally laser based) to record, read, or decode data.

Overlay. The technique of superimposing computer-generated text or graphics or both onto motion or still video.

Packet switching. The transfer of data by means of addressed blocks ("packets") of information in which a telecommunications channel is occupied only for the time of transmission of the packet. This allows more efficient use of channels, which ordinarily have periods of low use.

Pay per view (PPV). Program services purchased by cable TV subscribers on a per-program rather than per-month basis.

Peripheral equipment. Equipment that works in conjunction with a communications system or a computer but that is not integral to them (e.g., computer printers).

Personal electronic media. Networks serving the specialized information needs of their users, usually through electronic-mail exchanges. Eventually such personal networking will incorporate video capabilities.

Photon. The fundamental unit of light and other forms of electromagnetic energy. Photons are to optical fibers what electrons are to copper wires; like electrons, they have a wave motion.

Prodigy. A consumer-oriented data network based on personal computers and developed by IBM and Sears Roebuck. Prodigy is currently the largest of several national services. Eventually, these services will expand their present videotext and still-graphics capabilities to include interactive video services.

Protocol. A set of rules that defines procedures for the transfer of information in a communications system.

Qube. An interactive cable TV system developed in the 1980s by American Express and Warner Communications in Columbus, Ohio. Although unsuccessful at the time, it demonstrated the potential of interactive programming to homes.

Quicktime. A computer file format that enables Macintosh computers to compress and play digitized video without additional hardware.

Random-access memory (RAM). A computer memory, the contents of which can be altered at any time. It is the most commonly used method of defining computer capability (e.g., 64K RAM).

Read-only memory (ROM). A computer chip that stores data and instructions in a form that cannot be altered. It is thus distinguished from random-access memory, the contents of which can be changed.

Satellite master antenna television (SMATV). Broadcasting satellite systems designed to serve apartment houses and hotels.

Semiconductor. A material (e.g., silicon, germanium, gallium arsenide) with properties between those of conductors and insulators. Semiconductors are used to manufacturer solid-state devices such as diodes, transistors, integrated circuits, injection lasers, and light-emitting diodes.

Software. The detailed instruction or programs that tell the computer what to do byte by byte.

Squarial. A small earth terminal that is square or rectangular in shape and designed to be attached to the roofs or sides of houses and other, smaller structures.

Telecomputer. A combined television receiver and computer, which may be the central information and entertainment unit of homes in the new multimedia environment.

Teletext. One-way broadcast transmissions that piggyback digital data onto the regular television-broadcasting signal by inserting their messages into unused lines of the vertical blanking interval.

Television receive only (TVRO) terminal. A small earth station that receives video signals from a space satellite.

Transponder. A component in a satellite that receives and transmits television or data signals.

Ultra-high frequency (UHF). The radio spectrum from 300 megahertz to 3 gigahertz. It is the frequency band that includes TV channels 14–83, as well as cellular radio frequencies.

Value-added network (VAN). Data processing done as part of a transmission service package.

Very high frequency (VHF). The radio spectrum from 30 to 300 megahertz, which includes TV channels 2–13, the FM broadcast band, and various specialized services.

Very small aperture terminal (VSAT). A range of small earth station designs that are capable, due to advanced semiconductor technology, of receiving signals from space satellites. A newer generation of VSATS can also transmit signals to the satellites.

VHS. The technical standard that dominates videocassette use, following an epochal marketing battle with the Betamax standard in the 1980s.

Videotext. The transmission of information by television channels, FM frequencies, or telephone circuits to a TV or computer monitor. There are many variations of videotext services, the most advanced of which is full two-way transmission, in which a television receiver is equipped to function as a computer terminal.

Videotext publishing. An increasingly important market for supplying videotext materials from large databases to home computers and other terminals. Many newspapers and magazines now offer their printed products electronically in this manner.

Virtual reality. Software that produces multidimensional visual images. The computerized images can create "realities," which are manipulated in many different formats by a user wearing computerized gloves or helmet.

Wireless cable. See: Multichannel microwave distribution system.

Write once, read many (WORM). An optical storage medium that becomes readable only after data are written into the disk. It can store large amounts of information and has a long shelf life. Some WORM disks are analog and some are digital.

SELECTED BIBLIOGRAPHY

Abramson, Jeffrey B., Christopher Arterton, and Gary Orren, eds. *The Electronic Commonwealth.* New York: Basic Books, 1988.

American Newspaper Publishers Association. *The Media Landscape: The Next Five Years.* Reston, Va., 1989.

——. *Newspaper Electronic Information Services Directory.* Reston, Va., 1991.

——. *Facts About Newspapers—1991.* Reston, Va., April 1991.

American Society of Newspaper Editors. *Keys to Our Survival.* Reston, Va., July 1991.

Aspen Institute Program on Communications and Society. *Shaping the Future Telecommunications Structure.* Queenstown, Md., 1991.

——. *Electronic Media Regulation and the First Amendment.* Forum Report No. 14. Queenstown, Md., 1991.

Aziz, A. M. A. *A Pakistani Journalist Looks at America.* Dacca: Al-Helat, 1960.

Baer, Walter S. *Technology's Challenge to the First Amendment.* Report P-7773. Santa Monica, Calif.: Rand Corporation, 1992.

Bagdikian, Ben. *Media Monopoly.* Boston: Beacon, 1987.

Barnouw, Erik. *Tube of Plenty: The Evolution of American Television,* 2d ed. New York: Oxford University Press, 1990.

Bart, Peter. *The Calamitous Final Days of MGM.* New York: William Morrow, 1990.

Bell, Daniel. *The Coming of Post-Industrial Society.* New York: Basic Books, 1973.

Beniger, James. *The Control Revolution.* Cambridge, Mass.: Harvard University Press, 1986.

Benjamin, Gerald, ed. *The Communications Revolution in Politics.* New York: Academy of Political Science, 1982.

Bennett, W. Lance. *The Governing Crisis: Media, Money and Marketing in American Elections.* New York: St. Martin's, 1982.

Berger, Arthur Asa. *Media USA.* New York: Longman, 1991.

Besen, Stanley. *Misregulating Television: Network Dominance and the FCC.* Chicago: University of Chicago Press, 1984.

Bogart, Leo. *The American Media System and Its Commercial Culture.* Occasional Paper. Gannett Foundation Media Center, New York, March 1991.

Bolling, George H. *AT&T: Aftermath of Antitrust.* Washington, D.C.: National Defense University Press, 1983.

Brand, Stewart. *The Media Lab: Inventing the Future at MIT.* New York: Penguin Books, 1988.

Brown, Richard D. *Knowledge Is Power: The Diffusion of Information in Early America.* New York: Oxford University Press, 1989.

Carpentier, Michel, Sylviane Farnoux-Toporkoff, and Garric Christian. *Telecommunications in Transition.* New York: John Wiley & Sons, 1992.

Carter, Thomas. *The First Amendment and the Fifth Estate,* 2d ed. Mineola, N.Y.: Foundation, 1988.

Cate, Fred, ed. *Visions of the First Amendment for a New Millenium.* Occasional Paper. Annenberg Washington Program, Washington, D.C., 1992.

Clurman, Richard. *To the End of Time.* New York: Simon & Schuster, 1992.

Cohen, Stephen S., and John Zyzman. *Manufacturing Matters: The Myth of the Post-Industrial Economy.* New York: Basic Books, 1987.

Cook, Philip, Douglas Gomery, and Lawrence Lichty, eds. *The Future of the News.* Washington, D.C.: Woodrow Wilson Center, 1992. Distributed by Johns Hopkins University Press.

Corporation for Public Broadcasting. *Strategies for Public Television in a Multi-Channel Environment.* Washington, D.C., March 1991.

Cose, Ellis. *The Press.* New York: William Morrow, 1989.

Crandall, Robert W. *After the Breakup: U.S. Telecommunications in a More Competitive Era.* Washington, D.C.: Brookings Institution, 1991.

Dahlgren, Peter, and Colin Sparks. *Journalism and Popular Culture.* Newbury Park, Calif.: Sage, 1992.

Dates, Jannette L., and William Barlow. *Split Image: African Americans in the Mass Media.* Washington, D.C.: Howard University Press, 1900.

Dennis, Everette E. *Of Media and People.* Newbury Park, Calif.: Sage, 1992.

Dennis, Everette E., and John Merrill. *Media Debates: Issues in Mass Communication.* New York: Longman, 1991.

Dertouzos, Michael, and Joel Moses. *The Computer Age.* Cambridge, Mass.: Massachusetts Institute of Technology Press, 1979.

DeSonne, Marcia. *Spectrum of New Broadcast/Media Technologies.* National Association of Broadcasters, Washington, D.C., March 1990.

Deutsch, Karl. *The Nerves of Government.* New York: Free Press of Glencoe, 1963.

Dizard, Wilson P. *Television: A World View.* Syracuse, N.Y.: Syracuse University Press, 1966.

———. *The Coming Information Age,* 3d ed. New York: Longman, 1989.

Dizard, Wilson P., and Blake Swensrud. *Gorbachev's Information Revolution: Controlling Glasnost in a New Electronic Era.* Colorado Springs, Colo.: Westview, 1987.

Donlan, Thomas G. *Supertech.* Homewood, Ill.: Business One Irwin, 1991.

Dorfman, Ariel. *The Emperor's Old Clothes.* New York: Pantheon Books, 1983.

Dutton, William, Jay Blumler, and Kenneth Kraemer, eds. *Wired Cities: Shaping the Future of Communications.* Boston: G. K. Hall, 1987.

Economist (London). Special reports on communications and mass media: "The Entertainment Industry," 23 December 1989; "Netting the Future," 10 March 1990; and "The New Boys," 5 October 1991.

Egan, Bruce L. *Information Superhighways: The Economics of Advanced Public Communications Networks.* Norwood, Mass.: Artech House, 1991.

Eisenstein, Elizabeth. *The Printing Press as an Agent for Change.* New York: Cambridge University Press, 1980.

Ellul, Jacques. *The Technological Society.* New York: Alfred A. Knopf, 1964.

——. *Propaganda.* New York: Alfred A. Knopf, 1968.

Elton, Martin C. J. *Integrated Broadband Networks: The Public Policy Issues.* Amsterdam, Netherlands: Elsevier Science Publishers, 1991.

Flamm, Kenneth. *Creating the Computer: Government, Industry and High Technology.* Washington, D.C.: Brookings Institution, 1988.

Flournoy, Don M. *CNN World Report: Ted Turner's International News Coup.* Acamedia Research Monograph 9. London: John Libbey, 1992.

Fowles, Jib. *Why Viewers Watch.* Newbury Park, Calif.: Sage, 1992.

Freedom Forum Media Studies Center. *Media at the Millennium.* Report of the First Fellows Symposium on the Future of the Media and Media Studies. New York, 1992.

Geller, Henry. *Fiber Optics: An Opportunity for a New Policy?* Annenberg Washington Program, Washington, D.C., 1991.

Gilder, George. *Life After Television.* New York: W. W. Norton, 1992.

Goldman, William. *Adventures in the Screen Trade.* New York: Warner Books, 1983.

Grover, Ron. *The Disney Touch: How a Disney Management Team Revived an Entertainment Empire.* New York: Business One Irwin, 1991.

Gumpert, Gary. *Talking Tombstones & Other Tales of the Media Age.* New York: Oxford University Press, 1987.

Harlow, Alvin F. *Old Wires and New Waves.* New York: Appleton Century, 1936.

Horowitz, Irving Louis. *Communicating Ideas: The Politics of Publishing in a Post-Industrial Society.* New Brunswick, N.J.: Transaction, 1991.

Horowitz, Robert. *The Irony of Regulatory Reform: The Deregulation of American Telecommunications.* New York: Oxford University Press, 1989.

Innis, Harold A. *Empire and Communications.* Toronto: University of Toronto Press, 1972.

Institute for Information Studies. *Universal Telephone Service: Ready for the 21st Century?* Aspen Institute, Queenstown, Md., 1991.

International Encyclopaedia of Communications (4 vols.). New York: Oxford University Press, 1989.

Jackson, Charles, Harry Shooshan, and Jane Wilson. *Newspapers and Videotex; How Free a Press?* Modern Media Institute, St. Petersburg, Fla., 1981.

Johnson, Craig, ed. *The International Cable-Telco Tango.* International Communications Studies Program, Center for Strategic and International Studies, Washington, D.C., March 1991.

Johnson, Leland. *Development of High-Definition Television: A Study in US-Japan Trade Relations.* Report R-3921-CUSJR. Santa Monica, Calif.: Rand Corporation, 1991.

Johnson, Leland, and Deborah Castleman. *Direct Satellites: A Comparative Alternative to Cable Television.* Report R-4047-MF-RL. Santa Monica, Calif.: Rand Corporation, 1991.

Johnson, Leland, and David Read. *Residential Broadband Services by Telephone Companies? Technology, Economics and Public Policy.* Report R-3906-MF-RL. Santa Monica, Calif.: Rand Corporation, June 1990.

Jowett, Garth. *Movies as Mass Communication,* 2d ed. Newbury Park, Calif.: Sage, 1989.

Kellner, Douglas. *Television and the Crisis of Democracy.* Boulder, Colo.: Westview, 1990.

Kern, Montague. *30-Second Politics.* New York: Praeger, 1989.

Keyworth, George, and Bruce Abell. *Competitiveness and Communications: America's Economic Future—the House-to-House Digital Fiber Optic Network.* Hudson Institute, Indianapolis, Ind., 1990.

Kobrak, Fred, and Beth Leuy, eds. *The Structure of International Publishing in the 1990s.* New Brunswick, N.J.: Transaction, 1991.

Koch, Tom. *Journalism for the 21st Century: Online Information, Electronic Databases and the News.* New York: Praeger, 1991.

Laurie, Peter. *The Micro Revolution.* New York: Basic Books, 1980.

Leaming, Barbara. *Orson Welles: A Biography.* New York: Viking Penguin, 1985.

Lensen, Anton. *Concentration in the Media Industry: the European Community and Mass Media Regulation,* Washington Annenberg Program, Washington, D.C., 1992.

Levy, Mark, and Barrie Gunter. *Home Video and the Changing Nature of the Television Audience.* IBA Television Research Monograph. London: John Libbey, 1988.

Lichtenberg, Judith. *Democracy and the Mass Media.* New York: Cambridge University Press, 1990.

Lippmann, Walter. *Public Opinion.* New York: Harcourt Brace, 1922.

Lowenstein, Ralph, and John Merrill. *Macromedia: Mission, Message, Morality.* New York: Longman, 1990.

MacDonald, Greg. *The Emergence of Global Multi-Media Conglomerates.* Working Paper No. 70. International Labor Organization. Geneva, Switzerland, 1990.

MacDonald, J. Fred. *One Nation Under Television: The Rise and Decline of Network TV.* New York: Pantheon Books, 1990.

McGannon Communications Research Center. *Fiber Optics in the Home: What Does the Public Want and Need?* Fordham University Department of Communications, New York, May 1989.

Machlup, Fritz. *The Production and Distribution of Information in the United States.* Princeton, N.J.: Princeton University Press, 1962.

McLuhan, Marshall. *The Gutenberg Galaxy.* Toronto: University of Toronto Press. 1962.

———. *Understanding Media,* 2d ed. New York: New American Library, 1964.

McQuail, Denis. *Media Performance: Mass Communications and the Public Interest.* Newbury Park, Calif.: Sage, 1992.

Manheim, Jarol B. *All the People, All the Time.* Armonk, N.Y.: M. E. Sharpe, 1991.

Marvin, Carolyn. *When Old Technologies Were New.* New York: Oxford University Press, 1988.

Marx, Leo. *The Machine in the Garden.* New York: Oxford University Press, 1964.

Masuda, Yoneji. *The Information Society as Post-Industrial Society.* Tokyo: Institute for the Information Society, 1980. Reprinted in the United States by the World Future Society, Bethesda, Md., 1981.

Meyer, Martin. *Whatever Happened to Madison Avenue?* Boston: Little Brown, 1991.

Miller, Nod, and Rod Allen. *It's Live—But Is It Real?* Current Debates in Broadcasting 2. London: John Libbey, 1992.

Minow, Newton. *How Vast the Wasteland Now?* Freedom Forum Media Studies Center, Columbia University, August 1991.

Mintz, Morton, and Jerry S. Cohen. *America Inc.: Who Owns and Operates the United States?* New York: Dell Books, 1972.

Morrison, David E. *Television and the Gulf War.* Acamedia Research Monograph 7. London: John Libbey, 1992.

Mosco, Vincent. *The Pay-Per Society: Computers and Communications in the Information Age.* Norwood, N.J.: Ablex, 1989.

Mosco, Vincent, and Janet Wasco. *The Political Economy of Information.* Madison, Wis.: University of Wisconsin Press, 1988.

Moskin, Robert, ed. *Toward the Year 2000: New Faces in Publishing.* Gutersloh, Germany: Bertlesmann Foundation, 1989.

Naisbitt, John. *Megatrends.* New York: Warner Books, 1984.

National Telecommunications and Information Administration, U.S. Department of Commerce. *Telecom 2000.* Washington, D.C.: 1989.

————. *The Globalization of Mass Media Firms.* Washington, D.C., 1993.

Neuman, W. Russell. *The Future of the Mass Audience.* New York: Cambridge University Press, 1992.

Noam, Eli. *Television in Europe.* New York: Oxford University Press, 1991.

Nora, Simon, and Alain Minc. *The Computerization of Society.* Cambridge, Mass.: Massachusetts Institute of Technology Press, 1981.

Owen, Bruce, and Steven Wildman. *Video Economics.* Cambridge, Mass.: Harvard University Press, 1992.

Penzias, Arnold. *Ideas and Information.* New York: W. W. Norton, 1989.

Pool, Ithiel de Sola, ed. *The Social Impact of the Telephone.* Cambridge, Mass.: Massachusetts Institute of Technology Press, 1977.

Pool, Ithiel de Sola. *Technologies of Freedom.* Cambridge, Mass.: Harvard University Press, 1983.

————. *Technologies Without Boundaries.* Cambridge, Mass.: Harvard University Press, 1990.

Postman, Neil. *Amusing Ourselves to Death.* New York: Penguin Books, 1986.

————. *Technology: The Surrender of Culture to Technology.* New York: Alfred A. Knopf, 1992.

Postman, Neil, and Steve Powers. *How to Watch TV News.* New York: Penguin Books, 1992.

Quester, George. *The International Politics of Television.* New York: Lexington Books, 1990.

Read, William. *America's Mass-Media Merchants.* Baltimore: Johns Hopkins University Press, 1976.

Real, Michael R. *Super Media.* Newbury Park, Calif.: Sage Publications, 1989.

Reich, Robert. *The Work of Nations.* New York: Alfred A. Knopf, 1991.

Reid, T. R. *The Chip.* New York: Simon & Schuster, 1984.

Rheingold, Howard. *Virtual Reality.* New York: Summit Books, 1991.

Roof, Dana, Denise Trauth, and John Huffman. *In Pursuit of Diversity: An Argument for Structural Regulation of the Cable Television Industry.* School of Mass Communications, Bowling Green State University, Bowling Green, Ky., August 1991.

Rosen, Jay, and Paul Taylor. *The New News and the Old News: The Press and Politics in the 1990s.* A Twentieth Century Fund Paper. New York, 1992.

Rubin, Michael R., and Mary T. Huber. *The Knowledge Industry in the United States, 1960–1980.* Princeton, N.J.: Princeton University Press, 1986.

Scientific American. "Communications, Computers and Networks," special issue. September 1991.

Setzer, Florence, and Jonathan Levy. *Broadcast Television in a Multichannel Marketplace.* Office of Policy and Plans Working Paper No. 26. Federal Communications Commission, Washington, D.C., June 1991.

Shaughnessy, Haydn, and Carmen Fuente Cobo. *The Cultural Obligations of Broadcasting.* Media Monograph No. 12. European Media Institute, University of Manchester (Great Britain), 1990.

Shawcross, William. *Rupert Murdoch: Ringmaster of the Information Circus.* London: Chatto & Windus, 1992.

Slack, Jennifer D., and Fred Fejes, eds. *The Ideology of Information Age.* Norwood, N.J.: Ablex, 1987.

Smith, Anthony. *The Geopolitics of Information.* New York: Oxford University Press, 1980.

———. *Goodbye, Gutenberg.* New York: Oxford University Press, 1980.

———. *The Age of Behemoths: The Globalization of Mass Media Firms.* Report for the Twentieth Century Fund. New York: Priority, 1991.

Smith, Sally Bedell. *In All His Glory.* New York: Simon & Schuster, 1990.

Sterling, Christopher, and John Kitross. *Stay Tuned: A Concise History of American Broadcasting.* Belmont, Calif.: Wadsworth, 1990.

Stonier, Tom. *The Wealth of Information.* London: Thomas Methuen, 1983.

Sussman, Leonard. *Power, the Press and the Technology of Freedom: The Coming Age of ISDN.* Lanham, Md.: University Press of America, 1990.

Times-Mirror Center for the People and the Press. *The Age of Indifference: A Study of Young Americans and How They View the News.* Washington, D.C., June 1990.

Toffler, Alvin. *The Third Wave.* New York: William Morrow, 1980.

Traber, Michael. *The Myth of the Information Revolution: Social and Ethical Implications of Information Technology.* Newbury Park, Calif.: Sage, 1988.

Turow, Joseph. *Media Systems in Society.* New York: Longman, 1992.

Ulloth, Dana R., ed. *Communications Technology: A Survey.* Lanham, Md.: University Press of America, 1991.

U.S. Congress, House of Representatives. *Options Papers.* Prepared by the staff of the Subcommittee on Communications, Committee on Interstate and Foreign Commerce, 95th Congress, 1st Session. Committee Print 95-13. Washington, D.C., May 1977.

———. Office of Technology Assessment. *Critical Connections: Communications for the Future.* OTA Publication OTA-CIT-407. Washington, D.C., January 1990.

———. Office of Technology Assessment. *The Big Picture: HDTV and High-Resolution Systems.* Report OTA-BP-CIT-64. Washington, D.C., June 1990.

U.S. Department of Commerce, Office of Telecommunications. *The Information Economy.* Special Publication 77-12. Washington, D.C., 1977.

———. International Trade Administration. *1992 Industrial Outlook.* Washington, D.C., January 1992.

U.S. Department of Justice. *The Geodesic Network: Report on Competition in the Telephone Industry.* Anti-Trust Division. Washington, D.C., January 1987.

Veronis, Suhler & Associates. *Communications Industry Forecast: Industry Spending Projections 1992-1996,* 6th ed. New York, June 1992.

Wildman, S. S., and S. E. Siwek. *International Trade in Films and Television Programs.* Cambridge, Mass.: Ballinger Books, 1988.

Wilhelm, Donald. *Global Communications and Political Power.* New Brunswick, N.J.: Transaction, 1990.

Williams, Frederick, ed. *Measuring the Information Society.* Newbury Park, Calif.: Sage, 1988.

Wriston, Walter B. *The Twilight of Sovereignty: How the Information Revolution Is Transforming Our World.* New York: Scribner, 1992.

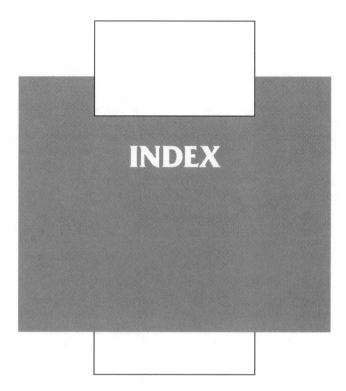

INDEX